Story Driven Modeling

Ulrich Norbisrath, Ruben Jubeh, Albert Zündorf

April 21, 2013

Print Version:
ISBN-13: 978-1483949253
ISBN-10: 1483949257
6" x 9"(15.24 x 22.86 cm)

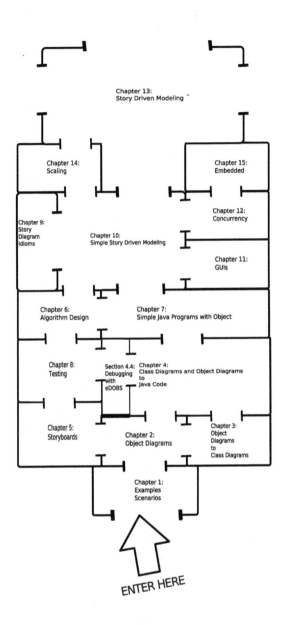

Figure 1: Book structure

Acknowledgments

We need to thank many people that supported us in writing this book:

- First of all, Marlon Dumas from University of Tartu was the one who permanently insisted that we had to write a book on Story Driven Modeling. All the authors were involved in teaching modeling with objects and we all used the story driven approach. These were somehow new ideas and thus we had no script or textbook to give to our students. Marlon repeatedly asked us to consider writing our own text book. Here it is. Thank you Marlon.

- As the class structure usually is the first thing you need to start programming, in former times all our software development started with class diagrams. And, our students (as all students) had significant problems in coming up with reasonable class diagrams at the beginning of our courses. Somehow, you need to be experienced to come up with a reasonable class diagram for your problem. Ira Diethelm did her PhD on Didactic for Computer Science and somehow she brought in the idea that we should start with objects instead of classes to facilitate the initial steps of software development. This turned out to be a generally very good idea. Thank you Ira.

- Leif Geiger has helped a lot in developing the ideas of Story Driven Modeling, and he has developed a lot of tool support for the whole process. In particular, Leif has matured the eDOBS tool that we use for debugging and enabled model level debugging, i.e. the stepping through our graphical story diagrams.

- Artjom Lind was one of Ulrich's first teaching assistants in Estonia and helped him executing the first story driven courses at the University of Tartu. He also helped out with countless other courses and duties and kept therefore Ulrich's back free when he was off writing this book. Artjom also worked a year directly together with Ruben and Albert in Germany taking on similar duties. Thank you Artjom for keeping the spirit up!

- Sabine (eagle eye) Zündorf did a great job in proof reading this book. You need to be brave to give your manuscript to Sabine for proof reading as she finds an enormous amount of typos and inconsistencies even when you think your manuscript is already pretty matured. In addition, Sabine supported us with marvelous boxes of food supply when we went to some huts for a week of book writing in seclusion several times. In addition, she and Tom Zündorf were very patient with Albert allowing to go off from the family for several weeks.

- Big thanks goes also especially to Ulrich's colleagues from Nazarbayev University Ben Tyler and Michael Lewis to support an early'ish finish of the book and covering in class while Ulrich was gone to seclusion to do the final writing. Special thanks for Ben: your comments made us feel that you have enjoyed parts of the book.

- Big thanks go to our host institutions University of Kassel, University of Tartu, and Nazarbayev University. They encouraged us to go on and provided the financial means or access to grants with such means to carry on. We are confident that this investment will pay off due to the beautiful course material, which we and our successors will now be able to use.

- This book was supported by the European Union Regional Development Fund through the Estonian Centre of Excellence in Computer Science.

- This book was also supported by the European Social Fund through the Estonian Doctoral School in Information and Communication Technology

- This book was supported by Castle Dagstuhl by hosting us for one week of book writing.

Contents

II Behavior   **91**

III Scaling Up   257

Part I

Object Models

Chapter 1

Introduction

If you would ask us, whether this is just another book about modeling, we would probably feel inclined to say: yes and no. Yes, it is a lot about modeling, but no, it is also about programming, methodological software design, and rapid prototyping via methods from model driven engineering. It will also be one of the first complete references and teaching guides for *Story Driven Modeling*. Story Driven Modeling is an agile software development method using objects and scenarios and special modeling steps to facilitate system analysis and design, [34, 21, 20]. Most parts of this book can be done with pencil and paper and with standard UML tools and standard software development environments. However, some steps are best supported by the rapid prototyping tool Fujaba [5] or the Story Driven Modeling library SDMLib [10].

The title of this book does not include Object Oriented Modeling on purpose. Object Orientation, Object Oriented Design, Object Oriented Analysis, and other object oriented methods all refer somehow to class diagrams and inheritance. Instead of this, we will actively use objects for modeling, analysis, and design. We will learn to think in objects.

This book is foremost planned to be a textbook for software modeling courses. It offers a very interactive and agile approach to modern software design. In this book, we introduce the Objects First principle which is the foundation of the Story Driven Modeling development method. This is not to be mistaken with an object oriented development method. You will see that the Object First method slightly differs from traditional object oriented methods.

With this book, we address a majority of readers dealing with or wanting to learn software development. This includes teachers and students for introduction to Object Orientation, Systems Modeling, Object Oriented Design, or Model Driven Engineering. This book should also be insightful for people interested in modeling and program design and beginning programmers. We expect from

3

the reader some very basic programming skills, preferable in Java, though most of the presented concepts in this book can be also applied in any other object oriented language. However, all the examples presented in this book focus on Java as the example language.

If you use this book for teaching, you might discuss at this point what your students expect from this course and why they are visiting you. If you are a student: yes this book explains the contents of your course in more detail. After each lecture, look-up the corresponding book chapter. This will help you doing your assignments in no time. If you are a software developer and just unhappy with the usual object oriented methods, it is not your fault: Most object oriented software development methods use class diagrams as the major means for modeling. As we show in this book, this is a very difficult approach. Instead, this book uses object diagrams and scenarios as the central means for modeling. This facilitates software development dramatically and solves a lot of confusing issues of software development.

There are multiple ways to read this book and few of them are linear. The floor plan of Figure 1.1 shows how the different sections of our book are connected. You correctly have started in the current section which introduces our notion of examples and scenarios, see below. This notion is pretty central to our ideas, so do not skip it. In this book we model with objects and thus Chapter 2 introduces our notion of object diagrams. From object diagrams the usual next step are class diagrams, cf. Chapter 3. From there you go to Java code in Chapter 4. Alternatively (or afterward) you might go from object diagrams to storyboards (Chapter 5) and testing (Chapter 8). For practical experiences with the elements achieved so far, a visit of the eDOBS tool in Chapter 4.4 is worthwhile. In software development we propose a test first approach where you do the tests before you do the methods. However, it is hard to write a test before you have an idea how the method to be tested looks like. As our methods focus on operations on object structures, visit the sections on algorithm design (Chapter 6) and on simple programs with object models (Chapter 7), first. Once you are familiar with this first part of the book, you are ready for complex algorithms with object structures. Chapter 9 illustrates how complex algorithms on object models may be developed with the help of object pattern search and rewrite operations. As a side, Chapter 11 shows how to combine object models with graphical user interfaces. GUI programming then leads you to concurrent programs (Chapter 12) which in turn opens the door for embedded applications (Chapter 15). The crown of all this is the Story Driven Modeling Chapter 13 that provides you with the software development methods that leverages all our techniques. If you still have doubts, visit Chapter 14 on scaling. Now you are ready to develop complex applications on a professional industrial level. Go, do magic.

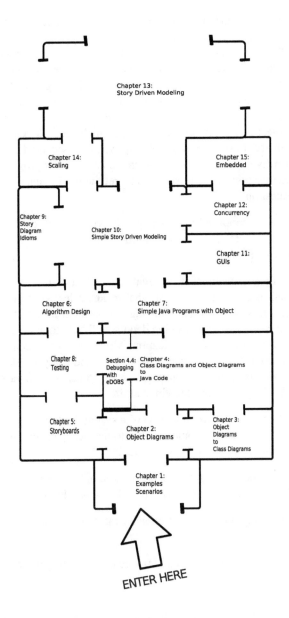

Figure 1.1: Book structure

1.1   Why Model?

Think for a minute, what was the biggest software project you have been involved in? How many lines of code did it have? How long have people been
working on it? If things took long, why did they take this much time?[1]

Usually, people thinking about these questions will recall some communication problems in the process of developing a specific program. These communication problems occur talking to the customer and between the programmers
and managers. Also, it should be observed that these problems are growing the
bigger the project is. As the title of this book includes "Modeling", modeling
might be an answer to some of the problems we just discovered.

However, why should we model, when we are all great programmers? This
is also a good question to ask to students to get them thinking. How would you
answer this question?

> "If you were supposed to understand it, we wouldn't call it code."
> – from a Federal Express promotion, reported by IS Survivalist
> Matthew O. Persico

Writing code already means that we create an artifact, which is not easy to understand, which is encrypted in a way that makes it less accessible for human
understanding. It is obvious that showing the problem in a particular context,
omitting some of the machine specific details, will help to understand this view
better and therefore foster communication. Models can show connections, relations, and context at once. This can help us to see and analyze risks and costs.

Many definitions of the term "model" (in the context of software) are related
to a system. Such as given by Bezivin et al. in

- [18]: "A model is a simplification of a system built with an intended goal
  in mind. The model should be able to answer questions in place of the
  actual system." or given by Seidewitz in

- [33]: „A model is a set of statements about some system under study
  [SUS]. Here, statement means expression about the SUS."

A definition focusing on aspects of a reality rather than systems is provided by
Pohl in

- [31]: "A model is an abstracting image of an existing or fictitious reality."

---

[1]There will be a lot of questions in this book, which ask you to think or do a small exercise. If
you are a teacher, you can easily use these questions as motivations in your lessons or lectures. If
you are a student, do your assignments yourself. We do not provide you with solutions for free. If
you read this book for yourself, we suggest you to take the time and do the little exercise.

This definition considers "abstracting images" from aspects of a (even fictitious) reality and not only systems, which is more suitable for early phases in a software process, when models are used for requirements engineering.

In our view

- A model is a simple description of relevant problem aspects with the purpose to communicate these aspects between stakeholders and the software developers and to ease software development.

In this definition, we put a special emphasis on the "ease software development" part. After all, we have to develop a piece of software, and we introduce models as an intermediate step because they make the overall effort much easier. Our models make software development easier by giving the developers a good idea of how their program is going to work, where which piece of information is represented, and how the software shall deal with it. Provided with this knowledge, the development of the algorithm part is a piece of cake (ideally :). In addition, the object models allow to discuss with customers on a simple example-based level. Thereby (ideally) the customer gets a good idea how the software will work. This helps the customer to use the software and to ensure that the software does what the customer wants.

Following these arguments, (data) modeling is a core competence in Computer Science. Initially, data modeling is not too simple. Internally, computers deal with numbers and characters only. Our challenge is to take important aspects of our problem and to map these aspects on numbers and characters such that the computer can compute something. Then we need to take the resulting numbers and characters and to map these results back to our problem. This means we have to interpret the computer results. Figure 1.2 shows the transfer we have to do as a developer to model a moon lander. The main properties which have to be taken into account for building a model here are mass (m), height (h), speed (v), amount of fuel (r), and the moon's gravitation (a). Luckily, it is easy to map onto numbers. Knowing these properties, we can program the behavior of the Lunar Lander. This means we take the physical laws for forces, masses, speed, and acceleration and turn them into computation rules. Luckily, these physical laws are already math equations easy to turn into a program. Using this, we can now compute, how the data of our Lunar Lander has changed after some seconds without breaking. We just compute some new values for the variables modeling height and speed in our program. Then, we interpret these numbers which is again easy for the Lunar Lander: For example, a height of -100 and a speed of 1000 means something like "major catastrophe".

We call here the way from the real world and actual physical objects or problem entities to the model "modeling" and the reverse way "interpretation".[2]

---

[2]We are of course aware that even in spite of the carefully selected screenshot from the Android

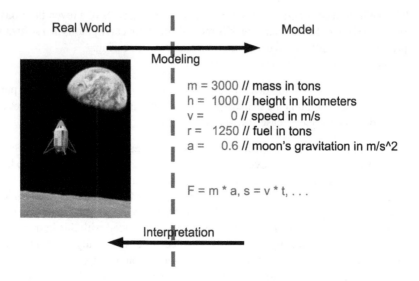

Real World | Model

Modeling

m = 3000 // mass in tons
h = 1000 // height in kilometers
v =   0 // speed in m/s
r = 1250 // fuel in tons
a =   0.6 // moon's gravitation in m/s^2

F = m * a, s = v * t, . . .

Interpretation

Figure 1.2: Modeling Lunar Lander

Figure 1.3 describes a little more complex example concerning the modeling of a map for the computation of short routes through a network of streets. Modeling a network of streets, i.e. representing the relevant aspects of a network of streets in the computer is hard at first sight, how are you going to represent the geometry of all these streets? However, for computing shortest paths you actually do not need the concrete geometry of the streets. It suffices to build a graph of nodes representing specific places and locations and connecting these and weighting their connections. Such a graph again is easily represented as a two-dimensional matrix showing the weights of the connections on the respective matrix position. The graph data structure we describe here is already much more complex than the simple numbers we were looking at in the Lunar Lander example. However, at the end, a graph is also just a somewhat organized collection of numbers a computer can deal with. With the help of this organized collection of numbers, the computer may easily compute the lengths of different paths in order to find the shortest path from node 1 to node 7 in our example graph. This shortest path

---

Lunar Lander the real world character of this image is questionable, but the authors agreed that this image would sufficiently inspire the reader to think about a real physical lunar lander arriving on the moon.

The Lunar Lander image is a modified version of work created and shared by the Android Open Source Project and used according to terms described in the Creative Commons 2.5 Attribution License. Reference: http://developer.android.com/resources/samples/LunarLander/

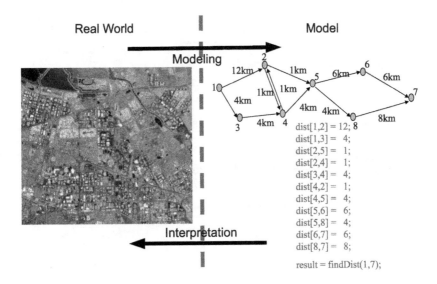

Figure 1.3: Modeling maps

will then be interpreted as "in 200 m turn left" within our navigation system.

By the way, can you find the shortest path from 1 to 7 in our graph? (Hint: you should not need more than 22 km.)

Figure 1.4[3] shows the example of modeling an ATM (Automatic Teller Machine). For modeling this we have to consider lists of numbers, multiple users and accounts, different locations, a central server or database and logging of the different payments made. This is the first example with multiple records of the same structure. This is therefore a first step towards object models, which is the main concept described in this book. In addition, it is an example where the effects of computations for the real world are easy to experience: an account total of -2000 has a clear meaning in the real world.

Overall, the Story Driven Modeling development method helps you to think very strictly in object models, it facilitates giving better lectures, to achieve better grades, and to write better and simpler programs faster. We will use storyboards and story diagrams to support this way of modeling. Using these modeling techniques, you will learn how simple it is to program with models and how to avoid plenty of standard programming mistakes.

---

[3]The satellite maps screenshot was taken with the NASA World Wind program (http://worldwind.arc.nasa.gov/).

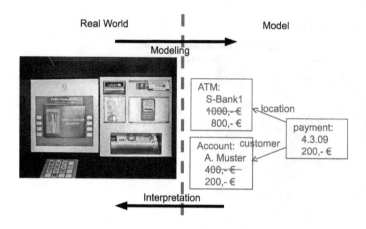

Figure 1.4: Modeling an ATM

1.2 Guiding Example: Study-Right University

Throughout this book we will use several guiding examples. The first example, which should inspire us, is developing a solution for the following problem:

The Perfect Exam[4]

We imagine a big university called "Study-Right University" with plenty of interconnected lecture halls as shown in the floor plan in Figure 1.5. The entrance to the university is from the lower edge through the math room. The exit is via the examination room in the upper left corner. The examination room hosts the examination board. To pass the exam for a degree, students need a specific amount of credit points, not more (who would do more anyway?) and not less. In every lecture hall a professor teaches students for the amount of credit points shown in the floor plan. Being taught costs the attending students the same amount of motivation points that they can earn as credit points in a class. The examination board only hands out a degree to the student if they have all their respective credit points and no motivation left to stay at the university and block other students. If students enter a lecture hall they will be automatically taught as long as necessary until their knowledge is worth the respective credit points of this class. Then they can move to the next room. If students have no motivation points left, they

---

[4]This motivating example is based on the "Rescue Princess Ada" scenario, described in [23], which is based on a task in a computer science competition for high school students in Poland.

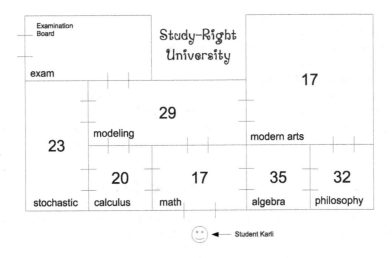

Figure 1.5: The Study-Right University

have to go on vacation and start over. All credit points earned so far will be lost. The students can visit lecture rooms multiple times. As the courses in Study-Right University are ongoing they can earn more credit points when they visit a room another time. However, after they have earned the credit points of a room, they first have to leave the room and be taught something different before they can come back and learn more.

The student Karli wants to achieve a degree at the Study-Right University. For a degree we need at the moment 214 credit points and Karli starts with 214 motivation points. The university is depicted in Figure 1.5. The amount of credit points (and hence the number of motivation points to be spent), which will be earned in each room are written as numbers in each room. The examination board is in the upper left corner. Each room has a topic, which is taught in it, and its name is written in the lower left corner of each room.

The task is now to develop a program that allows us to find a way for student Karli to pass the exam in the Study-Right University.

Well, do we actually need a program? Wouldn't it be faster to find a solution for Karli, manually? OK. Spend some 30 seconds and try it.

Not so easy? Yep. Still, finding a single solution is probably faster than programming a solver. Thus, programming the solver makes sense only, if you expect to use it over and over again. For example, the floor plan of the Study-

Right University might change. Or the number of credits required for an exam changes. Or the credits per topic change. Or you have to identify reasonably small yet interesting initial credits for new students that result in nontrivial paths through the university.[5]

The Study-Right University example has been used in modeling courses for years now and has proven to be an excellent start as it has the right complexity and it allows us to discuss many design and modeling and implementation alternatives. It is also easy to scale the problem up, e.g. by adding mandatory courses or by restricting the number of courses or by adding homework assignments.

1.3   From Concrete to Abstract to Objects

The concepts of concrete, abstract, and example are very important for this book. Therefore, let us start this section with a little exercise[6]:

1. Write down 3 things which are abstract.

2. Write down 3 things which are examples of concrete things.

3. Draw a table with two columns with the titles abstract and concrete. Now write down five rows, in the left column write one thing and in the right column write a thing which is more concrete than the one on the left.

You will get something like this:

1. heaven, color, zero

2. myself, this table, the green car

3.

abstract	concrete
color	green
table	desk
desk	this desk
tree	birch
class	object

4. Take a thing from the concrete column, add it to the abstract column and find an even more concrete thing for it.

---

[5]For example because you are writing a book on modeling and need interesting initial credits for your exercise.

[6]This exercise can be also carried out by small teams (of approximately three to four students) in a class.

5. Build a long chain of things starting with an abstract thing going down to more and more concrete things. (Can you do a chain of more than 10 things? Which team in your class has the longest chain?)

6. Now try to do a table with more abstract and more concrete activities / verbs. For example, start with "programming vs. programming in Java vs. programming a solver for Study-Right University vs. ... "

We can see several concepts from this example. First, we learn that a thing can be either abstract or concrete depending on the context. Therefore, the first task is a bit misleading. Even a thing like heaven can be seen as a concrete object of a set of religious concepts. "Zero" might lead to some discussion as it is very concrete as a number but very abstract in form of describing something physical and touchable of the real world.

Talking about abstract and concrete is a good base for starting a long philosophical discussion with no ends. If you look at the table in 3 you will see, that it is usually easy to agree about abstract and concrete in using them as comparative terms (as in more abstract or more concrete). The actual phenomenons of abstraction or concretion are the ones, which are really important to understand for software development and design.

The remaining question is, why are these two terms important for software development?

What might this have to do with modeling?

This book advocates that modeling and programming merely requires the skill and is the task to go from concrete real world examples to more abstract programs. Our programs should work not only for the example cases described in our problem statements and requirements documents but also for all related cases and related problems. We do not write a solver just to help Karli but generally to find paths. We find paths not only in universities but in general graphs. We find not only paths that consume motivation but general resources. Being more general makes our programs useful in more cases. Similarly, our models shall be general. They shall be able to represent not only one university but any floor plans or even more general mazes or search spaces. Thus, during modeling and programming we go from more concrete to more abstract things.

While very general and abstract models and programs are usable in many cases, they do a very poor job as means for communication. Only software people are able to discuss on the level of abstract concepts and models. And even software people manage to create disastrous misunderstandings while discussing program behavior with the help of abstract class diagrams. The same thing holds for abstract requirements descriptions like "Students study at universities. Universities offer courses. Courses give credits. Degrees require predefined credits. We want an automatic student." Such abstract descriptions do not help in communicating your requirements to the developers. They are just a source of misunderstandings. For requirements the problem is even more severe since requirements are negotiated with users or customers which may not be software people but experts in their own domain. People from other domains as e.g. social street workers, administrative people, or business people may have problems seeing a university just as a floor plan with topics and credits attached to it. University administrative staff might not like the idea of an automatic student. University administrative staff might not get nor like the idea to reduce their old, reputed, dignified institution to a graph with weighted nodes and undirected edges. Generally, non IT people have a problem to communicate in abstract concepts.[7] In addition, even if your users or customers are used to certain abstractions, these are most likely abstractions from their domain that you as an IT guy may have some difficulties with. Just think about strategies behind credit swap option derivatives.

To overcome these communication problems, this book advocates the usage of concrete examples. For most people, it is much easier to think in concrete examples than in abstract concepts. Using concrete examples, for example to speak about student Karli in the math room, is much easier than discussing about the young generation and the end of our civilization, at least if you try to identify software requirements. Thus, for requirements engineering, software people need the skill to be as concrete as possible, i.e. to find good examples that help to identify the relevant properties of the desired systems and the rules for the desired system behavior. With the help of concrete examples you will be able to communicate with non IT people, to identify their requirements, and to document requirements. Thereby you and your customer and your teammates are able to get the message and do your job.

To summarize, modelers and software developers need the skills to analyze concrete examples and to model and classify relevant aspects in an intuitive way. In addition, modelers and software developers need the skills to communicate their abstract models and programs via concrete examples to customers and team mates. Thus, the concepts of abstract and concrete and example are important for us.

1.4   The High Art of Giving Examples

We will find out that giving an example is a very important quality for a clean software design. Examples are an important means to help people understand each other.

Merriam Webster [8] defines *example* the following way:

---

[7]Well, we are not sure whether the problems with abstract concepts hold also for the professor of modern art in the Study-Right University.

1. one that serves as a pattern to be imitated or not to be imitated <a good example> <a bad example>

2. a punishment inflicted on someone as a warning to others; also : an individual so punished

3. one (as an item or incident) that is representative of all of a group or type

4. a parallel or closely similar case especially when serving as a precedent or model

5. an instance (as a problem to be solved) serving to illustrate a rule or precept or to act as an exercise in the application of a rule

- Synonyms: instance, model

In this definition you will note words like pattern, representative, group, type, case, model, and instance. These are all very important terms in the software modeling discipline. Especially remarkable is that an example can be a model.

As we see, giving examples is an integral part of modeling. However, when is an example feasible? How can we assess the quality of examples and how can we find examples?

Closely bound to the term example is the term *scenario* in the sense of a plot or a sequence of concrete events (for the exact definition look at Section 1.5). Finding a good scenario for a presentation, a paper, a monograph, or a project seems to be a skill rarely present in academia.[8] Teaching an Objects First course in a graduate program might often make you feel that you have to fight against all the abstract thinking students already have learned. You might ask yourself why is it harder for your students to be concrete than abstract? Obviously, computer science courses concentrate on skills required for going from concrete problems to abstract models and programs. This trains software people in using their abstraction skills and working with abstraction. However, the reverse skill of giving good concrete examples is seriously neglected. This book tries to close this gap in the set of student skills.

Why are examples important in software development? Like all other models we need these as a communication artifact. Examples are especially important for the communication with customers that might have problems with code or class diagrams.

---

[8]In our experience, grant applications often have very good examples while scientific papers frequently fail to give good examples. Thus, in principle academia can give good examples. Perhaps giving good examples is a skill you gain as a post-doc (writing now grant applications instead of papers). Another explanation is that papers address the peers of your own field and you might think these field experts get it without a good example while grant applications need to address reviewers with a more general background.

In the development method we will present and apply in this book, scenarios are the first models which have to be produced. They are one of the main means to be able to talk to the customer and making sure to achieve a mutual understanding.

But how can we give a good example? After reading the section on concrete and abstract, we already have a small idea what giving an example means: making something abstract more concrete. In the concrete-abstract pairs we described before, the concrete term is an example for the abstract value. If we have a variable in a description, giving the variable a value is also a form of giving an example. Nevertheless, it seems that especially in academia and educational settings the quality of giving good examples is less and less (or has never been) desirable. Presenting us abstract models, nicely closed formulas, and generic texts without their applications and useful contexts is common practice. This leads to bored students, misunderstanding, projects nobody wanted, and irrelevant papers. The question remains, how can we give a good example for a specific situation?

Let us consider here the "Perfect Exam" case of the Study-Right University from Section 1.2. We want to give an example addressing an important aspect of the case described.

Asking students for examples here often results in answers like this:

1. There is a university, where a student can move from room to room and earn credit points and lose at the same time motivation points. The student has to have a fixed number of credit points to be able to enter an exam room to pass the exam and graduate from the university.

2. A student is studying and has to get a number of credit points.

3. This case deals with a very specific curriculum.

4. Karli takes a fitting course.

These examples are not making us very happy. They are not really examples of the described Study-Right University case. Why not? They are not concrete, they are not showing any special facet of the described case. In contrast, they show some abstract concepts related with the case.

Example 1 describes in an abstract way, what is going on in the Study-Right University. In contrast to giving some concrete examples for rooms the student Karli moves from and to (like math room and algebra room), only the abstract term room is used. Instead of giving a concrete number of credit points like 17 only credit points is used. Instead of 214 "a fixed number" is used. Example 2 is even less concrete, it only talks about studying, not anymore about the rooms

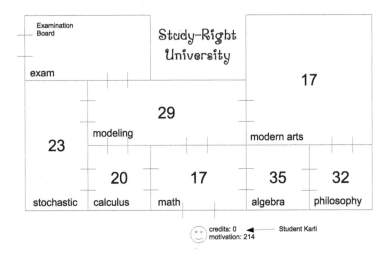

Figure 1.6: The Study-Right University

and their interconnections nor gives it an idea how points are earned. Example 3 gives a hint that it has to do with studying because it mentions curriculum. However it does not give any specific (even if it uses the same word) information explaining a concrete fact related to the Study-Right University case.

We want examples like the following:

1. The student Karli wants to achieve a degree at the Study-Right University. The initial situation is depicted in Figure 1.6. For a degree we need at the moment 214 credit points and Karli starts with 0 credit points and 214 motivation points. Karli is outside of the university and now enters the university into the math class. Karli attends the math lecture and automatically earns 17 credit points for it and loses at the same time 17 motivation points. Karli has now 17 credit points and 197 motivation points and can move on to the modeling class.

2. Karli has studied math and modeling and therefore has now 46 credit points and 168 motivation points. Karli tries to enter the examination room. This situation is depicted in Figure 1.7. When entering, the examination board asks for the study book containing the number of gained credit points as well as the visited courses. As Karli's number of credit points is smaller than 214 the examination board does not allow graduation and Karli has to leave the university and start over.

Instead of some student this example uses an individual student Karli. Instead of general courses it uses the math course and the modeling course. We do not start

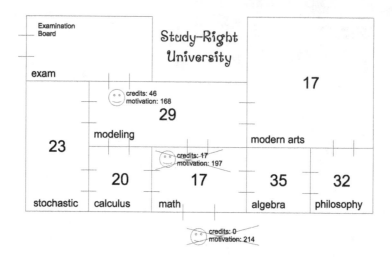

Figure 1.7: Karli in front of examination board.

with a certain amount of credits or motivation but with 214 credits required and
the math course gives you exactly 17 credits. After visiting math and modeling
Karli has earned 46 credits and it is pretty clear how earned credits are computed
from which values.

To give good examples one rule of thumb is to use things that have individual
names, e.g. "Karli" or "the math room". Using individual names ensures that
you have reached the level of concrete (individual) example objects. Still recall
that the example objects represent typical representative members of a group of
similar objects. Thus using an individual that represents some stereotype might
be a good choice. For example Joe the plumber or Gina the gossiping girl or
Steve the old man with hat in the slow old car in front of me might represent a
certain user group everybody has a good understanding of.

The example above even uses images to clarify things. Images can often
describe a situation much more condensed and effective than text and are therefore a good means to accompany such examples.[9] Two more good versions of
examples can be seen in the exercises (Section 1.6.2).

Examples are an extremely important means in communication to facilitate
understanding. They are especially allowing people from different domains talking with each other. Allowing your communication partners to develop a concrete idea of a case you are describing to them will allow them to share their
ideas with you the same way and therefore prevent a lot of modeling and design

---

[9]Well, can someone give a good example for an abstract image not clarifying anything? Hm, I
have seen presentations by economists that were close to it.

mistakes present in so much software today.

Caveat: while more concrete examples are easier to understand, they are harder to find than more general phrases.

1.5 Scenarios and Stories

When an example considers multiple steps where the underlying object model evolves over time, it becomes a *scenario*. In terms of language Merriam Webster defines scenario the following way:

1. a : an outline or synopsis of a play; especially : a plot outline used by actors of the commedia dell'arte
   b : the libretto of an opera

2. a : screenplay
   b : shooting script

3. a : a sequence of events especially when imagined; especially
   b : an account or synopsis of a possible course of action or events <his scenario for a settlement envisages ... reunification — Selig Harrison>

Point three mentions that it is "a synopsis of a possible course of action" or in 1 "an outline" or "a plot". This is exactly how we are going to understand scenarios: as an outline of steps which happen. We will define a scenario of executing a certain functionality of a system as a series of steps describing a concrete example of the *behavior* of the ready developed system in practice and interaction with potential users. We will use the term *story* synonymously with scenario.[10]

Scenarios will be refined and extended or broken into multiple scenarios in the course of the development project. We will also call the initial scenarios we will get from the users or the stakeholders of the system *user stories* – as the stories the potential users are telling us in the beginning.

To turn the example of the previous section into a scenario we just organize it with some more details. A scenario starts with a concrete title followed by the scenario description consisting of a list of concrete steps describing what is happening in this scenario, cf. Figure 1.8. These steps can describe the concrete status of the system and actions that change the status. Chapter 2 will cover how object diagrams can be derived from the different situations / steps described in a scenario, and Chapter 5 will describe how to derive storyboards from scenarios.

---

[10]Of course we prefer the term story to the term scenario as this is a book on Story Driven Modeling but for getting a good information from a potential user, often the word scenario triggers a better common understanding and leads to "better" stories.

Title: Karli tries to graduate directly and fails.
Description:

1. Initial situation:

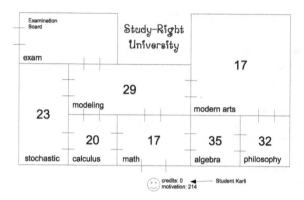

2. The student Karli wants to achieve a degree at the Study-Right University. For a degree we need at the moment 214 credit points and Karli starts with 0 credit points and 214 motivation points. Karli is outside of the university and now enters the university into the math class.

3. Karli attends the math lecture and automatically earns 17 credit points for it and loses at the same time 17 motivation points. Karli has now 17 credit points and 197 motivation points.

4. Karli enters the modeling class.

5. Karli attends the modeling lecture and receives 29 credit points and loses 29 motivation points. Karli has now studied math and modeling and therefore has now 46 credit points and 168 motivation points.

6. Karli tries to enter the examination room. When entering, the examination board asks for the study book containing the number of gained credit points as well as the visited courses. As Karli's number of credit points is smaller than 214 the examination board does not allow graduation and Karli has to leave the university and start over.

Figure 1.8: Scenario: Karli tries to graduate directly and fails.

At the beginning of a project scenarios will usually correspond to user stories. Later on the project may revisit and refine and reorganize scenarios to reflect restructurings of functionalities. In addition you may add scenarios for complex operations within certain components of your system. Such scenarios are not driven by users but they are an aid for team discussions and design.

At the beginning of a project, scenarios will usually correspond to user stories. Later on, the project may revisit and refine and reorganize scenarios to reflect restructurings of functionalities. In addition, you may add scenarios for complex operations within certain components of your system. Such scenarios are not driven by users but they are an aid for team discussions and design.

This chapter has introduced examples and scenarios. Chapter 2 will cover how object diagrams can be derived from the different situations / steps described in a scenario and Chapter 5 will describe how to derive storyboards from scenarios.

1.6 Exercises

Most of the exercises in our book are targeted at groups from 2 to 5 people, maximum. You might give different roles to the members of such groups. Pretend that one member of such a group is the customer. One could be a designer, several could be developers. At least one person should always write a log noting observations and generating keywords for the exercise results.

1.6.1 Abstract vs. Concrete

1.6.1.1 Terms and Definitions

1. Discuss in your group the terms "abstract" and "concrete". Give for each term 10 examples.

2. Create a table with the columns abstract and concrete. Find at least 10 sample pairs and add them to the table.

3. Have a contest on the most concrete example e.g. for a car.

4. Based on the discussions of the first two exercises, create definitions for "abstract", "concrete", and "example". Examples from the book / lecture are not allowed. Write one paragraph about what these terms could have to do with modeling.

1.6.1.2 Chess

Consider the game chess.

1. Give 10 concrete terms describing elements of a chess game.

2. Give 10 abstract terms describing elements of a chess game.

Variations

You can change the number of examples or sample pairs. If done in class, something like 5 for each can be sufficient.

1.6.2   Giving Examples

In this exercise, you have to give examples for situations which can occur in a specific case. For a reference, take a look again at the two examples mentioned in the end of Section 1.4.

1.6.2.1   Mau Mau

Consider the game Mau Mau. We have a deck of 32 cards, consisting of 4 suits (diamonds, hearts, spades, clubs). In each suit we have 7, 8, 9, 10, Jack, Queen, King, and Ace.

We abbreviate these cards like the following

- DA: Ace of diamonds

- S10: 10 of spades

- H7: 7 of hearts

We will assume the following rules in Mau Mau:

- Whoever gets rid of their cards first wins the game.

- In the beginning of a game the deck of cards is shuffled and five cards are dealt (to each player).

- You can play a card, if either its suit corresponds to the suit played before or its value corresponds to the value played before. On a 9 of spades, you can play only another spades or another 9 of a different suit.

- If a player cannot play a card, the player has to draw one card from the drawing stack. If this card can be played, the player may do so or keep the card and pass the turn.

- If the drawing stack is empty, the playing stack excluding the topmost card is shuffled and turned over.

- When a 7 is played the following player has to draw two cards from the drawing stack.

- When a Jack is played, a suit which has to be played next can be announced. On top of a Jack any card of the announced suit (with any value) can be played. A Jack itself can be played on top of any other card (suit and value do not have to match, a Jack can especailly also played on top of another Jack).

- When an 8 is played the following player passes a turn.

- There are plenty of different rules for Mau Mau. Check them out at Wikipedia and add four more to this list.

Give eight examples for Mau Mau situations. They should be reasonably different and target different situations in the game explaining different rules.

1.6.2.2 Battleships

In the two player game Battleships[11], each player plays on two grids. A primary and a recording grid. Each grid is 10x10 fields big. The cells of the grids are identified by letters (A-J) and numbers (1-10). For game setup, each player arranges their ships in secret on their primary grid. Each ship has a specific length and covers this length amount of neighboring cells in one direction (horizontal or vertical) on the grid. The ships are not allowed to overlap. Each player has the same number (and respective lengths) of ships. A usual selection of ships is given in the following table:

ship	size
aircraft carrier	5
battleship	4
submarine	3
destroyer	3
patrol boat	2

After setting up the positions of the ships, the game starts. In alternating turns each player announces a target cell (with letter and number). The other player checks on their primary grid, if this cell is part of a ship. If it is and this hit marks the last part of a ship the player being shot at answers "sunk". If it is not the last cell of a ship, the player answers "hit". If a cell with no ship on it is hit the player answers "water". If a ship was hit or sunk the shooting player gets another shot. If a water field was hit, the turn changes to the other player.

The game ends when all ships of one player have been sunk. The player, who still has ships, wins.

---

[11] The name Battleship® is a trademark by Hasbro, Inc.

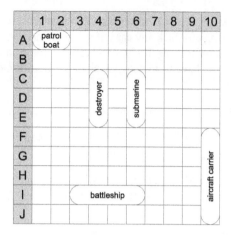

Figure 1.9: Initial primary grid setup in Ruben's Battleships game.

We assume that we want to design a single-player computer version of Battleships. We want to give various examples for in-game situations: The following two answers would be correct.

1. Ruben plays a computer version of the game Battleships. After starting the game and entering his name, he positions his patrol boat on {A1, A2}, his submarine on {C6,D6,E6}, his destroyer on {C4,D4,E4}, his battleship on {I3,I4,I5,I6}, and his aircraft carrier on {F10,G10,H10,I10,J10}. He clicks a button "ready" and the game begins. The initial field is depicted in Figure 1.9.

2. Ruben plays a computer version of the game Battleships. The boats are positioned as mentioned before, his submarine is destroyed. It is Ruben's turn. Ruben has shot at G1, G3, G5 and F2, but he only hit water. He selects F4 and hits. It is his turn again. The chart Ruben makes for keeping track of his hits is shown in Figure 1.10.

Give four more examples for the Battleships game. They should be equal in complexity, length, and concreteness to the just given examples.

1.6.2.3 Mancala

Mancala is a game for two persons. It is played on a Kalah board with 36 pebbles. A Kalah board has six small pits, called houses, on each side for each player. Therefore, there are two rows of six pits each. To the left and the right of these rows are one big pit each, called the Kalah or store. The game starts with 3 pebbles in each house. For the game setup compare Figure 1.11 The game is

	1	2	3	4	5	6	7	8	9	10
A										
B										
C										
D										
E										
F		-		X						
G	-		-		-					
H										
I										
J										

Figure 1.10: Ruben's recording grid for keeping track in his Battleships game.

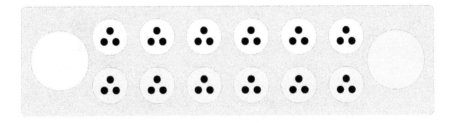

Figure 1.11: Mancala setup.

played in turns. In each turn the player selects one of his six houses containing pebbles and takes all the pebbles from this pit. The player then redistributes the pebbles counter clock-wise into the following pits treating the Kalah as a pit itself. If the last pit ends in the Kalah, the player gains another turn. If the last pit lands in an empty pit, the player can move all the pebbles from the opposite pit (from the other row) into the own Kalah. When the players sit opposite the own Kalah is the one to the right.

As one exercise in this book, we want to develop a multiplayer computer version of the Mancala game.

- To get started play a couple of rounds of Mancala to get familiar!

- While playing write down four examples of different situations.

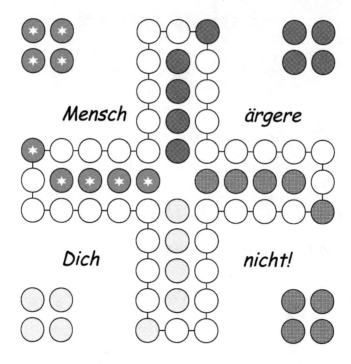

Figure 1.12: "Mensch ärgere dich nicht" game board.

1.6.2.4   Mensch Ärgere Dich Nicht

"Mensch Ärgere dich nicht" is a very similar game to the game played in UK called Ludo, Pacheesi and Trouble or Sorry! in the US, or Pachisi from India. The title literally means "Don't get angry", which usually is not successful as the game is a lot about kicking pegs out of the game to prevent the other players finishing earlier than yourself. A game board is depicted in Figure 1.12.

It can be played with 2-4 players. Each player gets 4 game pawns, which are on the home fields in the corners of the game board in the beginning. The goal is to bring them into the player's home row – the colored fields inside the cross on the board. The colored cross is surrounded by a ring of interconnected game fields. The player's pawns move in clockwise direction via this ring starting on the colored start field. The one field before the start field leads into the "home" row. The first player with all pieces in their "home" row wins the game. Also the turn order is clockwise. On a player's turn, the player throws a dice. If the player has no pawns inside the game (i.e. all on the home fields in their corner) the player can throw up to three times to get a pawn into the game. When the

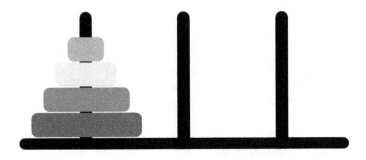

Figure 1.13: Towers of Hanoi

die shows a six, the player can move a pawn onto the start field (if not occupied by their own pawn) and throw the dice once more. The player can advance any of their pawns in the game by the number thrown. If a pawn lands on a pawn of another player the pawn is thrown out of the game and has to be brought in by a six again on the other player's turn.

Consider the game "Mensch ärgere dich nicht": give eight examples for in-game situations.

1.6.2.5 Towers of Hanoi

The "Towers of Hanoi" puzzle usually incorporates three poles and a number of differently sized disks with a hole in the center, cf. Figure 1.13. Usually all the disks are on one of the poles with the smallest disk on top and the largest disk on the bottom. The goal is to move the pile of disks one by one from the current pole to another pole. It is never allowed that a bigger disk lies on a smaller disk. For this exercise let us assume that we have three poles and four disks. The four disks should have different colors blue, red, yellow, and green.

Describe four example situations of an interactive computer version of the depicted Towers of Hanoi game.

1.6.2.6 ATM Money Withdrawal

Consider the software for an automated teller machine (ATM). Take especially a closer look at the parts being triggered when withdrawing money from an account. Give eight examples of situations in this process.

1.6.2.7   Borrowing Electronic Books from a Library

Consider the computer system for borrowing electronic books from a library. Take into account that users wanting to borrow books have eReader software installed. Address the digital rights management issues (how can you allow borrowing a book and getting the rights to read it revoked after a specific time). Give eight examples of situations here.

1.6.2.8   Trouble Ticket System

Lots of service institutions have Trouble Ticket Systems. They record a service request from a person and assign it to one or more employees. Some of these employees manage this service request and some go out to fix the problem recorded in this request. The service request has some different properties like its urgency or its status (indicating if it is still pending or solved). The persons working on the tickets might be out fixing problems at some customers' so we have to record where they are and if they are available. As a reference, take the trouble ticket system of your local phone or Internet provider.

Give twelve examples of different situations here.

1.6.2.9   Webshop

Let us assume that you want to sell a selection of your last amazing products or services via a website. Therefore, you need a webshop. You will have to deal with products, customers (their shipping and billing address), orders, and the workflow from receiving the order to shipping out or delivering the product to the customer.

As a reference think of Amazon, Google Play, or the last online shop, you have used.

Give twelve examples of different situations here.

Notes to instructors

Adding images to the examples is optional. There should be images, if they can clarify the situation. However, if the text is concrete enough, the task should be graded as passed.

Of course, the games can be easily modified with more rules, or the associated example companies for the trouble ticket system, or webshop can easily be modified to create some variance in the tasks.

1.6.3   User Stories / Scenarios

1.6.3.1   Mau Mau

Read the introduction from Section 1.6.2.1. Let's now assume that there are three players: Eero, Ulno, and Artjom. Eero sits right of Ulno, Ulno right of Artjom, and Artjom right of Eero. They play Mau Mau.

As an example consider the following user story:

Title: Eero deals one round of two cards each for Eero, Ulno, and Artjom.

1. Given is the situation as just described and the top of the deck is DK, HK, HQ, HJ, DJ, DA, H10, CA, HA, H7, C7, C8 (DK is top card). Eero holds the deck. Eero is dealer.

2. Eero takes the top two cards and gives them to Ulno, the next two to Artjom, the next two to himself. Each player takes the given cards on their hands.

3. Eero has now on his hand DJ, DA, Artjom has HQ, HJ, and Ulno has DK, HK. The top of the deck shows H10, CA, HA, H7, C7, C8.

Write down user-stories for the following titles:

- Eero deals three more rounds of cards.

- Artjom plays the DJ and announces as new suit clubs.

- The game starts with Ulno playing a seven forcing Artjom to draw.

- Ulno cannot follow suit nor value, draws a card and has to pass.

1.6.3.2   Battleships

Extend the two initial examples and your own four examples from Section 1.6.2.2 into user-stories.

1.6.3.3   Mancala

- Extend the four examples from Section 1.6.2.3 to scenarios.

- Come up with two (conceptually different, not only different names) scenarios for Mancala.

- Give a scenario for trying to make an invalid move and the system rejecting this.

- Give a scenario for describing the last three turns of a Mancala game making the game ending in a tie.

1.6.3.4 Mensch Ärgere Dich Nicht

Extend the eight examples from Section 1.6.2.4 to scenarios.

1.6.3.5 Towers of Hanoi

Extend the four examples from Section 1.6.2.5 to scenarios.

1.6.3.6 ATM Money Withdrawal

Extend the eight examples from Section 1.6.2.6 to scenarios.

1.6.3.7 Borrowing Electronic Books from Library

Extend the eight examples from Section 1.6.2.7 to scenarios.

1.6.3.8 Trouble Ticket System

Extend the twelve examples from Section 1.6.2.8 to scenarios.

1.6.3.9 Webshop

Extend the twelve examples from Section 1.6.2.9 to scenarios.

Chapter 2

Object Diagrams

In this chapter, we will learn how to model an example situation with an object diagram.

Figure 2.1 shows the floor plan of our Study-Right University introduced in Chapter 1. The task is to write a program that computes a course schedule that uses up our motivation points, gathers enough credits, and ends in the exam hall. How would you model this problem? Take some time and add your model into Figure 2.2.

If you have a background in programming languages, you might get the idea to model the floor plan as shown in the listing in Figure 2.3. (If the listing in Figure 2.3 does not tell you anything, you are safe. Just skip the corresponding paragraphs. If this listing from Figure 2.3 is what you were thinking about, you are on the wrong track, keep reading.)

We consider the listing in Figure 2.3 evil. In line 2 of this listing, it uses an array roomCredits of size 8 to model the credits you get in each room. Similarly, in lines 3 through 5 the topics array assigns the topics to the rooms. In lines 6 through 13 we use a two dimensional array to model which room is connected to which other room. For example, the first 1 in line 6 models that room 0 (the math room) is connected to room 1 (the calculus room). Note, two dimensional arrays are somehow the standard way to model graphs. An entry w on index i, j models that node i has an edge with weight w leading to node j. However, if you look at the listing in Figure 2.3, do you really think this is an intuitive model of our floor plan? By the way, there is a bug in the doors array initialization. Can you spot it? As an exercise, try to add a door connecting the algebra room with the modern arts room. Or add another room to the floor plan.

The point we want to make is that arrays are a poor modeling construct. Arrays are an ancient technology from the early 70s. In early imperative program-

31

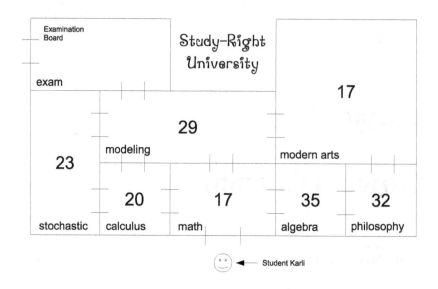

Figure 2.1: Study-Right University floor plan

ming languages, arrays (and structs) were the only means to build data structures. This was then complemented by pointers which actually enable you to build complex structures. But, pointers opened a can of worms with many kinds of tricky problems like memory leaks and dangling references. Actually, the lack of appropriate data structures in imperative programming languages may have been a strong motivation to use functional programming languages like Lisp. Lisp has built-in constructs for lists. Lists might even be nested to form trees. Graphs may easily be modeled as lists of nodes which have lists of neighbors. These built-in lisp data structures are such a great help that people even stand the clumsy syntax of lisp and the hard to understand mathematical style of functional languages. However, these days we have object oriented programming languages available. One contribution of modern object oriented programming languages is that they provide you with elegant means to model complex data structures. Accordingly, we propose to model our Study-Rights University with objects and links between objects, i.e. with *object diagrams*.

Our modeling with scenarios approach proposes to use objects to model the relevant elements of a given problem. For our example, we may introduce objects to model the rooms of our floor plan, the topics, and our student Karli. Relations between the elements may be modeled using links, e.g. we might use connected links to model which rooms are connected and pos links to model the current position of our student Karli. With objects, attributes, and links we

Figure 2.2: Your model here

```
1   public class StudyRight {
2       int[] roomCredits = {17,20,23,29,17,32,35,0};
3       String [] topics = {"math", "calculus",
4       "stochastic","modeling", "modern arts",
5       "philosophy", "algebra", "exam"};
6       int[][] doors = {{0,1,0,1,0,0,1,0},
7                        {1,0,1,1,0,0,0,0},
8                        {0,1,0,1,0,0,0,0},
9                        {1,1,1,0,1,0,0,1},
10                       {0,0,0,1,0,1,0,0},
11                       {0,0,0,0,1,0,1,0},
12                       {1,0,0,0,0,0,0,0},
13                       {0,0,0,1,0,0,0,0}};
14      int[] mandatoryRooms = {1, 3};
15      int studPos = -1;
16      int examPos = 7;
17      float motivation = 214.0;
18      int[] hasMandatoryTopic = {0,0};  . . .
```

Figure 2.3: Evil modeling with arrays

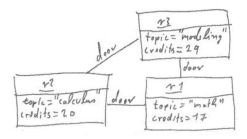

Figure 2.4: Sketching a first object diagram

may build object diagrams that model concrete example situations. This approach is embedded into a modeling approach called *Story Driven Modeling*.

As a start, we might try to model the floor plan of our Study-Right University with objects shown in Figure 2.4. It shows already three *objects*, one for the math room, one for the calculus room, and one for the modeling room. Following the UML notation for object diagrams [16], we use boxes to represent objects. Each object is named, in our case r1, r2, and r3. Object *names* are used e.g. for reference in text or group discussions. According to international conventions, object names start with lower case letters, always. In UML notation, object names are underlined to distinguish objects from other things also drawn as boxes. As you can see, the object boxes are split into two compartments. The upper compartment is the *name compartment*. The lower compartment is the so-called *attribute compartment*. The attribute compartment is used to model simple properties like names, short texts, or numbers. In our case, each room has two *attributes*, one for its topic and one for its credits. Relationships between objects are drawn as lines or arrows. In UML they are called *links*. Object links should be named, e.g. door in our example. Thus, the object diagram in Figure 2.4 shows already three objects for the math, the calculus, and the modeling room of our Study-Right University. We have also modeled the credits of each room and the doors connecting the three rooms to each other.

As an exercise,

- please add the remaining rooms of our Study-Right University to Figure 2.4 now. (Well add at least some rooms and some of their properties and doors.)

- Now let us do some more modeling. How would you add our student Karli to Figure 2.4?

- Please, model the name as an explicit attribute.

- Please model that Karli is in the math room.

- Please model that Karli has passed the math exam and has earned 17 credits.

Great, you have done your first Object Oriented Modeling. Perhaps you might compare your object oriented model with the model of the listing in Figure 2.3, now. Which one do you reckon as more intuitive? Where would you spot a wrong door more easily? How difficult is it to add e.g. a new door connecting the algebra room with the modern arts room?

Well, to be honest, while our object diagram is quite intuitive, the model of the listing in Figure 2.3 has the advantage of being closer to the implementation. To achieve an implementation, too, we will do some additional steps in the next sections.

Some final remarks. The model we have developed in Figure 2.4 is not the one and only truly right model for our example problem. In fact, there are many design alternatives. For example, we might have modeled the doors of our Study-Right University with explicit door objects instead of the simple door links, cf. Figure 2.5. Deciding between an explicit object and a plain link is a fairly typical design tradeoff. Generally, both solutions work well and thus both are good choices. Plain links are somewhat easier to handle and require somewhat less runtime memory. However, explicit objects may carry additional attributes as e.g. whether a door is open or closed. In addition, an explicit door object would facilitate to model the entrance and exit doors of our Study-Right University in the math and the exam room, respectively. Since a plain link always needs a source and a target object, modeling a door to the outside is hard with plain links, only. On the other hand, if we use explicit door objects, such an explicit door object usually has two rooms attached to it. However, the entrance and exit doors have only one room attached to it. Thus, the entrance and exit doors are exceptional cases independent from our modeling. Another rule of thumb for creating object diagrams is to identify the nouns of the scenario and turn them into objects. In our intial situation in our scenario we have the floor plan of the Study-Right University (Figure 2.1). Possible nouns, we can extract from here

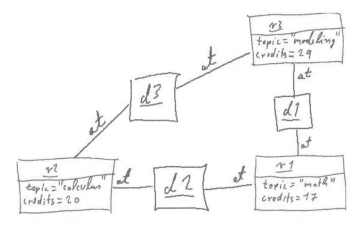

Figure 2.5: Alternative model with explicit door objects

are Karli and the various room names like math or calculus, which are elements we just used in our first object diagrams.

As another example, in Figure 2.4 we model the topic taught in a room as a string attribute of that room. We might also have chosen to use explicit objects for the topics. Explicit topic objects would e.g. allow student objects to refer to the topics they have already completed. In the model of Figure 2.4 we might use a visited link from e.g. the object representing our student Karli to the room object r1. However, such a visited link would need to be redirected if a topic moves from one room to another. Using explicit topic objects, a topic might have a link to the room where it is taught and for moving a topic we would only need to redirect this link. In addition, we might want to introduce explicit exam objects that model that a student has mastered a certain topic or has visited a certain room. Such exam objects might be organized as a linked list in order to model the route that a student took through the university.

Confronted with so many modeling alternatives, how should we decide on the best one? How can we tell if a model is good or bad? Frankly speaking, there is no simple answer to this question. Generally, a model is good if it serves its *purpose* well. The purpose of a model is to ease the implementation of the desired program. A good model has all the information at hand that you need during the implementation of a certain functionality. Unfortunately, it is some-what hard to already know at modeling time which information details you will need in later implementation steps. The answer to this problem is *iterative development*. This means, you start with a certain functionality. You develop an object model that fits for that functionality, then you implement that functionality. During implementation you might have ideas for improving your object model in order to facilitate things. Do this. Once you are done with a functionality, go for the next. Check whether your model already works for the new functionality, extend and adapt it otherwise. Implement the new functionality and extend and adapt your model again, when appropriate. And so on. Such an iterative approach has the problem that a later change to the model might affect a previous implementation. However, due to our experience, usually the required model changes do not affect existing implementation in an unbearable way and the iterative approach works smoothly. Perhaps, this depends a little bit on the experience of the modeler. The general message is: models are not done in a single shot. If something is not optimal in the first attempt, you get chances for improvement later when you have better knowledge of requirements and implementation needs.

Another important property of a good model is that it is *intuitive*. Intuitive means, everybody understands it easily and everybody finds each piece of information where they expect it. It is modeled in a way they would have modeled it themselves. During implementation, the object model serves as a means for orientation. If, for example, you have to sum up all credits offered by our example university, it is important to know how this information is modeled and where it is stored. To achieve a common understanding, an object model and its design alternatives should be discussed in team meetings with the people that are going to work with it. If there is a design trade-off that is hard for you to decide, you may ask the team members to vote for what the majority likes more. If there is a good argument for one alternative this will come up during the discussion and the team members will vote for it. If the alternatives are equally good, the choice probably does not matter or it will be revised during later steps anyhow. Asking the team members for their vote at least achieves that the majority of the team members will find the information as they would have modeled it themselves, and even the others will know how it has been modeled. Thus, such team discussions and votes achieve a lot of mutual understanding. Finally, the development team will work with the model and rely on it for building the implementation. Therefore, the development team should feel comfortable with the model. This is achieved by involving the team in the modeling activities.

There is one issue where we give clear modeling advice: sometimes, somebody might have the idea to store just a list of names of completed topics inside the student object. This is evil. Such an evil variant and a corresponding correct one is depicted in Figure 2.6. Using names or any other kind of id instead of an explicit reference, link, pointer between objects is a well known source of change anomalies causing runtime failures and bugs. If there happens to be a typo in a topic name and therefore someone changes the name, all students that have already completed that topic still use the old spelling to refer to it. Either you update all student records (with a high likelihood to miss some) or you introduce aliases i.e. the old name still works in identifying the topic. This increases the likelihood of name clashes. Name clashes are another typical source of bugs

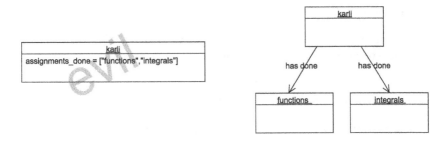

Figure 2.6: Evil and correct way to refer to objects.

caused by the usage of names or simple ids. It is just hard to guarantee that no two different topics have the same name. Having one name referring to two different things is a direct way to malfunction. Thus, we recommend links instead of names whenever possible.

2.1 Exercises

2.1.1 Mau Mau

- Draw object diagrams for the start situation and for the situations after each step of each user story built for the Mau Mau exercise in Section 1.6.3.1.

- Specify all hands!

As an example, let us assume the small user story presented in 1.6.3.1. For the given task, we would need one object diagram for the start situation after point 1. In point 2, we need three diagrams: one for Ulno received cards, one for Artjom received cards, one for Eero received cards (maybe a fourth for showing that players picked up their cards). The last situation is already the end situation described in point 3. Therefore, we would expect four or five object diagrams as a solution for this user story.

2.1.2 Battleship

- Draw object diagrams for the start situation and for the situations after each step of each user story built for the Battleship exercise in Section 1.6.3.2. Use only a small, but relevant section of the respective board.

2.1.3   Mancala

- Draw object diagrams for the start situation and for the situations after each step of each user story built for the Mancala exercise in Section 1.6.3.3.

2.1.4   Mensch Ärgere Dich Nicht

- Draw object diagrams for the start situation and for the situations after each step of each user story built for the Mensch ärgere dich nicht exercise in Section 1.6.3.4.

- Most of the time, you will need only a small part of the overall board to be represented

2.1.5   Towers of Hanoi

- Create an object diagram for the initial setup of the game, showing all disks and poles.

- Create an object diagram showing the situation after moving the first disk.

- Create object diagrams for the next three turns.

2.1.6   ATM Money Withdrawal

- Draw object diagrams for the start situation and for the situations after each step of each user story built for the ATM money withdrawal exercise in Section 1.6.3.6.

2.1.7   Borrowing Electronic Books from Library

- Draw object diagrams for the start situation and for the situations after each step of each user story built for the borrowing electronic books from library exercise in Section 1.6.3.7.

2.1.8   Trouble Ticket System

- Draw object diagrams for the start situation and for the situations after each step of each user story built for the trouble ticket system exercise in Section 1.6.3.8.

2.1.9 Webshop

- Draw object diagrams for the start situation and for the situations after each step of each user story built for the webshop exercise in Section 1.6.3.8.

Chapter 3

From Objects to Classes

3.1 Introduction

So far, we have sketched the first object model for our problem, i.e. for the Study-Right University. This is already good, but our target is to program the Study-Right University solver. In order to derive a program from the object model, the first step is the derivation of the class structure that implements the object model. This class structure will be represented by a UML class diagram[1]. The development of the first class diagram for a new application is usually a challenging task. An experienced programmer is needed to come up with a reasonable class diagram for a non trivial application. Unfortunately, it is very hard to teach experience, especially in a textbook. It is also hard to gain such experience other than by going through a lot of painful failures until you develop the right skills. Even if you have done this, and you come up with good class diagrams for a problem, your teammates will not get the idea behind your design and will start a lot of fruitless discussion with you. The problem here is that class diagrams model only the static structure of programs. Class diagrams tell you which classes are used to realize your program and how these classes use each other. In addition, a class diagram may tell you, which features may possibly be contained in your object structures. However, class diagrams tell you very little about how these features will be used at runtime to represent certain aspects of your problem state. Thus, even if you come up with a splendid class diagram design, it will not provide you with the most important information on your runtime system states and how they evolve over time.

We have attended numerous design meetings, where people tried to discuss design aspects with the help of class diagrams. Frequently, the discussion be-

---

[1]We will learn about class diagrams by simply using them. For a systematic introduction and complete features, see [16]

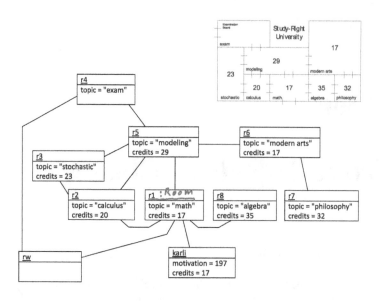

Figure 3.1: Assigning types to objects

comes heated and people start shouting at each other. Usually, the problem is a misunderstanding of ideas. From our experience, such misunderstandings arise from the usage of class diagrams instead of object diagrams or storyboards. Because class diagrams show only static program structure, they are not suitable for the discussion of runtime behavior. Thus, misunderstandings are provoked. Therefore, we always use object diagrams and storyboards for design discussions.

3.2 Deriving Class Diagrams from Object Diagrams

Although class diagrams do not work for design discussions, they are valuable for documenting the results of design discussions and as input for the implementation phase. Thus, once we have created a number of object diagrams modeling certain aspects of our application, we may start to derive a class diagram from the object diagrams. Fortunately, the derivation of the part of the class diagram that realizes the runtime object structures is quite straightforward and easy to learn.

As an example, consider Figure 3.1 showing a more elaborated object diagram modeling our Study-Right University. We start by assigning types to objects. This can be done in a team discussion on a whiteboard. To allow this, we have left justified the object names and left space for the addition of type names behind the object names. Let us start with object r1 in the center of Figure 3.1. Object r1 models room 17 of our Study-Right University (where math is taught). Thus, you and your team mates may easily agree to introduce e.g. the type Room for this object. Note, any other name like Space, Area, or LectureHall would have done the job, either. Note, due to international conventions, type and class names start with capital letters while object names start with lower case letters. Stick to it. Note, in UML object diagrams the name of objects and the colon and the type name are completely underlined. This is necessary to distinguish objects from classes. Actually, the colon already suffices to distinguish an object from a class. However, sometimes we use objects without giving the type. Therefore, underlining the whole object name line is taken seriously in UML (i.e. doing wrong you will lose points in grading).

Once you have decided on the type of object r1 you may go through the object diagram of Figure 3.1 and look for similar objects. Objects r2, r8, r7, r3, r5, and r6 look pretty similar to object r1 and thus we might also assign type Room to these objects. You might do so using a pencil on Figure 3.1.

Next, decide on the type of the karli object. How do you like Student? Add your choice to Figure 3.1. (Do not forget to underline the whole name line.)

As you might have noticed, we have skipped object r4. Object r4 represents the exam room. This room is somewhat different from the other rooms. In Figure 3.1 we use attribute topic with value "exam" to mark the room as examination room. However, "exam" is not really a study topic. While you might still be ready to accept this, the exam room is the only room that has no credits attached to it. Thus, there are good reasons to consider object r4 as a different kind of room and to introduce a new type for it, e.g. type ExamRoom. This might allow you to drop the topic attribute as the purpose of the room is now clear from its type. If we look closer on object r4 and on the other Room objects, you might notice that all the Room objects have a common feature: rooms may have doors to other rooms. In our example this is represented by the links between objects.

As the ExamRoom object r4 and the normal Room objects equally may be source or target of such a link, you may want to declare this feature only once. For this you can either just accept the fact that ExamRoom teaches as subject "exam" with 0 credits or you use a concept called inheritance. If you have not heard about inheritance before, mark the following paragraph and just skip over to the next for the moment. Come back here, when you have encountered or tried out inheritance. For the flow of the book it is not important. You can practice Story Driven Modeling without the concept of inheritance.

However, as you did not skip this paragraph, you may achieve the re-use of having doors between Room objects in making the link declaration a part of class ExamRoom and by letting class Room inherit from class ExamRoom. Our students generally do not feel comfortable with making a usual Room class a subclass of a special ExamRoom class. Thus, frequently this discussion leads to the proposal to factor out the link property into a new common superclass of these two types. Because we have already used the general term room for the lecture halls, we might use an even more general name like Space for the new superclass. Alternatively, we might change our Room class to a more specific term like LectureHall and then use Room for the new superclass. If we do so, we need to change the types of our lecture hall objects in Figure 3.1, accordingly. This inheritance design uses many classes that will need to be implemented. Thus this design violates the goal of a model to simplify implementation. On the other hand this design meets the expectation of many programmers that are used to object oriented inheritance. Therefore, it meets the goal of being intuitive.

While the just described optional design is an interesting case for the usage of object oriented inheritance, you might alternatively also go for a simpler class structure using one class Room for both, for the lecture halls and for the examination room. Going for this option means that each room has the topic and the credits property. While we may use a special topic value like "exam" to distinguish the examination room from the lecture halls, using the credits property within the examination room makes no sense. Still, this may be resolved by assigning credits = 0 to the examination room. This design alternative uses only one class and therefore is simpler. On the other hand, it stresses the intuition of the team members a little bit to think of the examination room as a lecture hall with topic "exam" and zero credits. In addition, during the implementation phase the special value for the topic property will most likely result in if statements handling this special case. Thus, the simple design also causes some code complexity which is against the purpose of a model. You may decide for yourself whether the solution using inheritance or the simple solution is harder to implement.

As a third alternative, we might again consider to separate the courses from the rooms. This means, we might introduce explicit course objects having the topic and the credits properties. Course objects are then attached to rooms. This would allow to move topics from room to room, easily. The examination room is then just a room that has no course attached to it. This is again a pretty intuitive design. Furthermore, we could introduce a certain subclass of either Room or Course for Exam to strongly indicate it, but we strongly discourage using inheritance unless you know exactly what you are doing. Another less complex, but also type safe variant is to use a boolean attribute isExamRoom. See Figure 3.2 for various modeling alternatives. For the last alternative, you could either implicitly model that no associated course means the room is the exam room, or, if

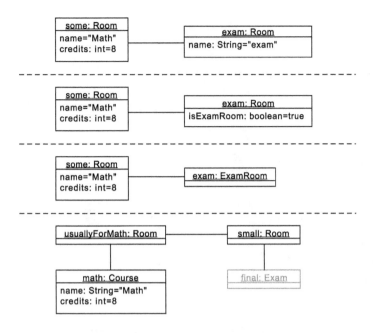

Figure 3.2: Modeling alternatives for rooms, credits and the exam

you expect to have multiple rooms without courses, use a marker object of type Exam (which might be a subclass of course to reuse the association). This design alternative comes for the costs of an additional course class that we will most likely need anyhow. Still our code will need if statements to handle the special case of the examination room having no course attached to it. In addition, the general task of the Study-Right University solver is to find a route through the rooms that collects enough credits without losing too much motivation. This task becomes more complicated if our design allows that courses may move to other rooms while a student is studying.

As you can see, assigning types to our objects may yet again raise interesting design discussions. However, with the help of object diagrams, it is much easier to solve these issues since object diagrams allow us to discuss the representation of problem aspects at runtime. Therefore, it is somewhat easier to judge the effects of design decisions and their influence on the purpose of an object model: to ease implementation and to meet intuition. Having a team discussion on these aspects (with the help of object diagrams) will foster common understanding of the design and thus the goal of an intuitive model. Similarly, the team members will most likely be able to judge the implementation efforts required by the dif-

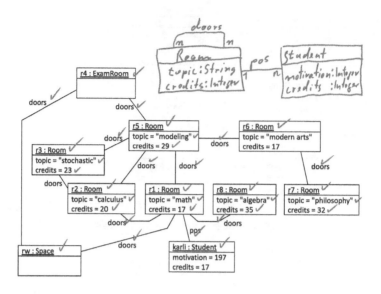

Figure 3.3: Deriving a UML class diagram

ferent design decisions more easily with the help of their intuitive understanding of the common model.

Let us come back to the task of deriving the class structure that we will use to implement our Study-Right University solver. As mentioned in the beginning of this section, we will use a UML class diagram to draw the program structure. Thus, we should start doing so. Figure 3.3 shows the object diagram for our Study-Right University again, now with types attached to objects. In addition, we have attached types to links. And we draw the class diagram in the upper right corner. The figure actually shows the end result of this step. However, we imagine that we start without the handwritten notes and now first discuss the drawing of the Room class.

Therefore, to derive a class diagram from an object diagram, one possible method is to do the following: Start assigning types to objects (e.g. type Room to r1) and keep an eye on the class diagram and compare if the corresponding class is already present (e.g. when adding a type to the next room like r2). If not, add a new class to the class diagram (e.g. when assigning a type to karli). In UML a class is drawn as a box with the class name in it near to the top. In contrast to objects, the class name is not underlined and per convention, the class name starts with an upper case letter. We propose to put a check mark next to or on

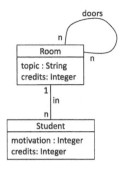

Figure 3.4: Deriving a UML class diagram

top of each object that has got a type (and the type has become part of the class diagram). Thereby, we ensure to cover all parts of the object diagram.

Next we deal with properties. For each property of an object, we introduce an attribute declaration in the corresponding class. For example the topic = "math" property of object r1 (and of the other Room objects) is represented by the topic : String attribute declaration within the box of class Room. Note, for the attribute declaration we need an attribute type which is a basic type like String or Integer or Boolean. Note, within a class box, the class name and the attribute declaration compartment are separated by a horizontal line. This line must not be confused with the underlining of the object name in an object box. (Which might easily happen in a hand drawing. Also here points might not be given.) Again, we put a check mark next to the object attribute values that are covered by attribute declarations in the class diagram to ensure full coverage.

A somewhat more tricky issue are the links between objects. Links in the object diagram are mapped to associations between the corresponding classes in the class diagrams. Associations are drawn as lines between classes with an association name close to the line. As an example consider the pos link between objects karli and r1. This link creates a pos association between the corresponding classes Student and Space, cf. Figure 3.3. For associations one needs also to provide cardinalities. For deciding on cardinalities, you have to ask yourself the question "at how many spaces may a student be at a given time" resulting in the 1 at the association end close to class Space. Similarly, the question "how many students may stay at one place at a given time" may result in the answer n, i.e. any number. (Note, instead of n, an asterisk * is also commonly used.) We also use the check mark at the links to indicate that a link is covered by our association in the class diagram.

3.3   About Cardinalities

In the example above, we use cardinalities that only provide upper bounds for the association ends. Generally, UML allows to provide also lower bounds. Thus, you might use the cardinality 0..1 or 1..1 for the left end of the pos association in Figure 3.3. In our example, this lower cardinality would describe the minimal number of Room objects attached to a given Student object at a given time.

In the following, we will now reason why it does not make sense to use 1..1 or even a higher number as a lower bound nor a fixed number (like 4 for tires of a car or 32 for number of playing cards) as an upper bound. This will reference some very specifics of Java as well as inheritance. For a new reader with little programming experience we suggest to fast forward directly to the exercises or the start of the next chapter and therefore also skip Section 3.4. Make sure however to note down that the pos link has to be able to exist between each of the lecture halls and the student as well as between the exam room and the student. If these are of the same type as modeled in Figure 3.3, this is no problem and we obtain the class diagram with cardinalities depicted in Figure 3.4.

If we a fixed lower cardinality of 1, it would mean that a student is always attached to a space. In principle this is a valuable information that is worth to be added to the class diagram. A lower cardinality of 1 for the pos association would mean that one may at any time ask students for their position with the guarantee that this query results in a valid Space object. Thus, during implementation we would not need to check for null pointer results. Great.

Unfortunately, relying on such guarantees for lower cardinalities is a frequent source of program crashes. Actually, in a programming language like Java, it is pretty hard to guarantee a lower cardinality "at any time". At least after creating an object during the execution of the constructor, for some instructions the attribute is not yet initialized. In unlucky cases, these instructions call a method. This method may later be changed to call yet another method passing the object under construction as a parameter. The called method may have been written under the assumption that the passed object has been initialized properly, i.e. that the student has a pos. Using this uninitialized pos will lead to a crash. Note also, before the constructor of the current class is executed, the constructors of its superclasses are executed. These may invoke methods that may be overwritten by the current class. This may again call a method that assumes that the object is properly initialized, leading again to a crash. See Listing 3.1 and its output in Listing 3.2 for an example of such a situation in code: try to track down the reason why null appears in the output, although we enforce all string attributes to be non-null by requiring them in the constructors and the override implementation of toString() is clearly correct. To avoid these problems, it is a common practice not to rely on lower cardinalities but to check a pointer always before you dereference it[2]. We conclude that the lower cardinality has merely no advantage for the implementation and advise to use no other lower bounds than 0.

Next, to guarantee that a student always has a pos, you might require that an initial Space object is passed as a parameter to the constructor of class Student. Constructors with mandatory parameters are somewhat uncomfortable for later programming. In our case you need a Space object to construct a Student object. This is a problem if e.g. you want to use some kind of Factory design pattern[3] to construct the Student object in one subsystem while Space objects are handled in another subsystem. Thus, instead of easing the implementation, a design using lower cardinalities may complicate the implementation i.e. violate the goal of modeling.

In the other direction, our pos association uses cardinality n, i.e. a Space may have any number of students. In many cases, one may want to express an exact number or an upper limit for such to-many associations. For example, a car might be modeled to have exactly 4 wheels or a card deck might have exactly 32 cards or a course should not have more than 42 students. However, an exact cardinality number imposes a lower cardinality bound and we have just discussed this. What is about upper cardinality bounds?

In contrast to lower bounds, upper bounds are easy to enforce in programming languages like Java. You encapsulate the addition to the to-many association in a method and this method throws an exception if the upper bound is violated. In addition, such upper bounds might meet your intuition and thus ease the understanding of the design. Good.

Well, in ancient times upper cardinalities have been used to determine the sizes of arrays used to implement to-many associations. Arrays have been considered to be very efficient implementations of to-many associations or more generally of collections. While this holds to a certain extent, old-fashioned arrays have a static size. Static size means, e.g. a room has a fixed capacity of 42 students. Even if only some students are in the room, the full array size is allocated. Thus, in frequent cases static arrays waste memory. In addition, in some cases a 43rd student may show up which cannot be stored due to capacity restrictions, i.e. in some cases the static array that wastes so much memory is still too small. To overcome these problems modern programming languages like Java provide dynamic collections that may shrink and grow over time to fit their usage. Such dynamic collections help to avoid unnecessary memory consumption and are at the same time able to deal with unannounced large numbers of entries. For such modern dynamic collections, an upper association cardinality

---

[2] Another lesson learned is: do not put initialization code in constructors when using inheritance, use separate init methods instead.

[3] We will not elaborate very deeply on design patterns in this book and forward the interested reader to the classic book for design patterns by the Gang of Four [26].

```
 1   public class Address {
 2
 3     String street; // street address, name ommitted
 4     String zipTown; // postal code + city/town/
            locality
 5
 6     public Address(String street , String zipTown) {
 7       this.street = street;
 8       this.zipTown = zipTown;
 9       System.out.println("new_Address_" + this + "_
            created_for_DB.");
10     }
11
12     public String toString() {
13       return street + "|" + zipTown;
14     }
15
16     public static void main(String[] args) {
17       Address adr = new Address("Main_St._1", "
            09101_Sao_Paulo");
18       Address iadr = new InternationalAddress(
19           "Main_St._1", "09101_Sao_Paulo", "Brazil"
              );
20       System.out.print("Oops,_again:_" + iadr);
21     }
22   }
23
24   class InternationalAddress extends Address {
25
26     String country;
27
28     public InternationalAddress(String str , String
            zt , String country) {
29       super(str , zt);
30       this.country = country;
31     }
32
33     public String toString() {
34       return super.toString() + "|" + country;
35     }
36   }
```

Listing 3.1: Example: lower cardinalities and constructors clash

```
1  new  Adress  "Main  St.  1I09101  Sao  Paulo"  created
      for  database.
2  new  Adress  "Main  St.  1I09101  Sao  PauloInull"
      created  for  database.
3  Oops,  again:  Main  St.  1I09101  Sao  PauloIBrazil
```
Listing 3.2: Console output of code in Listing 3.1

is no major help or requirement. Enforcing an upper cardinality for a dynamic collection would just restrict the offered flexibility. Thus, we rarely use limited upper cardinalities.

3.4 Correct Use of Inheritance

Let us come back to the derivation of class diagrams from object diagrams in our example. In Figure 3.3 we have not yet handled the doors links. The doors links are a special case: a doors link usually starts from a Room object and ends in a Room object. Thus, the corresponding association starts at class Room and ends in class Room, cf. Figure 3.4. Obviously, a given room might have multiple doors leading to neighbor rooms, thus we use cardinality n. However, the doors association shown in Figure 3.4 does not properly reflect the object diagram of Figure 3.3. In Figure 3.3 there is a doors link connecting object r4 and r5. The problem is that r4 is of type ExamRoom. To implement such a doors link, we need a doors association connecting class ExamRoom and class Room. Similarly, the doors link between objects r4 and rw requires a doors association between classes ExamRoom and Space. To cover all these different cases, we could introduce an inheritance hierarchy as shown in Figure 3.5 and introduce the doors association as self-association from class Space to class Space. Then the classes ExamRoom and Room inherit the property to have a doors association and all doors links in Figure 3.3 could be mapped to this doors association.

An alternative modeling would assign the type Room to the examination room r4 and even to the "real world" object rw. This would lead to the situation that these objects would have a topic and a credits attribute value. While this might be somewhat counter intuitive, it is pretty easy to find appropriate dummy values for these attributes. Using such dummy values for the attributes allows us to use a common type Room instead of the class hierarchy of Figure 3.3. Thus, our class diagram and thus the program structure and thus the implementation becomes accordingly simpler as shown in Figure 3.4.

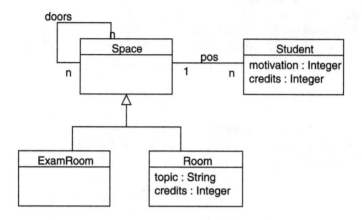

Figure 3.5: Deriving a UML class diagram

3.5 Exercises

3.5.1 Mau Mau

- Derive a class diagram from the objects diagrams created in exercise 2.1.1.

- For each association, explain the cardinalities you have chosen.

3.5.2 Battleships

- Derive a class diagram from the objects diagrams created in exercise 2.1.2.

- For each association, explain the cardinalities you have chosen.

3.5.3 Mancala

- Derive a class diagram from the objects diagrams created in exercise 2.1.3.

- For each association, explain the cardinalities you have chosen.

3.5.4 Mensch Ärgere Dich Nicht

- Derive a class diagram from the objects diagrams created in exercise 2.1.4.

- For each association, explain the cardinalities you have chosen.

3.5.5 Towers of Hanoi

- Derive a class diagram from the objects diagrams created in exercise 2.1.5.

- For each association, explain the cardinalities you have chosen.

- Draw a new object diagram that conforms to your class diagram and where two posts have two disks, each.

3.5.6 ATM Money Withdrawal

- Derive a class diagram from the objects diagrams created in exercise 2.1.6.

- For each association, explain the cardinalities you have chosen.

3.5.7 Borrowing Electronic Books from Library

- Derive a class diagram from the objects diagrams created in exercise 2.1.7.

- For each association, explain the cardinalities you have chosen.

3.5.8 Trouble Ticket System

- Derive a class diagram from the objects diagrams created in exercise 2.1.8.

- For each association, explain the cardinalities you have chosen.

3.5.9 Webshop

- Derive a class diagram from the objects diagrams created in exercise 2.1.9.

- For each association, explain the cardinalities you have chosen.

3.5.10 Matching

Which object diagrams from Figure 3.7 conform to the class diagram given in Figure 3.6?

- Mark the object diagrams in that are allowed.

- For the forbidden object diagrams, mark the invalid elements.

- Add the missing link names to the object diagrams where possible.

- Draw an object diagram that conforms to the class diagram of Figure 3.6 and that has one B that contains four Ds where each D has one C.

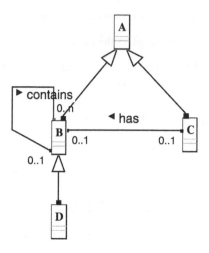

Figure 3.6: Generic class diagram

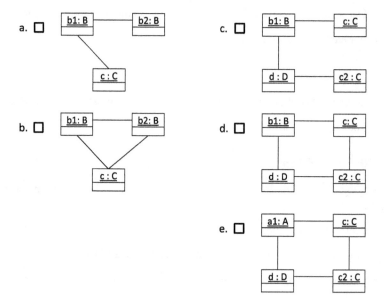

Figure 3.7: Corresponding object diagrams

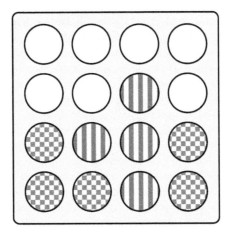

Figure 3.8: Connect Four Game

3.5.11 Deriving Object- and Class Diagrams

The following situation is given:

On a table there are a number of things: a pencil, a pen, and a sheet of paper. Both writing tools write in black color. The paper sheet is not wrinkled. All things belong to Paul.

- Draw an object diagram modeling the above situation. Try to address all object properties, either by attributes or by links.

- Derive a class diagram from your object diagram. Discuss the usage of inheritance for the various things on the table.

3.5.12 Connect Four Game

We want to program the Connect Four[4] game. For simplicity reasons, the game board shall provide just four by four fields. The game is for two players. Each player has eight stones either all red (checkerboard pattern) or all green (striped). In alternating turns, each player puts one stone in one column with at least one vacant field. The stone drops to the bottom. As soon as one player has 4 stones in one row, column, or diagonal this players wins.

Now Bob is playing Connect Four with Alice, cf. Figure 3.8. Bob owns the red stones, Alice's owns the green stones.

- Draw an object diagram that reflects the situation depicted in Figure 3.8. Fields shall be represented as objects.

---

[4]The name Connect Four® is a trademark by Hasbro, Inc.

- Derive a class diagram from the object diagram developed in the previous step. Discuss the association cardinalities.

Chapter 4

Translating Diagrams to Java Code

So far we have learned to look into example situations and scenarios and to derive object diagrams that model how situations shall be represented within our computer. From the object diagrams we derive class diagrams that model how our program shall be structured to be able to deal with the desired objects. With the help of these diagrams we will now implement the classes that will allow us to deal with the desired objects and we will learn how to use this implementation to work with object structures at runtime.

Source code can be derived from class diagrams and object diagrams (and later from storyboards and story diagrams) in several ways:

1. Implementing the modeled structures in a programming language of your choice, manually. This can be done in a systematic way with guidelines. In order to create objects, which are runtime structures, statically typed programming languages like Java require types in form of class definitions. Deriving the structural code (classes, their references and method declarations) is part of this chapter. Once we have implemented classes, we can create object patterns by instantiating objects, which will be covered in Section 4.2.

2. Using a Code generator. There are numerous tools that allow you to draw a UML class diagram and then generate e.g. Java classes from such diagrams. However, there are dramatic differences in the quality of the generated code especially if it comes to the implementation of bidirectional associations. This book proposes to use the Fujaba tool [5], SDMLib [10], or the UML Lab tool [12] for this purpose.

3. Another possibility to create running programs out of your diagram artifacts is not covered by this book, but we want to mention its existence
and properties here: diagrams could be interpreted, or translated into other
textual forms than directly executable code. For example, an XML serialization of UML models could be either interpreted by a UML tool,
or could be directly executed by some framework code, that creates objects and even their type information at runtime. This approach is usually
slower [1] or more complex than translating diagrams directly into code. In
the following, we will just discuss the translation of diagram types used in
this book to Java code with just dependencies to the JDK classes.

4.1   Class Diagrams to Java Code

Translating class diagrams to Java code is a task usually performed by a code
generator. In this chapter, we will take a deeper look how this is systematically
done and do the translation manually. We start with a simple class, not containing
any attributes or methods. The class Student will be translated to the following
basic code block within a file named Student.java:

```
              ┌─────────────────────┐
              │      Student         │
              ├─────────────────────┤
              └─────────────────────┘
```

```
public class Student
{
}
```

Now we add the name attribute to the Student class. An attribute gets translated to a member variable and its corresponding accessors. The access methods,
one getter and one setter, encapsulate the name field and make sure that the setter is the one and only central point where the name field is assigned. Compared
to directly accessible public fields, inconsistencies are unlikely. The translated
code looks like this:

```
              ┌─────────────────────┐
              │      Student         │
              ├─────────────────────┤
              │    name : String     │
              └─────────────────────┘
```

---

[1] In certain cases, interpreting could be faster, as it is not bound to static/compile time structures
and optimizations can be applied at runtime.

```java
public class Student
{
    private String name;

    public void setName(String name)
    {
        this.name = name;
    }

    public String getName()
    {
        return name;
    }
}
```

The setter can also be used to perform certain checks on the parameter value, so an alternative looks like this:

```java
public void setName(String name)
{
    if (name == null)
    {
        throw new IllegalArgumentException(
            "Student name must not be null!");
    }
    this.name = name;
}
```

Translating associations is more complex, let's start with a simple example:

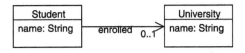

This is simply a reference from a student to the corresponding university, so the Student class gets an appropriate field and accessor methods. Class University remains unchanged:

```java
public class Student
{
    private University university;

    public void setUniversity(University
        university)
```

```
{
        this.university = university;
}

public University getUniversity()
{
        return university;
}

        ...

}
```

A unidirectional to-many association in the reverse direction cannot be translated with a simple reference. It requires a container object, something that can hold *multiple* references to the other association end. Such a container class is usually part of your programming language API. At simplest, an array will do the job, but lacks type safety and we still have to deal with the limited capacity of such. So, we use java.util.LinkedHashSet[2]. The following example shows an one-to-many association between Student and Course.

A course refers to multiple students. The corresponding code will not feature a get/set method pair, instead we use an add method to add a new student to the course and a remove method to remove a student from the course and a get method to get the set of students that attend the course:

```
import java.util.LinkedHashSet;

public class Course
{

        private LinkedHashSet<Student> students
            = new LinkedHashSet<Student>();

        public void addStudent(Student student)
        {
                students.add(student);
```

---

[2]Other container classes are feasible as well, but we use LinkedHashSet because it preserves addition order and still retains set semantic.

```
    }

    public void removeStudent(Student student)
    {
        students.remove(student);
    }

    public LinkedHashSet<Student> getStudents()
    {
        return students;
    }
}
```

Although the accessor methods aim for protecting the container object from arbitrary outside modifications, this goal is not reached. Possible callers can still do the following:

```
Course course = ...;
course.getStudents().clear();
// now all student references are gone
course.getStudents().add(new EvilStudent());
// possible parameter check of addStudent()
    circumvented!
```

Thus, we recommend the following accessor methods to have a robust implementation:

```
import java.util.Collections;
import java.util.LinkedHashSet;
import java.util.Set;

public class Course
{

    private Set<Student> students
        = new LinkedHashSet<Student>();

    public boolean addStudent(Student student)
    {
        // you might want to check the parameter
            here
        return students.add(student);
    }
```

```
public boolean removeStudent(Student student)
{
    return students.remove(student);
}

// don't expose the concrete container class
public Set<Student> getStudents()
{
    return Collections.unmodifiableSet(
        students);
}
}
```

Note that we just use `java.util.Set<Student>` in the public interface, which is sufficient and allows changing the concrete container class later in a simple way. As explained above, `getStudents()` just returns a readable set and forbids direct modifications like `clear()` or `add(...)`, but allows read access, e.g. `getStudents().size()`.

4.1.1   Bidirectional Associations: Managing Referential Integrity

So far we discussed just unidirectional associations. Bidirectional associations, the more common case, require references on both ends of the association, meaning that both classes should have a member field, pointing to an instance of the opposite class. First, let us have a look at a bidirectional one-to-one association, see top of Figure 4.1.

This example allows only one course in one lecture hall at one time, so we use a one-to-one association here. Class `LectureHall` has a reference to `course` and class `Course` has a reference to its associated lecture hall. As both references belong to the same association, we have to ensure that they are pointing to the opposite object. It would be an inconsistent implementation state, when a course refers lecture hall, but this lecture hall instance refers to a completely different course or no instance at all. We need some code that manages the references to match, and the best place to do so is in the reference-encapsulating setter access method. We have to write code for both classes. This looks similar to the unidirectional case, but now also manages the back-reference. `LectureHall` and `Course` are depicted next to each other to see the back-reference management in Figure 4.1.

```
LectureHall                              Course
                0..1  lectureHall  course  0..1
```

```java
public class LectureHall                 public class Course
{                                        {
    private Course course;
                                             private LectureHall
    public void setCourse(Course                 lectureHall;
        course)
    {                                        public void setLectureHall(
        if (this.course !=                       LectureHall lectureHall)
            course)                          {
        {                                        if (this.lectureHall !=
            Course oldValue =                        lectureHall)
                this.course;                 {
            this.course = course                 LectureHall oldValue
                ;                                    = this.
            if (oldValue != null                     lectureHall;
                )                                this.lectureHall =
            {                                        lectureHall;
                oldValue.                        if (oldValue != null
                    setLectureHall               )
                    (null);                      {
            }                                        oldValue.
            if (course != null)                          setCourse(
            {                                            null);
                course.                          }
                    setLectureHall               if (lectureHall !=
                    (this);                          null)
            }                                    {
        }                                            lectureHall.
    }                                                    setCourse(
                                                         this);
    public Course getCourse()                    }
    {                                        }
        return course;                   }
    }
}                                        public LectureHall
                                             getLectureHall()
                                         {
                                             return lectureHall;
                                         }

                                     }
```

Figure 4.1: LectureHall and Course code with mutual references

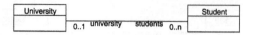

```java
public class Student
{
    private University university;

    public void setUniversity(University university)
    {
        if (this.university != university)
        {
            University oldValue = this.university;
            this.university = university;
            if (oldValue != null)
            {
                oldValue.removeStudent(this);
            }
            if (university != null)
            {
                university.addStudent(this);
            }
        }
    }

    public University getUniversity() { return university; }
}

public class University
{
    private Set<Student> students = new LinkedHashSet<Student>();

    public boolean addStudent(Student student)
    {
        boolean changed = students.add(student);
        if (changed && student != null)
        {
            student.setUniversity(this);
        }
        return changed;
    }

    public boolean removeStudent(Student student)
    {
        boolean changed = students.remove(student);
        if (changed && student != null)
        {
            student.setUniversity(null);
        }
        return changed;
    }

    public Set<Student> getStudents()
    {
        return Collections.unmodifiableSet(students);
    }
}
```

Figure 4.2: Manual code of bidirectional association between Student and
University

The set method is used to manage integrity: from the point of view of one association end object, someone calls the setter method to change the link from this object to another one. When the reference changes, the previously referred object has to be notified that it is no longer associated with ourselves, this is done by the `oldValue.setCourse(null)` method call. Furthermore, the new associated object has to be informed that we are its new partner: `lectureHall.setCourse(this)` does the job. Beware of null pointer references, as both the old and new value might be null, we have to check those. Both setters look like siblings and are calling each other recursively. The first check, `(this.foo != value)`, makes sure that there won't be an infinitive recursion. It's important that both setter methods do call the opposite side, as we cannot know which association end or setter will be used to create a link, but both should be valid.

Bidirectional to-many associations will combine both techniques we learned so far: the implementation should manage referential integrity as well as provide appropriate accessor methods. As example we use the association between `Student` and `University` shown at the top of Figure 4.2. The implementation is shown in the same figure.

Note that the add/remove-methods delegate the decision whether the to-many set has changed to the collection implementation of the `LinkedHashSet`. By calling the corresponding add/remove method in the `Student.setUniversity(...)` setter, we ensure that one student is always associated with just one university; without that, one student might be referred by multiple universities, which breaks our specification of the one-to-many association.

4.1.2 Choosing the Right Container Class for To-Many Associations

The Java Collection implementation contains basically three different types of containers[3]:

- `java.util.Set` - The most general and efficient choice, but managing set semantics: it ensures that an object does not get added twice to the set and usually does not retain the given order. That means, that the element order while iterating over the set might be different from the order the elements have been added and the order may differ from program run to program run. `java.util.HashSet` is an concrete implementation, but `java.util.TreeSet` might be also handy. The latter sorts objects, either if the objects implement the `java.lang.Comparable` interface or

---

[3]`java.util.Deque` is left out, because it only provides access methods for first and last objects of a list, not random access as we want it

when a `java.util.Comparator` is given. If you need a stable and repeatable order (e.g. the order in which elements have been added), use `LinkedHashSet`, as we did in the examples before. It will pay off when testing or debugging your code, as test runs will be deterministic and repeatable.

- `java.util.List` - stores an arbitrary size of elements in the given order. Different implementations are available, the most popular are `java.-util.ArrayList`, `LinkedList`, and `Vector`, which differentiate in implementation details. A list allows to implement access methods with index numbers easily, as it allows random access to elements of the list by index number.

- `java.util.Map` - choose this if you want efficient access to a certain element by providing an associated key instead of being forced to iterate over all elements each time you want to access a certain one. Compared to a list, a map is more general as it allows arbitrary objects as keys. Those keys are unique, there can be only one element per key. This allows to implement access methods with those keys as parameter.

4.1.3   Generated Code

When doing the exercises, you will get some experience in manually implementing all these support methods and structures for classes, their attributes, and their different types of associations. It will feel kind of repetitive and tedious. You will probably wonder if there are no tools being able to create these support methods and structures for us. As mentioned in the beginning of this chapter, existing tools are very sparse in creating support code. Stubs for the classes can be generated by most of the tools and most tools can do getters and setters. However, most tools do a very poor job in generating code for associations. A University prototype used (and developed) by the authors is the *Fujaba* tool suite [5] and another is SDMLib. The code generated by Fujaba for an initial Study-Right University is shown in Listing 4.1.

As you see the code starts with a "visual" description of the considered association (lines 4-10). It also generates annotation information to allow other tools to extract model information from the source code (lines 13, 17, 41). This book does not exploit such annotations. Also the methods `setUniversity`, `withUniversity`, `getUniversity`, and `removeYou` are generated. `setUniversity` comes with a lot of support code for handling the associated objects. It also takes care of changes and removal. Therefore, it is also called by `removeYou`.

You will also notice that the method `withUniversity` is generated and returns the this-object. With the help of this method you can build

```
1    public class Student
2    {
3
4       /**
5        * <pre>
6        *              0..*        studiesAt        0..1
7        * Student ——————————————————————— University
8        *              student                university
9        * </pre>
10       */
11      public static final String PROPERTY_UNIVERSITY="university";
12
13      @Property(name=PROPERTY_UNIVERSITY, partner=University.
          PROPERTY_STUDENT, kind= ReferenceHandler.ReferenceKind.TO_ONE,
14          adornment=ReferenceHandler.Adornment.NONE)
15      private University university;
16
17      @Property(name=PROPERTY_UNIVERSITY)
18      public boolean setUniversity (University value)
19      {
20          boolean changed = false;
21
22          if (this.university != value)
23          {
24              University oldValue = this.university;
25              Student source = this;
26              if (this.university != null)
27              {
28                  this.university = null;
29                  oldValue.removeFromStudent (this);
30              }
31              this.university = value;
32              if (value != null)
33              {
34                  value.addToStudent (this);
35              }
36              changed = true;
37          }
38          return changed;
39      }
40
41      @Property( name = PROPERTY_UNIVERSITY )
42      public Student withUniversity (University value)
43      {
44          setUniversity (value);
45          return this;
46      }
47
48      public University getUniversity ()
49      {
50          return this.university;
51      }
52
53      public void removeYou()
54      {
55          this.setUniversity (null);
56      }
57  }
```

Listing 4.1: Code Generated by Fujaba

```
Player  tom  =  new  Player ()
          . withName ( "Tom" )
          . withColor ( "blue" ) ;

Player  sabine  =  new  Player ()
          . withName ( " Sabine " )
          . withColor ( "red" ) ;

Dice  dice  =  tom . createDice ()
          . withValue (6) ;

Pawn  p2  =  tom . createPawns ()
          . withColor ( "blue" ) ;

Field  tomStartField  =  tom . createStart ()
          . withColor ( "blue" )
          . withKind ( " start " ) ;

Field  tomBase  =  tom . createBase ()
          . withColor ( "blue" )
          . withKind ( " base " )
          . withPawns ( p2 ) ;

Pawn  p9  =  sabine . createPawns ()
          . withColor ( "red" )
          . withPos ( tomStartField ) ;
  [ . . . ]
```

Listing 4.2: Example of fluent object creating code

a so-called *fluent* interface (cf. http://www.martinfowler.com/bliki/
FluentInterface.html). A fluent interface allows to chain multiple method
calls, usually setter methods, to the same object sequentially in the same code
statement. Fluent accessor methods are simply setter methods returning the
this-Object, so that multiple setter calls on the same subject can be chained
in a single statement. We suggest to add fluent accessor methods as well, as this
allows very readable, concise code for building object structures. Listing 4.2
shows some test setup code that makes extensive use of fluent accessor methods. It consists of just seven statements, but invokes 20 individual create- and
set-operations. Our code uses one line for each operation in order to allow you
to stop the debugger on any of the operations, easily.

As you see, modeling tools with code generation can actually save a lot of programming effort and also protect you from errors in taking care of the mutual handling of objects of associated classes.

There are different code generators available (this list is not exhaustive and its order is purely random):

- UML Lab[4]

- Fujaba with CodeGen2, as described above `http://seblog.cs.uni-kassel.de/projects/fujaba/`

- SDMLib has also a very light weight template-based code generator.

- EMF has great tools, but requires some learning effort. See `http://www.eclipse.org/modeling/m2t/` for the available code generators.

- Even the Eclipse editor templates might already help you. Someone should come up with a good set of such templates.

4.2 Object Diagrams to Java Code

Object diagrams describe runtime structures and cannot be expressed in static structures like classes. Therefore, we need code blocks, usually methods, which will build or match object structures by creating instances of classes, assign attributes values and link the objects. One obvious place for the creation of an initial object structure is a main method with the signature: `public static void main(String[] args) { ... }`

Note that a main method has to be declared static, that means the Java Virtual Machine is calling it from a static context where no objects have been created yet. Therefore, this is the place were we will create the first object instance. It is good practice to create just the main application instance there and leave the static context as soon as possible, as static means the referred language construct is unique in the Java Virtual Machine. This will lead to problems almost every time your program evolves and grows. Thus, a good start for our main method is:

```
public class University
{
  public static void main(String[] args) {
    University university = new University();
  }
  ...
}
```

---

[4]`http://www.uml-lab.com/`

When you run this code, it creates a `University` object instance and calls the constructor, where more code or method calls can be placed. That is it, we have created our first object!

Unfortunately, that code is not (yet) that useful, the main method terminates and the university instance dies. If we want to invoke some code actually doing something useful, our basic example needs to be extended for example like this:

```java
public class University
{
    public static void main(String[] args) {
        University university = new University();
            university.run(); // leave static context
                as soon as possible
    }

    public void run()
    {
        createFaculties();
        loadStudents();
        assignCourses();
    }

    ...
}
```

Let us now take a simple object diagram from Figure 4.3 and create the object structure at runtime.

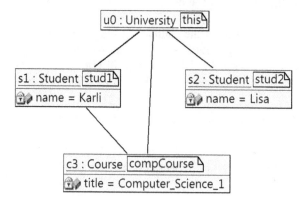

Figure 4.3: University object diagram (taken from eDOBS – see Section 4.4)

```
1   public class University
2   {
3     public void run ()
4     {
5       Course compCourse = new Course ();
6       compCourse.setTitle ("Computer_Science_1");
7
8       Student stud1 = new Student ();
9       stud1.setName ("Karli");
10
11      Student stud2 = new Student ();
12      stud2.setName ("Lisa");
13
14      this.addToStudents (stud1);
15      this.addToStudents (stud2);
16
17      this.addToCourses (compCourse);
18
19      compCourse.addToStudents (stud1);
20
21      System.out.println ();
22    }
23
24    public static void main (String [] args) {
25      University university = new University ();
26      university.run ();
27    }
28  }
```

First, we create the instances and set their attributes (lines 5-12). Then, we link the instances by calling accessor methods (line 14-19), which guarantees referential integrity, as shown in the previous section. In this example we have generated the model implementation classes with Fujaba and Fujaba uses addTo methods instead of just add methods. Note that the variable names used in your code do not need to match the object names in the object diagram. Object names and variable names are just two different things. In some programs there may exist multiple variables that refer to the same object. Similarly, at different points in time one variable may refer to different objects.

We have added a println statement in line 21 of our code. This statement just enables you to set a breakpoint after the model creation code and to stop the debugger at that line and to browse the created object structure with our eDOBS tool. This way we have created Figure 4.3. eDOBS is explained in more detail in Section 4.4.

```
 1   public class University
 2   {
 3     public void run ()
 4     {
 5       Course compCourse = this . createCourses ()
 6         . withTitle ("Computer_Science_1");
 7
 8       Student stud1 = this . createStudents ()
 9         . withName ("Karli")
10         . withCourses (compCourse);
11
12       Student stud2 = this . createStudents ()
13         . withName ("Lisa");
14
15       System . out . println ();
16     }
17
18     public static void main (String [] args) {
19       University university = new University ();
20             university . run ();
21     }
22   }
```

Listing 4.3: Fluent object diagram implementation

We can improve the previous code by using the fluent API (see Listing 4.3). In this code, we have extended the fluent API of class University with methods createCourses and createStudents. Method createCourses consists of the single line: return withCourses(new Course());. Method createStudents is implemented, accordingly. Thus, these methods may be used to create new neighbor objects. Compared to the listing above, some setter methods in Listing 4.3 use the reverse role of their association: for example, compCourse.addToStudents(stud1) from the previous listing has been replaced with stud1.[...].withCourses(compCourse). As the corresponding association is bidirectional and as our access methods update each other mutually, both directions work well.

4.3 Generic Implementations of Object Diagrams

In Chapter 2 we have learned to model example situations with object diagrams. In Chapter 3 we have learned to derive a class diagram from our object diagrams and Section 4.1 explains how to implement first the class diagrams and then Section 4.2 explains how to implement object diagrams with the help of the class diagram code. Deriving an application specific class diagram and implementing it in Java might look quiet tedious to you. Why can we not implement the object diagram directly? If you know some Java Collection classes, you might get the idea to represent an object by a HashMap that stores key-value pairs for the object's attributes. Such a HashMap may even store key-pointer pairs to realize links to other objects. Let's look at this in more detail.

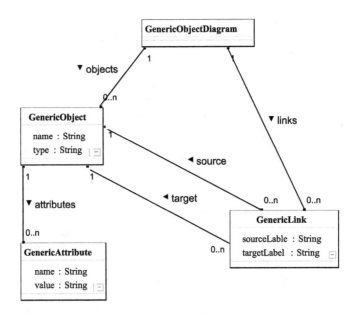

Figure 4.4: Generic classes for object diagrams

Figure 4.4 shows a class diagram for generic object diagrams[5].

---

[5]Weird, to get rid of class diagrams, we start with yet another class diagram. Perhaps we (the authors) are following this track to long, already

Figure 4.4 proposes a `GenericObject` that holds a set of `GenericAttributes`.
`GenericAttributes` are name-value pairs. In addition, we deploy
`GenericLinks` that connect `GenericObjects`. Compared to our initial
HashMap idea, `GenericLinks` will help us to maintain referential integrity.
These classes needs to be implemented only once and they may be provided
by some library. With this library we are then able to implement arbitrary object
structures.

Listing 4.4 shows how to implement the object structure of Figure 4.3. Figure 4.5
shows the actual object structure that is created by this code. If we compare the
generic implementation with the application specific implementation given in
Listing 4.3 you easily spot close correspondence:

- To create an object, we e.g. use
  `new GenericObject().withType("University")` instead of
  `new University()`.

- To assign an attribute value we use e.g.
  `.withAttributes("title", "Computer Sciene I")` instead of
  `.withTitle("Computer Sciene I")`.

- To create a link we use e.g.
  `.withLink("university", university, "lectures")` instead of
  `.withUniversity(university)`.

Yes, the generic solution is slightly, longer especially for links, but this is not
a major problem. Yes, at runtime we use much more generic objects as the
application specific solution, but as software engineers we do not worry about
memory consumption that much. However, the generic implementation uses
string literals for types, attribute names, and role names. If we do a typo, the
compiler will not catch this bug but we will have to test and debug. This is a
problem from the software engineering point of view. To mitigate this, we might
use explicit String constants like:
`public static final String STUDENTS = "students";`

Eclipse even provides a method that allows you to replace all occurrences
of a certain string literal by a constant with the same content. If you use such
constants on all places, you avoid the problem of undetected typos and in Eclipse
you even get completion: you type just some characters of the desired constant
and then the key combination Ctrl-blank either finishes the name or proposes a
list of possible completions.

Well, to some extend the constants we have just introduced are just a poor

```
1   public class GenericUniversity {
2      public void run(){
3         GenericObject university = new
              GenericObject()
4         .withType("University");
5
6         GenericObject 10 = new GenericObject()
7         .withType("Lecture")
8         .withAttributes("title", "Computer_Sciene_I
              ")
9         .withLink("university", university, "
              lectures");
10
11        GenericObject s0 = new GenericObject()
12        .withType("Student")
13        .withAttributes("name", "Karli")
14        .withLink("university", university, "
              students")
15        .withLink("lectures", 10, "students");
16
17        GenericObject s1 = new GenericObject()
18        .withType("Student")
19        .withAttributes("name", "Lisa")
20        .withLink("university", university, "
              students")
21        .withLink("lectures", 10, "students");
22     }
23
24     public static void main(String[] args) {
25        GenericUniversity university = new
              GenericUniversity();
26        university.run();
27     }
28  }
```

Listing 4.4: University object diagram with generic classes

replacement for real application specific classes. The major problem we still have with the generic solution is the lack of type information. When you later on create a new object of a certain type to hold a certain information, you will soon have forgotten which type of object you should use, which attributes you should set, which links are mandatory, and where to put these things in your overall model. Your object model is complex by itself. To navigate within this object model and to have in mind where you find which information and how it is organized is already difficult in an application specific class model. If you throw away all this type information you lose a lot of valuable programming aids not to mention that your compiler looses the ability to catch silly errors that you will now need to track down with tests and debugging. After all, a model has the task to facilitate software development. Generic models do not help you a lot and thus generic models are poor in comparison to application specific models.

Note, Java is a strongly typed language and thus, type information is available and exploited in your code. Having application specific classes is thus very well supported in Java. This strong typing also enables for example Eclipse to give you rich code completion functionality. These days scripting languages like Python, PHP, Ruby, and JavaScript are popular. These languages provide you with much more flexibility by throwing away static typing. In JavaScript an object is by default just a generic HashMap. Such a generic HashMap allows you to add any object using any key you want. On the other hand, there will be no help telling you which entries you should add to a HashMap that should for example represent a student. Similarly, editors for script languages usually provide only little code completion functionality. As discussed: no type information no orientation aids. Thus, scripting languages are poor in comparison to strongly typed languages with application specific classes.

Still there are cases where generic models are helpful. There is a number of tools that deal with object models as a whole: for example persistent object storage, object model serialization, or object model visualization tools. These tools deal with object models that are not even known to the tool at the development time. Thus, for these tools a generic object model is the only choice. However, development of such tools is a task for advanced programming (as you need to deal with the lack of type information) and thus not content of this book.

4.4   eDobs as Runtime Model Explorer

In this chapter, we will learn how to use the eDOBS as graphical model explorer at program runtime. eDOBS is an Eclipse plugin which visualizes the Java object storage of a running Java application. This enables the developer to browse and explore the object structure to get an idea of the object graph representing the runtime space of the virtual Java machine. Class structures can be interactively

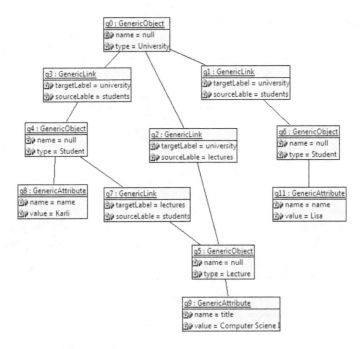

Figure 4.5: Generic objects representing the University object diagram

tested by testing objects and their relations at runtime. To do so, we have to create instances of our classes. After that, we can assign attribute values to these objects and we may link objects, when corresponding associations are available. Usually, this is done in some method code, like the main()-method. But if you forgot something, you would have to change the method, recompile your code, and restart into runtime again[6]. Or you would have to write sophisticated methods with parameters and more, so the code depends on actual runtime data. This is a disproportionate effort for just testing your class structure.

To circumvent this, you can use the eDOBS debugger environment to inter-actively build object structures. eDOBS is a graphical tool visualizing the Java in-memory heap objects. eDOBS stands for (eclipse) Dynamic Object Browsing System. It can also be used as graphical debugger. Here we use it as an inter-active, graphical tool showing and modifying "online" object diagrams of the program under test. It analyzes complete object structures, starting at a certain object, reads its attribute assignments and links to other objects. When initially started, the runtime environment does not contain any objects yet. We can create

---

[6]Or use the Java Hot Code Replacement debugger feature. This lets you modify your code with no need to restart it, within certain limits, e.g. changing the class structure is unsupported.

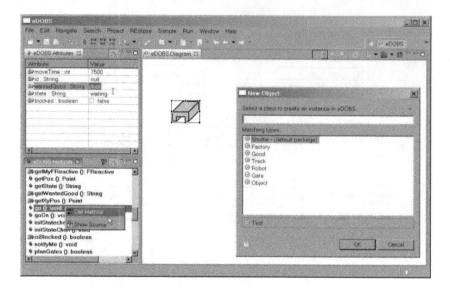

Figure 4.6: eDOBS Screenshot

one by using the "Create new object" function (cf. Figure 4.7). After selecting the desired class/type, eDOBS shows the object in the same notation we have seen in the object diagrams chapter. This object now can be modified interactively by assigning attributes using the eDOBS attribute view. Methods can be called. When having created multiple objects, we can link them using the "Link" functionality. By clicking on a link, the link labels show role names, so it is clear which association this link represents.

4.5   Exercises

4.5.1   Study-Right University

- Take the class diagram of our Study-Right University example from Figure 3.4 and implement it in Java, e.g. using Eclipse [4]. Take special care to achieve bidirectional references and referential integrity.

- Start the eDOBS Debugging environment. Create the following object structure by using the eDOBS "Create New Object" and "Link" functionality. Create four Rooms and Karli. Assign meaningful attribute values, so that objects can be identified without just the object name.

- Implement an additional class University with a main method. This

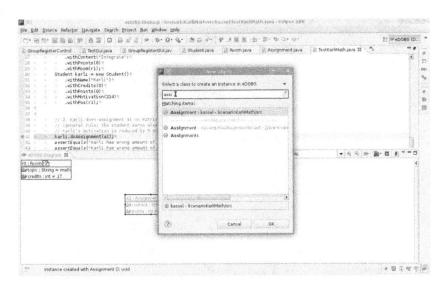

Figure 4.7: eDOBS new object

main method shall create an University object and invoke method run
on it. Implement the run method of the University class to build the
object structure shown in Figure 3.1.

- Debug the run method of the University class and step through the construction of the object structure. Use the variables view to check the referential integrity of your bidirectional references. Use eDOBS to visualize
  the object structure during construction.

- Extend your University.run() method to move karli from the math
  Room to the algebra Room. Check the referential integrity.

4.5.2 Mau Mau[7]

- Take the class diagram from exercise 3.5.1 and implement it in Java, e.g.
  using Eclipse [4]. Take special care to achieve bidirectional references and
  referential integrity.

- Start the eDOBS Debugging environment and create an object structure
  taken from an object diagram from exercise 2.1.1 by using the eDOBS

---

[7]To a large extend, the following exercises are just copies of the previous section. We give
full copies of the exercise descriptions for the convenience of instructors that may take any of the
exercises and just copy them into their slides.

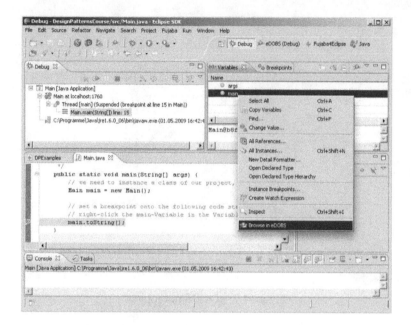

Figure 4.8: Invoke eDOBS on debugger variables

"Create New Object" and "Link" functionality. Assign meaningful attribute values, so that objects can be identified without just the object
name.

- Implement an additional class Main with a main method. This main
  method shall create a Main object and invoke method run() on it. Implement the run() method of the Main class to build the object structure
  you have built in the eDOBS step above.

- Debug the run() method of the Main class and step through the construction of the object structure. Use the variables view to check the referential
  integrity of your bidirectional references. Use eDOBS to visualize the
  object structure during construction.

- Extend your Main.run() method to change some links. Check the referential integrity.

4.5.3   Battleships

- Take the class diagram from exercise 3.5.2 and implement it in Java, e.g.
  using Eclipse [4]. Take special care to achieve bidirectional references and

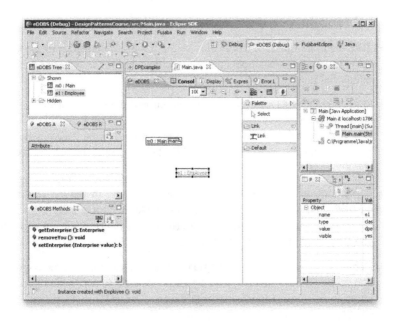

Figure 4.9: Debugging or exploring with eDOBS

referential integrity.

- Start the eDOBS Debugging environment and create an object structure taken from an object diagram from exercise 2.1.2 by using the eDOBS "Create New Object" and "Link" functionality. Assign meaningful attribute values, so that objects can be identified without just the object name.

- Implement an additional class Main with a main method. This main method shall create a Main object and invoke method run() on it. Implement the run() method of the Main class to build the object structure you have built in the eDOBS step above.

- Debug the run() method of the Main class and step through the construction of the object structure. Use the variables view to check the referential integrity of your bidirectional references. Use eDOBS to visualize the object structure during construction.

- Extend your Main.run() method to change some links. Check the referential integrity.

4.5.4   Mancala

- Take the class diagram from exercise 3.5.3 and implement it in Java, e.g. using Eclipse [4]. Take special care to achieve bidirectional references and referential integrity.

- Start the eDOBS Debugging environment and create an object structure taken from an object diagram from exercise 2.1.3 by using the eDOBS "Create New Object" and "Link" functionality. Assign meaningful attribute values, so that objects can be identified without just the object name.

- Implement an additional class Main with a main method. This main method shall create a Main object and invoke method run() on it. Implement the run() method of the Main class to build the object structure you have built in the eDOBS step above.

- Debug the run() method of the Main class and step through the construction of the object structure. Use the variables view to check the referential integrity of your bidirectional references. Use eDOBS to visualize the object structure during construction.

- Extend your Main.run() method to change some links. Check the referential integrity.

4.5.5   Mensch Ärgere Dich Nicht

- Take the class diagram from exercise 3.5.4 and implement it in Java, e.g. using Eclipse [4]. Take special care to achieve bidirectional references and referential integrity.

- Start the eDOBS Debugging environment and create an object structure taken from an object diagram from exercise 2.1.4 by using the eDOBS "Create New Object" and "Link" functionality. Assign meaningful attribute values, so that objects can be identified without just the object name.

- Implement an additional class Main with a main method. This main method shall create a Main object and invoke method run() on it. Implement the run() method of the Main class to build the object structure you have built in the eDOBS step above.

- Debug the run() method of the Main class and step through the construction of the object structure. Use the variables view to check the referential integrity of your bidirectional references. Use eDOBS to visualize the object structure during construction.

- Extend your `Main.run()` method to change some links. Check the referential integrity.

4.5.6 Towers of Hanoi

- Take the class diagram from exercise 3.5.5 and implement it in Java, e.g. using Eclipse [4]. Take special care to achieve bidirectional references and referential integrity.

- Start the eDOBS Debugging environment and create an object structure taken from an object diagram from exercise 2.1.5 by using the eDOBS "Create New Object" and "Link" functionality. Assign meaningful attribute values, so that objects can be identified without just the object name.

- Implement an additional class `Main` with a `main` method. This `main` method shall create a `Main` object and invoke method `run()` on it. Implement the `run()` method of the `Main` class to build the object structure you have built in the eDOBS step above.

- Debug the `run()` method of the `Main` class and step through the construction of the object structure. Use the variables view to check the referential integrity of your bidirectional references. Use eDOBS to visualize the object structure during construction.

- Extend your `Main.run()` method to change some links. Check the referential integrity.

4.5.7 ATM Money Withdrawal

- Take the class diagram from exercise 3.5.6 and implement it in Java, e.g. using Eclipse [4]. Take special care to achieve bidirectional references and referential integrity.

- Start the eDOBS Debugging environment and create an object structure taken from an object diagram from exercise 2.1.6 by using the eDOBS "Create New Object" and "Link" functionality. Assign meaningful attribute values, so that objects can be identified without just the object name.

- Implement an additional class `Main` with a `main` method. This `main` method shall create a `Main` object and invoke method `run()` on it. Implement the `run()` method of the `Main` class to build the object structure you have built in the eDOBS step above.

- Debug the run() method of the Main class and step through the construction of the object structure. Use the variables view to check the referential integrity of your bidirectional references. Use eDOBS to visualize the object structure during construction.

- Extend your Main.run() method to change some links. Check the referential integrity.

4.5.8   Borrowing Electronic Books from Library

- Take the class diagram from exercise 3.5.7 and implement it in Java, e.g. using Eclipse [4]. Take special care to achieve bidirectional references and referential integrity.

- Start the eDOBS Debugging environment and create an object structure taken from an object diagram from exercise 2.1.7 by using the eDOBS "Create New Object" and "Link" functionality. Assign meaningful attribute values, so that objects can be identified without just the object name.

- Implement an additional class Main with a main method. This main method shall create a Main object and invoke method run() on it. Implement the run() method of the Main class to build the object structure you have built in the eDOBS step above.

- Debug the run() method of the Main class and step through the construction of the object structure. Use the variables view to check the referential integrity of your bidirectional references. Use eDOBS to visualize the object structure during construction.

- Extend your Main.run() method to change some links. Check the referential integrity.

4.5.9   Trouble Ticket System

- Take the class diagram from exercise 3.5.8 and implement it in Java, e.g. using Eclipse [4]. Take special care to achieve bidirectional references and referential integrity.

- Start the eDOBS Debugging environment and create an object structure taken from an object diagram from exercise 2.1.8 by using the eDOBS "Create New Object" and "Link" functionality. Assign meaningful attribute values, so that objects can be identified without just the object name.

- Implement an additional class Main with a main method. This main method shall create a Main object and invoke method run() on it. Implement the run() method of the Main class to build the object structure you have built in the eDOBS step above.

- Debug the run() method of the Main class and step through the construction of the object structure. Use the variables view to check the referential integrity of your bidirectional references. Use eDOBS to visualize the object structure during construction.

- Extend your Main.run() method to change some links. Check the referential integrity.

4.5.10 Webshop

- Take the class diagram from exercise 3.5.9 and implement it in Java, e.g. using Eclipse [4]. Take special care to achieve bidirectional references and referential integrity.

- Start the eDOBS Debugging environment and create an object structure taken from an object diagram from exercise 2.1.9 by using the eDOBS "Create New Object" and "Link" functionality. Assign meaningful attribute values, so that objects can be identified without just the object name.

- Implement an additional class Main with a main method. This main method shall create a Main object and invoke method run() on it. Implement the run() method of the Main class to build the object structure you have built in the eDOBS step above.

- Debug the run() method of the Main class and step through the construction of the object structure. Use the variables view to check the referential integrity of your bidirectional references. Use eDOBS to visualize the object structure during construction.

- Extend your Main.run() method to change some links. Check the referential integrity.

4.5.11 Connect Four Game

- Take the class diagram from exercise 3.5.12 and implement it in Java, e.g. using Eclipse [4]. Take special care to achieve bidirectional references and referential integrity.

- Start the eDOBS Debugging environment and create an object structure taken from an object diagram from exercise 3.5.12 by using the eDOBS "Create New Object" and "Link" functionality. Assign meaningful attribute values, so that objects can be identified without just the object name.

- Implement an additional class Main with a main method. This main method shall create a Main object and invoke method run() on it. Implement the run() method of the Main class to build the object structure you have built in the eDOBS step above.

- Debug the run() method of the Main class and step through the construction of the object structure. Use the variables view to check the referential integrity of your bidirectional references. Use eDOBS to visualize the object structure during construction.

- Extend your Main.run() method to change some links. Check the referential integrity.

4.5.12   Derive Classes from Code

- Derive a class diagram from Listing 4.5. Implement this class diagram in Java.

- Execute the main()-Method from Listing 4.5 and browse the resulting object structure in eDOBS.

- Alice and Bob are divorced now. Extend the main method from Listing 4.5 such that both Alice and Bob have their own bank account and share the account balance of the existing ab-account between Alice and Bob.

4.5.13   Referential Integrity Templates

- Build new Eclipse editor templates to ease the implementation of to-one and to-many associations. To add a template to eclipse use Window -> Preferences -> Java - > Editor -> Content Assist -> Templates. Take an existing template as example. Copy an example implementation for a to-one / to-many association from one of the previous exercises. Insert this code into your new template. Replace program specific names with appropriate template variables.

- Test your new templates on some of the previous class diagram implementation examples.

```
1   public static void main(String[] args)
2   {
3     Bank b = new Bank();
4     Customer alice = new Customer("Alice");
5     Customer bob = new Customer("Bob");
6     Customer charlie = new Customer("Charlie");
7     Account ab = new Account(b, "32442545");
8     Account ac = new Account(b, "44543214");
9     alice.setAccount(ab);
10    bob.setAccount(ab);
11    charlie.setAccount(ac);
12    ab.deposit(20000);
13    ac.deposit(10000);
14    println("Total Assets: "
15        + b.getTotalAssets()); // <- prints 30000
16  }
```

Listing 4.5: Main Method for Bank Application

Part II

Behavior

Chapter 5

Storyboards

In the first part, we have learned how to model a situation or a snapshot of a moment of a running system. For this we use object and class diagrams. However, a program usually goes through many such moments as it usually runs a longer time. Therefore, we have to somehow address these changes of the system status. We have to start modeling behavior. If we go back to the introduction we might remember that we have talked already about behavior as part of the scenario and story definition. Therefore, we already have information in the scenario about the behavior. We will now analyze how to identify and analyze these behavior-elements of our stories and capture them in different models. We will learn in this chapter how to transfer our scenarios into storyboards by amending them with object diagrams. This will lead to a model, the storyboard, of the specific behavior of our system for the given scenario. The next chapter will use these storyboards to derive the general behavior and algorithm amending the existing storyboard with pseudo code and therefore creating a model for the generic behavior. The subsequent chapters will then show how to model this behavior.

Within our Study-Right University example, our final goal is to program a solver that computes a route through our University that allows us to earn sufficient credits to pass the examination without using up too much of our motivation. For a first programming exercise this goal is too complex. We rather would like to do something easier inside a room. For such an exercise, we will extend our Study-Right University example a little bit adding assignments that have to be completed in order to earn the credits of a visited room or course. For this, we assume the following change-request situation:

In our Study-Right University, the professors now think that it is too easy to get credits. Therefore, they introduce mandatory assignments. For example Figure 5.1 shows a list of assignments a1 through a3 attached to the math room of our Study-Right University. As shown in Figure 5.1, each assignment addresses

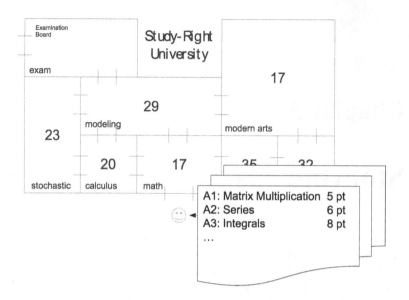

Figure 5.1: Study-Right University with math assignments

a certain math topic. As also shown, each assignment offers a certain number of points achievable. Unfortunately, the professors have no time to grade the assignments. Thus, if Karli does, for example, the assignment on Integrals, Karli will just get all 8 points of the Integrals assignment.

Assuming that the professors are our customers, we ask them if the students always get full points if they do an assignment. They actually confirm that this is a general rule. The professors state, when Karli has done all three assignments shown in Figure 5.1 Karli will get the 17 math credits since the sum of assignment points (19) is higher than the credits Karli earns. This is again a general rule, meaning it applies also for the other rooms. The professors explain, if Karli goes on to the modeling room, does the assignments there and achieves the modeling credits and if Karli then revisits the math course, then Karli may not just do the three assignments shown in Figure 5.1, again. That would be too easy. Instead, the professors would provide new assignments on new math topics. Thus, on the second visit Karli needs to do more complex assignments justifying giving Karli additional credits on math.

To model these extensions to our Study-Right University, we start with the scenario/story shown in Scenario 5.1. In this story, our student Karli starts in the math room. In three steps, Karli does one assignment after the other. Finally, Karli has collected enough assignment points in order to earn the math credits.

Scenario 5.1 Story for Karli doing the first math assignments

---

Karli does math assignments

1. Karli enters the Study-Right University in the math room. Karli has no credits yet and still a motivation of 214.

2. Karli does assignment a1 on Matrix Multiplication and earns 5 points (general rule: the student earns always full points for doing an assignment). Karli's motivation is reduced by 5 points to now 209.

3. Karli does assignment a2 on Series and earns another 6 points. Thus Karli has 11 points now. Motivation is reduced to 203.

4. Karli does the third assignment on Integrals, earns another 8 points and thus Karli has now 19 points and a motivation of 195.

5. Since 19 points are more than the 17 points required for the 17 math credits, Karli hands the points in and earns the credits. (General rule: if the points earned by the assignments are higher than the credit points, the credit points will be awarded to the student.)

6. Karli has completed the math topic.

The next step is the creation of object diagrams modeling our example situations. To derive a class diagram for our model, a single object diagram modeling a representative situation would probably suffice. However, this chapter deals with the modeling of behavior. Therefore, we will use a series of object diagrams modeling the steps of our scenario and how our object structure evolves during scenario execution. In addition, we add new elements to our object diagrams to express changes to the object structures like attribute assignments, object or link creation, or object or link deletion. A scenario with such object diagrams for each of its steps is called a *storyboard* and the activity of creating such a storyboard is called *storyboarding*.

Figure 5.2 shows the first two steps of the storyboard of our example scenario. The object diagram for the first step is derived from the text as usual. We use a Room object r1 to model the math room and a Student object karli to model Karli. We also have three Assignment objects a1, a2, and a3 attached to the room. These three assignments are not mentioned in the textual description of the first step, but they are mentioned in later steps. We have added them to the first object diagram, already, since the first object diagram of a storyboard has the task to model the start situation of a scenario. If later steps require the existence of a certain object, this object shall be modeled explicitly in the first step. Usually, you start with a small object diagram for the first step and then you go on with the next steps. When you recognize in a later step that you would like another object to exist, go back to the initial (or previous) object diagram(s) and add it there.

The object diagram for the second step in Figure 5.2 shows how our model reflects that karli does the first assignment. First of all, there is a new done link connecting karli and assignment a1. This done link models that karli has now completed assignment a1. This is necessary if karli revisit the math room later on. Then, only new assignments that are not yet connected to karli will be available for a second round on math.

Note, unchanged elements of the object diagram that have just been copied from previous steps are shown in black. New elements are shown in green color. In addition, new objects and links are marked with the stereotype «create». Elements that are deleted are shown in black with the stereotype «destroy» in red color. Assignments are distinguished from attribute values using a := operator and green color. In addition, objects that are known from previous steps do not show their type.

In step 2 of Figure 5.2 we also change the motivation of karli to motivation-a1.points which is 214-5 resulting in 209. This models that doing the assignment was some effort for karli and how this effort is computed.

To sum up the points that karli has accumulated in this visit to the math room, we have extended the Student object with a points attribute. In the first step of our storyboard, karli's points are 0. In step 2 this is changed to 5. Here we have omitted the computation since it is trivial. However, in step 3 of our storyboard shown in Figure 5.3 we show that points are accumulated with the attribute assignment points become points+6 which is 11. In that step Assignment a2 is added to karli's done list and motivation is reduced to 203.

Similarly, step 4 of our storyboard handles the completion of assignment a3. Step 5 of our storyboard shown in Figure 5.4 models a more interesting case. As modeled in the step before, karli has now 19 points which suffices to complete the math topic. Therefore, karli's credits become 17. Here we might have added the computation rule credits+r1.credits to document how this value is determined. In addition, we reset karli's points attribute in order to be ready for the next topic.

For completeness reasons, step 6 of our storyboard shows the object structure after the execution of the scenario. This will become important for deriving tests from storyboards as shown in Chapter 8.

In general, we design our storyboards with Fujaba or SDMLib. However, you can also use the whiteboard or paper or a mixture of MS Word [29], MS Visio [28], LibreOffice [24], UMLet[11], Inkscape [6], and MagicDraw[30] for it. The advantage of using Fujaba [5] or SDMLib [10] is the option to generate

Karli does math assignments

1. Karli enters the Study-Right University in the math room. Karli has no credits yet and still a motivation of 214.

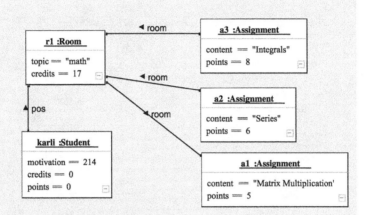

2. Karli does assignment a1 on Matrix Multiplication and earns 5 points. Karli's motivation is reduced by 5 points to now 209.

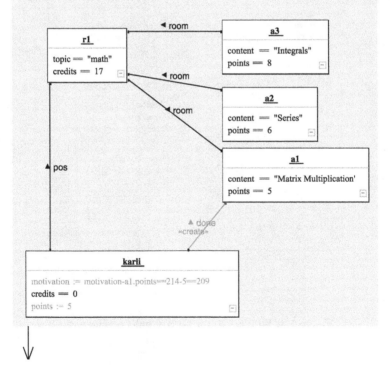

Figure 5.2: Storyboard for steps 1 and 2 of Figure 5.1

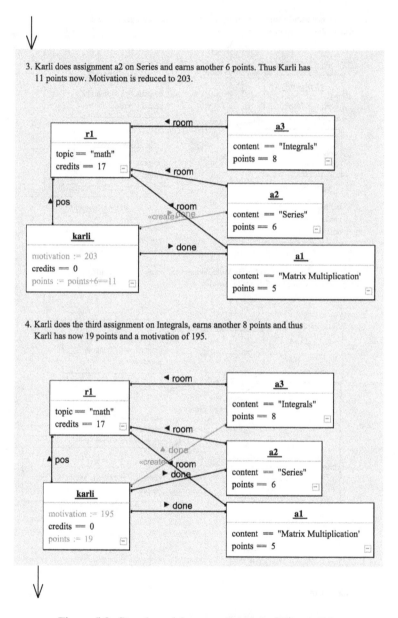

3. Karli does assignment a2 on Series and earns another 6 points. Thus Karli has 11 points now. Motivation is reduced to 203.

4. Karli does the third assignment on Integrals, earns another 8 points and thus Karli has now 19 points and a motivation of 195.

Figure 5.3: Storyboard for steps 3 and 4 of Figure 5.1

5. Since 19 points are more than the 17 points required for the 17 math credits, Karli hands the points in and earns the credits.

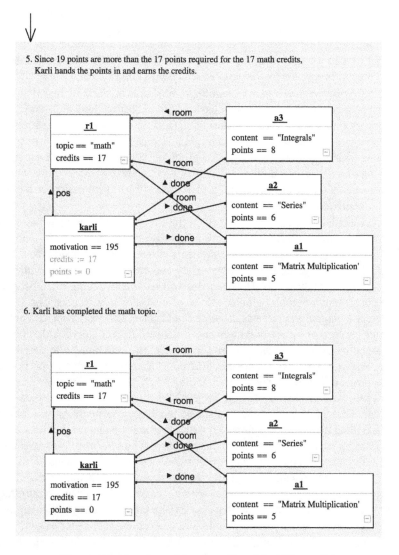

6. Karli has completed the math topic.

Figure 5.4: Storyboard for steps 5 and 6 of Figure 5.1

code directly from the story diagram or in the case of SDMLib while creating it.

Creating storyboards is really easy: As a first step copy the scenario text into your choice of Story Driven Modeling tool. For each step add an object diagram. Leave some space in the margin for later notes on creating the generic behavior. In our experience, creating storyboards covers the major part for building up a solid understanding of how the future program should work either for the developer as also the potential stakeholders. Even if it is data structures based, it offers a good base to derive the generic behavior as described in the next chapter.

While software developers generally prefer simple boxes to represent objects in storyboards, your customer might have a different background and many other disciplines find simple boxes too abstract. Thus, to discuss your scenarios and storyboards with your customers you might use some icons instead of your object boxes or within your object boxes, cf. Figure 5.5. Such icons do not change the meaning of our storyboard but your customer will much easier recognize what is represented by a certain object, and it therefore will be much easier for them to discuss with you.

It can actually make sense to work on the class diagram design while creating the storyboards. Some tools like Fujaba will require the design of the class diagram in advance to specifying any objects of one of the designed types. This brings the advantage of a lot of type safety and completion support while designing the object diagrams. However this will require switching often between different abstraction levels, which might be an obstacle for beginners. The design of the class diagrams is done as discussed in Chapter 3. As storyboards contain a larger number of object diagrams and because different storyboards may be developed by different team members in parallel, we recommend to derive the class diagram quite early. This class diagram is shared between all storyboards of the project. During further storyboarding work, the common class diagram serves as a kind of glossary for the project. Whenever you have to decide how a certain element of your scenario shall be modeled, you might have a look at the class diagram, whether it already provides modeling elements that serve your needs. If you reuse a model element that you are not familiar with, you might use cross references to look-up other storyboards that use these elements. This will provide you with valuable information about the intentions behind these model elements and whether they fit for your scenario or whether you need to introduce new model elements. For these reasons, Fujaba enforces that you declare any model element in your class diagram before you can use it in a storyboard.

Figure 5.6 shows the class diagram that we have created during the development of our storyboard. From this class diagram we now generate the implementation for our object model. Later on, this model implementation is the basis for the implementation of tests and for the implementation of model behavior.

We have seen that deriving the storyboard from the scenario is not too difficult as it mainly demands finding respective object diagrams for the different

Karli does math assignments

1. Karli enters the Study-Right University in the math room. Karli has no credits yet and still a motivation of 214.

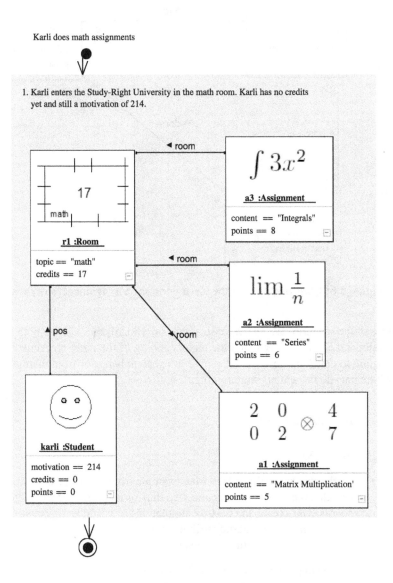

Figure 5.5: Storyboard with icons

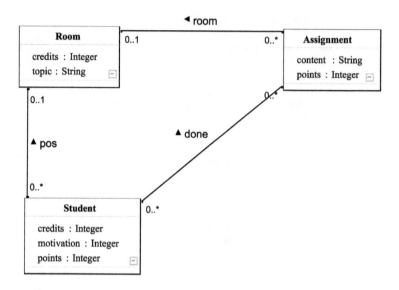

Figure 5.6: Class diagram for the Karli does `math` assignments storyboard

steps of the scenario. We also have seen that storyboards facilitate on both of the developer's and customer's side the understanding of the inner workings of the program to develop. Now we will derive the generic behavior from them, which will help us do the actual programming.

5.1   Exercises

5.1.1   Mau Mau

- Take the scenarios of our Mau Mau example from Section 1.6.3.1 and add object diagrams for each scenario step thus turning the scenarios into storyboards. Use create and destroy annotations to visualize object structure modifications. Cross out old attribute values and use attribute assignments to visualize changing attribute values.

- Take the implementation of our Mau Mau example from Section 4.5.2. Change method `Main.run()` to implement one storyboard after the other (or use different `runXY()` methods for the different scenarios):

  - Implement the creation of the initial object structure of the current scenario.

– For later scenario steps, implement the modeled object structure modifications and attribute changes.

– Debug through the execution of the storyboard and use eDOBS to visualize the object model at each scenario step.

5.1.2 Battleships

Take the scenarios of our Battleships example from Section 1.6.3.2 and add object diagrams for each scenario step thus turning the scenarios into storyboards. Use create and destroy annotations to visualize object structure modifications. Cross out old attribute values and use attribute assignments to visualize changing attribute values.

- Take the implementation of our Battleships example from Section 4.5.3. Change method Main.run() to implement one storyboard after the other (or use different runXY() methods for the different scenarios):

    – Implement the creation of the initial object structure of the current scenario.

    – For later scenario steps, implement the modeled object structure modifications and attribute changes.

    – Debug through the execution of the storyboard and use eDOBS to visualize the object model at each scenario step.

5.1.3 Mancala

- Take the scenarios of our Mancala example from Section 1.6.3.3 and add object diagrams for each scenario step thus turning the scenarios into storyboards. Use create and destroy annotations to visualize object structure modifications. Cross out old attribute values and use attribute assignments to visualize changing attribute values.

- Take the implementation of our Mancala example from Section 4.5.4. Change method Main.run() to implement one storyboard after the other (or use different runXY() methods for the different scenarios):

    – Implement the creation of the initial object structure of the current scenario.

    – For later scenario steps, implement the modeled object structure modifications and attribute changes.

    – Debug through the execution of the storyboard and use eDOBS to visualize the object model at each scenario step.

5.1.4   Mensch Ärgere Dich Nicht

Take the scenarios of our Mensch Ärgere Dich Nicht example from Section
1.6.3.4 and add object diagrams for each scenario step thus turning the scenarios
into storyboards. Use create and destroy annotations to visualize object structure
modifications. Cross out old attribute values and use attribute assignments to
visualize changing attribute values.

- Take the implementation of our Mensch Ärgere Dich Nicht example from
  Section 4.5.5. Change method `Main.run()` to implement one storyboard
  after the other (or use different `runXY()` methods for the different scenarios):

  - Implement the creation of the initial object structure of the current
    scenario.

  - For later scenario steps, implement the modeled object structure
    modifications and attribute changes.

  - Debug through the execution of the storyboard and use eDOBS to
    visualize the object model at each scenario step.

5.1.5   Towers of Hanoi

Take the scenarios of our Towers of Hanoi example from Section 1.6.3.5 and
add object diagrams for each scenario step thus turning the scenarios into storyboards. Use create and destroy annotations to visualize object structure modifications. Cross out old attribute values and use attribute assignments to visualize
changing attribute values.

- Take the implementation of our Towers of Hanoi example from Section
  4.5.6. Change method `Main.run()` to implement one storyboard after the
  other (or use different `runXY()` methods for the different scenarios):

  - Implement the creation of the initial object structure of the current
    scenario.

  - For later scenario steps, implement the modeled object structure
    modifications and attribute changes.

  - Debug through the execution of the storyboard and use eDOBS to
    visualize the object model at each scenario step.

5.1.6   ATM Money Withdrawal

Take the scenarios of our ATM Money Withdrawal example from Section 1.6.3.6
and add object diagrams for each scenario step thus turning the scenarios into

storyboards. Use create and destroy annotations to visualize object structure modifications. Cross out old attribute values and use attribute assignments to visualize changing attribute values.

- Take the implementation of our ATM Money Withdrawal example from Section 4.5.7. Change method Main.run() to implement one storyboard after the other (or use different runXY() methods for the different scenarios):

    - Implement the creation of the initial object structure of the current scenario.

    - For later scenario steps, implement the modeled object structure modifications and attribute changes.

    - Debug through the execution of the storyboard and use eDOBS to visualize the object model at each scenario step.

5.1.7 Borrowing Electronic Books from Library

Take the scenarios of our Library example from Section 1.6.3.7 and add object diagrams for each scenario step thus turning the scenarios into storyboards. Use create and destroy annotations to visualize object structure modifications. Cross out old attribute values and use attribute assignments to visualize changing attribute values.

- Take the implementation of our Library example from Section 4.5.8. Change method Main.run() to implement one storyboard after the other (or use different runXY() methods for the different scenarios):

    - Implement the creation of the initial object structure of the current scenario.

    - For later scenario steps, implement the modeled object structure modifications and attribute changes.

    - Debug through the execution of the storyboard and use eDOBS to visualize the object model at each scenario step.

5.1.8 Trouble Ticket System

Take the scenarios of our Trouble Ticket System example from Section 1.6.3.8 and add object diagrams for each scenario step thus turning the scenarios into storyboards. Use create and destroy annotations to visualize object structure modifications. Cross out old attribute values and use attribute assignments to visualize changing attribute values.

- Take the implementation of our Trouble Ticket System example from Section 4.5.9. Change method `Main.run()` to implement one storyboard after the other (or use different `runXY()` methods for the different scenarios):

  - Implement the creation of the initial object structure of the current scenario.

  - For later scenario steps, implement the modeled object structure modifications and attribute changes.

  - Debug through the execution of the storyboard and use eDOBS to visualize the object model at each scenario step.

5.1.9 Webshop

Take the scenarios of our Webshop example from Section 1.6.3.9 and add object diagrams for each scenario step thus turning the scenarios into storyboards. Use create and destroy annotations to visualize object structure modifications. Cross out old attribute values and use attribute assignments to visualize changing attribute values.

- Take the implementation of our Webshop example from Section 4.5.10. Change method `Main.run()` to implement one storyboard after the other (or use different `runXY()` methods for the different scenarios):

  - Implement the creation of the initial object structure of the current scenario.

  - For later scenario steps, implement the modeled object structure modifications and attribute changes.

  - Debug through the execution of the storyboard and use eDOBS to visualize the object model at each scenario step.

5.1.10 Connect Four Game

Take our Connect Four Game example from Sections 3.5.12 and 4.5.11 and develop four scenarios for different phases of the game. Add object diagrams for each scenario step thus turning the scenarios into storyboards. Use create and destroy annotations to visualize object structure modifications. Cross out old attribute values and use attribute assignments to visualize changing attribute values.

- Take the implementation of our Connect Four Game example from Section 4.5.11. Change method `Main.run()` to implement one storyboard after the other (or use different runXY() methods for the different scenarios):

- Implement the creation of the initial object structure of the current scenario.
- For later scenario steps, implement the modeled object structure modifications and attribute changes.
- Debug through the execution of the storyboard and use eDOBS to visualize the object model at each scenario step.

Chapter 6

Algorithm Design

Programming is a major intellectual challenge. Programming requires us to classify things and to identify general rules about how things work. Deriving rules from the recognition of example behavior or from experimental results or from user scenarios is one of the most demanding intellectual activities in general. This holds for the scientist Newton, recognizing an apple falling from a tree and deriving the physical laws of gravitation. This holds for Albert Einstein sitting in his office thinking about spacecrafts traveling at almost light speed and deriving the Theory of Relativity. This holds for engineers developing new mechanisms. This holds for software developers developing new programs.

To facilitate the ever challenging task of programming, our story driven modeling method offers all kinds of stepping stones for reducing its complexity. Basically, all story driven modeling steps try to reduce the complexity of the programming task. First, we separate the modeling from the programming. For the modeling step, we focus on concrete scenarios. Compared to the general case, concrete scenarios reduce complexity by discussing / modeling just one case at a time. Scenarios start at the domain level with some textual scenario step descriptions. These textual scenario steps allow the storyboarding or the object diagram modeling to look at one scenario step at a time, again reducing complexity. The scenarios, storyboards and object models derived from these phases are now input for the programming task.

So far, we have learned to identify concrete scenarios (Section 1.5) for a system and to derive object diagrams (Chapter 2) and class diagrams (Chapter 3) from these scenarios. We are able to derive storyboards from scenarios (Chapter 5) and related object diagrams. After these steps, we have a concrete case describing what is happening for this case in terms of changes of the participating objects. However, we do not know how our program should look that works for the current example situation. The program shall also work for other cases, it shall work for the general case. The program shall even cover corner cases. One major difficulty in developing a program is to change the perspective from a scenario developer having a bird's eye view over all objects, to a computer executing a program having a very local view restricted to the (local) variables visible within the current method. This change of perspective is a difficult abstraction step being the direct base for the method implementation. To facilitate this change of perspective, the next sections present two methods, one for using in a self-study or lecture environment called *Model Exploration* (Section 6.1) and one called the *Object Game* (Section 6.2) which fits especially well for a group of persons (and for interactive teaching). With the help of the new perspective, we go through the storyboard again and try to derive general program execution rules, i.e, abstract program steps. We call this phase storyboard abstraction.

When we take a look at the Study-Right University with assignments, we know its scenario (Figure 5.1), the storyboard (Figure 5.2-5.4), and that we want to implement this functionality as part of our program. Now, our task is to figure out how to program this functionality. In Java, nearly all code resides in methods. Thus, we first need to define a method that hosts the code for the desired functionality and we need to find a class to host that method. We will name the method doAssignments and locate it in the class Student for now.[1] Looking at the storyboard, we can see that probably no extra information is needed apart from the room and assignments which are connected via associations to the student. Therefore, we keep the signature empty. We can also just leave it empty in the beginning and fill it on demand, if the Model Exploration or Object Game reveals that we need some more input. We know what is happening for the specific case that Karli is in the math room. To help us get an idea of what will happen in the general case of a random student in a random room with random assignments, we will now try to allow the exploring person of the Model Exploration or the participants of the Object Game to experience a shift of perspective. This shift in perspective means leaving the bird's eye perspective of a scenario developer and to take the perspective of a computer executing a program. A computer executing a program has a restricted view on the current object model. The computer sees only the elements of the object model that are reachable via the (local) variables of the currently executed method.

6.1 Model Exploration

Model Exploration is suited to help a single developer to do the just mentioned shift in perspective. To take the view of a computer as a single person, we start

---

[1]In regard of separation of concern, adding such functionality to the model is usually not a good choice. As moving this method to another class with so called refactoring methods is relatively easy, we will ignore this warning here.

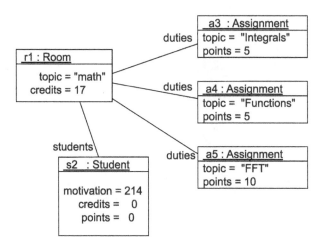

Figure 6.1: Object diagram for start situation for a student doing math assignments

with the object diagram of Figure 6.1.

We want to go through an invocation of method doAssignments on object s2. When the computer enters the execution of this method, at the beginning it just knows that it is inside some object. Thus, from the computer's point of view, the current object diagram looks as shown in Figure 6.2.

To simulate the computer's view, we may put the full object diagram aside and take a blank sheet of paper and draw an empty box for the invocation target and a small arrow pointing to it. We label the arrow with the method invocation statement.

Alternatively, you may print the object diagram and take a pencil and gray out the parts of the object diagram that the computer does not yet see, cf. Figure 6.3. During the following execution steps, we may use an eraser to reveal the discovered parts of the object diagram to the computer.

Following the "blank sheet of paper" approach of Figure 6.2, in the next step, the computer may ask the current object for its type and look-up the class diagram to find out which attributes and references the current object carries, cf. Figure 6.4

So, with this limited information at hand, what shall the computer try next in order to do the student's assignments? With our knowledge of the overall object model, we might advice the computer to look up the pos attribute of the current object. This reveals, the room object where the student is currently located. After identifying the type of the reached object and after retrieval of its attributes, the

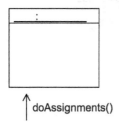

doAssignments()

Figure 6.2: Object diagram from computer's point of view on invocation

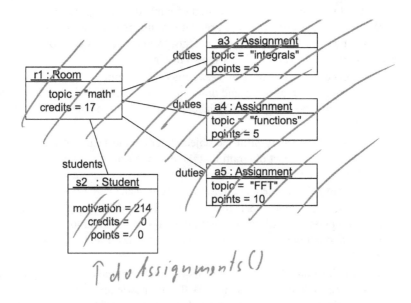

Figure 6.3: Object diagram with fog of oblivion

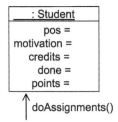

Figure 6.4: Object diagram with fog of oblivion

computer's view of the current situation is shown in Figure 6.5. Each time we do such an exploration step, we should ask ourselves whether this operation works only for the given situation or whether it is a general operation that works in many or all situations. If it is a general step, we log it as one step of the general program that we want to write. In our example, for a Student object seeking to do assignments, looking up the current room is a general step that should be executed in all cases. Thus we protocol this operation as step 1 of our algorithm on our paper sheet, cf. Figure 6.5. Well, for students outside the university this step may fail. We keep that in mind as a possible corner case and go on with the algorithm exploration.

So, our computer knows a little bit about the current student and the student's current location. How shall we go on to do the assignments? With our background knowledge, we advice the computer to look up the room's assignments, cf. Figure 6.6.

In our example situation, the room has three Assignment objects attached to its assignments attribute. Thus, we might advice the computer to visit the first, second, and third assignment. However, if we think of the general case, the assignments attribute may hold an arbitrary number of assignments, 3, 4, 10, or none at all. Thus, a more general advice to our computer is to loop through the set of available assignments. Actually, this is a quite general rule of thumb: "if you explore a to-many association, use a loop". Thus, we add to our algorithm

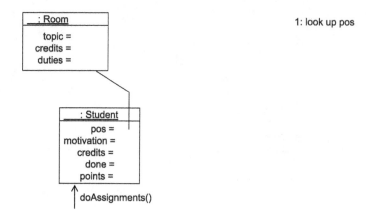

Figure 6.5: Object diagram with room explored

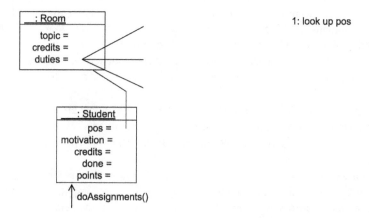

Figure 6.6: Object diagram with room's assignments explored

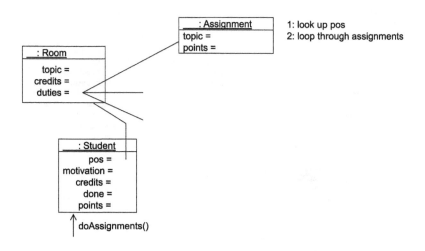

Figure 6.7: Object diagram with first assignment explored

protocol as step 2 "loop through assignments". And, in order to go on with our exploration, we enter the loop and retrieve the first assignment of our example, cf. Figure 6.7.

OK, the computer has found an assignment it might "do". Hm, how is an assignment done by the computer? From the storyboard step 4 we recall, that for the topmost assignment the student's `points` go up to 19 and the `motivation` drops down to 195. In addition, the assignment is added to the students `done` links. Well, are 19 and 195 the general case? No, in general, we read the assignment's points and add the result to the student's points and subtract it from the motivation. Thus we instruct the computer accordingly, cf. Figure 6.8. Following these advices, the computer explorers that the current assignment has 5 points and that the student has had no points yet and thus ends up with 5 points. The student has had a motivation of 214 which is thus changed to 209, now. In addition, the done link is created.

So, the computer is done with this assignment. What's next? Next assignment? Why not. Just add to the protocol that we go back to step 2 of our algorithm in order to look up the next assignment and then actually redo the exploration for steps a) through d). We end up in Figure 6.9.

Note, the computer has a very limited short term memory. Actually, the computer recalls / knows only things that are stored in the local variables of the current method. Thus, if we use a loop variable to store the current assignment, the content of this variable is overwritten in each loop iteration. Thus, although the computer has just visited the first assignment at the beginning of the second

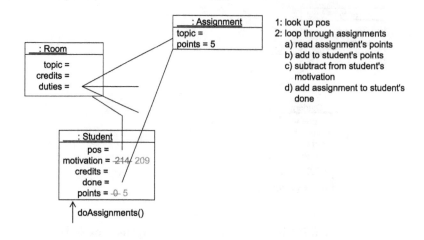

Figure 6.8: Object diagram with first computations

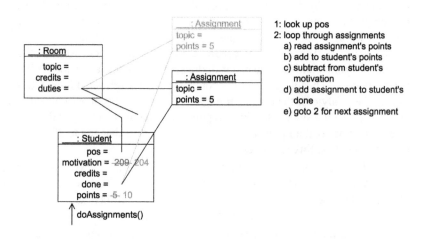

Figure 6.9: Object diagram with second computations

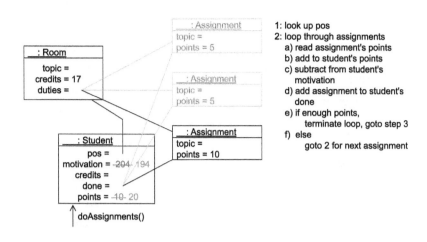

Figure 6.10: Object diagram with third computations

iteration, it has already forgotten the first assignment and now focuses on the second one. To make you aware of this focus change, the just forgotten assignment is grayed out in Figure 6.9.

Ok, second iteration done. Hm, how many iterations shall we do? From the storyboard, we know that in our example situation we need three iterations. Is this the general case? No. Thus, do we usually iterate through all assignments of a room? No. As already mentioned in the textual story for our example and as mentioned in the comments to our storyboard, we stop acquiring points as soon as we have enough points to get the credits of the current room, i.e. we stop iterating when the student's points are equal or greater than the credits of the current room. Thus, we change step e) of our algorithm protocol and insert a check for loop termination, cf. Figure 6.10. Note, due to the new advice in step e) of Figure 6.10, the computer now has to look up the value of the credits of the current room. Thus, the credits attribute shows its value (17). In Figure 6.10 we have already done the third iteration and the computations for the third assignment. In this iteration the check of step e) of our algorithm is successful and the loop terminates.

So, the loop has terminated and in our example we have acquired enough points to earn the credits. Hm, is this generally true? Well, as our story comments tell, we have asked our customer, the professors of the Study-Right University whether there will always be enough assignments available. They assured this. We have explicitly asked for it and it's in the protocol and they have signed the protocol. They are professors! They know their business! You can trust them! Well, no. If the program crashes on this, they will blame you anyhow. Thus, we

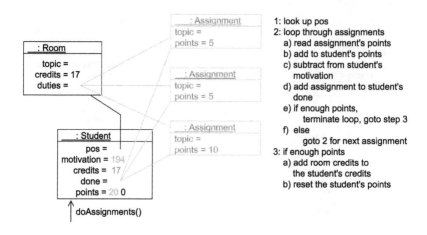

Figure 6.11: Earning the credits

better double check the points earned. If we have enough points, we shall earn the credits and reset the points, cf. Figure 6.11.

Victory! We have earned the credits. We have successfully explored our model and developed the algorithm that realizes the general behavior of the doAssignments method. With this algorithm outline, we can go for method implementation, testing, deployment, victory party, and vacation. Hm, did we really catch all cases? Well, there was this corner case that the student has no room. Not yet handled. And, yes step 3 of our algorithm double checks that we have enough credits, but we have not yet specified the failure case. And, our story mentions that students may visit rooms multiple times and they shall do new assignments each time. Therefore, the student's done association stores the already done assignments. Good. But our loop does not check whether an assignment has already been done. To cover these extra cases, we should extend our scenario and storyboard or come up with alternative scenarios. We might either develop these alternative scenarios and storyboards now, or we might create a todo item and go for implementation and testing of our current algorithm outline first. There is no strict rule here. It might depend on the complexity of the cases or just on your preferences.

This section explains the model exploration method in very detailed and tiny steps. Our goal was to equip you with an actual systematic method for algorithm design. Therefore, we went through all the tiny steps of the model exploration. This detailed model exploration describes the following method for the design of simple algorithms: from the start object, look-up neighbors and neighbor's neighbors until you reach all necessary information. Be aware of the computer's limitations / capabilities. To deal with overwriting of variable contents, accumulated (e.g. sum up) information during loops. On each exploration step ask for the general case. If an attribute is changed, ask for the computation rules. If you look up a to-one reference, consider that it might be null. If you look up a to-many reference, use a loop. Ask for termination conditions. After a loop, ask whether it has terminated normally. Do the termination conditions you expect hold in all cases? This approach is guided by the example object models you consider. Be sure to consider all relevant examples. While the object models are a valuable help for the design of simple algorithms with the model exploration method, this also limits the kind of algorithms that might be developed with this method. More complex algorithms will most likely need additional creative ideas, developer knowledge, and experiences. Still, due to our experiences, starting with concrete example object diagrams and storyboards is a tremendous help for algorithm development.

6.2 Object Games

The Object Game is suited to experience the shift in perspective as a group in a game. We want the participants of this game to think like or think in objects. For this we will select several players with different roles:

Processor: We select a person, we call the processor. This person will be blindfolded and interact with physical objects (like bowls or boxes) representing the objects of the initial object diagram of the storyboard. Blindfolding achieves the effect of simulating the limited view of the processor, similar to the fog of oblivion in the Model Exploration.

Processor-assistant: This person represents actually the memory and helps the processor to remember positions of physical objects and marks these on demand with sticky-notes.

Logger: This person will take notes of questions, actions, and memory assignments the processor does, but tries to write it down in a generalized form (which should be discussed amongst the team members). This log will be in the end a pseudo code-like input for the actual implementation of the method. Therefore, the logger and the supporting team have always to discuss here what could change for a similar scenario and how could this different scenario also be supported by the same actions.

Other participants will be advisers and can help the players making decisions. It is advisable to have the class diagram and storyboard at the whiteboard or printed out while playing the Object Game. In class it makes sense to have a student recording this game with a video or mobile phone camera. There are

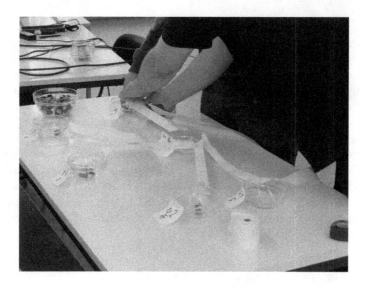

Figure 6.12: Object Game setup with bowls and strips.

various materials you can use to play the game. In one case we have used bowls
as objects, paper strips as associations (very easy to label), pebbles for simulating
the attributes (see Figure 6.12), and sticky-notes for variables. In another case we
have used LEGO® TECHNIC elements building boxes and detachable LEGO®
arms as associations, small LEGO® bricks for the attributes (see Figure 6.13),
and sticky-notes for labels of the associations variables. With enough open-
minded participants the Object Game can also be carried out with persons as
objects and their arms as associations (see Figure 6.14).

After setting up the start situation for the Object Game, the selected processor
player is given access to the object of the class of the invoked method. This object
should be named this. This naming process is done by asking the processor
assistant to provide a sticky-note labeled this and attaching it to the start object.
We (the processor assistant) record this step. The start object is in our example
here the object representing Karli of the class Student. The person playing the
processor must now think what will be the next step. Usually, the first steps
will be inferring the relevant context for executing the task. In our case this
will mean finding the current room and giving it a name like r. For finding
the room, the processor player will have to de-reference the pos-association.
We record this step. The next step will be trying to do one of the assignments.
The players will however discover that there are several assignments attached
to the room. They will discuss that in the general case they have to somehow
address that the number of the attached assignments is not known in the general

Figure 6.13: Object Game with LEGO® TECHNIC.

Figure 6.14: Object Game with persons as objects. Image taken from [22].

case. From the annotations in the storyboard we know that we have to address here several assignments to gain enough assignment points. So there we will find out that we have to do something here with all assignments attached to the room. We have discovered that we have to use a loop when we try to follow a to-n association (compare with class diagram). We record this loop. This discussion for the finding of the general rule is a main point of the Object Game and most important step. This is the actual abstraction. It helps a lot to ask the questions here, what can change in the future. What are other scenarios to be covered by the same rules we are currently deriving. After finding the loop, we can discuss how the selection of one of the assignments takes place. Mainly, we are only concerned that the assignment is not yet done. We will write this down as the selection criteria. We will now pick one assignment and assign it a name like a. We record this step. We will now collect the assignment points located in this assignment and add it to the local assignment points of the student marked by the this object. We will also deduct the assignment points from the motivation points. We record this step. Maybe we will actually discover here, that some corner cases like motivation drops under zero or being smarter in selecting an assignment with lower motivation points might have been necessary, we will omit this discovery at this point. Then we will go back to a and create an association to the student marked by this to remember that this assignment has already been done. We record this step. If the number of assignment points is now higher or equal to the credit points which can be earned (can be read in the room r) then the student receives the credit points and sets the assignment points back to 0. We record this step. If there are not enough assignment points gathered the student will now go back to the room r and find the next assignment which has not yet been done (has not yet an association to the student) and move the sticky-note with the a to the new assignment. We record the loop end. We will most likely discover here that we have not covered the case that happens if there is no assignment left for achieving enough assignment points (it might be also already noted in the storyboard). This will eventually (not in this simple case) trigger the development of another scenario and if already present now also play an Object Game amending the log we created for this current Object Game. Also the case of re-visiting a room will be omitted here for simplicity reasons, but should be covered in a real world setting - we can leave the changes for this as an exercise to the reader.

This game will lead to a protocol which will look similar to the one in Figure 6.15. The protocol is the pseudo code or algorithm description we can use for implementing the method.

As we are mainly dealing in this method with doing assignments one possible name choice for it is doAssignments. This is what we will use for this book.

Also Model Exploration can be carried out in a group as an alternative to the Object Game. We call it then the Sticky-Notes Test. In general this requires

1. Label start object with `this`.

2. Find current room in following `pos` association and label it `r`.

3. Loop over the following

   (a) Pick an (the first found) assignment reachable via a room association and not being connected to the student `this`

   (b) Label this assignment as `a`.

   (c) Take assignment points and add points and link to student `this`.

   (d) Use up motivation (deduct assignment points) from it.

   (e) This is done until we have enough points to earn the credits of the current topic or no assignments are left.

4. If we have enough points, we earn the credits.

Figure 6.15: Example log of Object Game.

less resources and players. We just need paper, blackboard, or whiteboard, and sticky-notes. Also here it is advisable to have the class diagram and storyboard on the whiteboard or printed out as a reference. As a preparation we have to copy the start situation to our choice of writing mean. If we have multiple people, the roles are as before: processor, processor assistant, logger. If we have only one person, all roles have to be carried out by this person. We will mark the object corresponding to our selected class with a sticky-note labeled `this` and gray out[2] the rest of the objects. This grayed out part is the fog of oblivion. It simulates the blindfoldedness of the processor in the Object Game. The rest works just as in the Object Game, just that the fog of discovered objects is removed from them. The Sticky-Notes Test can also be used as a real test for validating a previously derived pseudo code or algorithm. It can be used to simulate the actual method being called on a computer or on paper or on the blackboard and uncover possible misbehavior.

---

[2]This graying out can be realized either with paper covering the grayed out object or on the black- and whiteboard with striking through the object or really graying it out.

6.3 Exercises

6.3.1 Mau Mau

Take the storyboards of our Mau Mau example from Section 5.1.1 and develop pseudo code algorithms for:

- dealing cards,

- playing a seven and letting the next player draw two cards,

- playing a Jack and changing the current color,

- computing the set of cards the current player could play,

- not being able to play a card and thus drawing one card from the deck and passing on.

6.3.2 Battleships

Take the storyboards of our Battleships example from Section 5.1.2 and develop pseudo code algorithms for:

- checking the placement of ships for overlap,

- firing on the other players board, checking for a hit, and checking for sinking ships and checking for the end of the game.

6.3.3 Mancala

Take the storyboards of our Mancala example from Section 5.1.3 and develop a pseudo code algorithm for:

- selecting one house and taking the pebbles and redistributing them,

- and considering the case to end in your own Khala and having another turn,

- and possibly earn opposite pebbles or have another turn.

6.3.4 Mensch Ärgere Dich Nicht

Take the storyboards of our Mensch Ärgere Dich Nicht example from Section 5.1.4 and develop a pseudo code algorithm for moving a pawn once the player has rolled the dice

- address a simple move,

- address kicking another player's pawn from the field,

- address not being allowed to kick your pawn from the field,

- address entering the landing fields,

- address putting a pawn from the base field to the starting field.

6.3.5 Towers of Hanoi

Take the storyboards of our Towers of Hanoi example from Section 5.1.5 and develop pseudo code algorithms for:

- moving a tower of disks from the left to the right pole,

- in an intermediate situation giving the user a hint which disk should be moved next and where to move it.

6.3.6 ATM Money Withdrawal

Take the storyboards of our ATM Money Withdrawal example from Section 5.1.6 and develop pseudo code algorithms for:

- computing a "nice" combination of bills of different values for the customer,

  - Some 5, 10, and 20 Euro bills, mostly 50 Euro bills.
  - Sometimes you may run out of e.g. 20 Euro bills.

- computing the sum of withdrawals per day. You may also print the list of withdrawals,

- printing an account statement, i.e. printing the withdrawals for a given account for e.g. one month.

6.3.7 Borrowing Electronic Books from Library

Take the storyboards of our Library example from Section 5.1.7 and develop pseudo code algorithms for:

- identifying the favorite book category of a given user,

- recommending new books to some user,

- finding two users that own "similar" books and propose to make contact which each other.

6.3.8   Trouble Ticket System

Take the storyboards of our Trouble Ticket System example from Section 5.1.8 and develop pseudo code algorithms for:

- identifying the "trouble maker" of the month, i.e. the customer that has filed the most trouble tickets,

- identifying the "trouble shooter" of the month, i.e. the employee that has closed the most tickets,

- identifying the 100 most urgent tickets, i.e. the tickets that have not been reacted on for the longest time.

6.3.9   Webshop

Take the storyboards of our Webshop example from Section 5.1.9 and develop pseudo code algorithms for:

- identifying your 10 best customers,

- identifying your 10 best selling products,

- computing your monthly shipping costs.

6.3.10   Connect Four Game

Take the storyboards of our Connect Four Game example from Section 5.1.10 and develop pseudo code algorithms for:

- checking whether one player has won,

- checking whether the other player can win with his next move and whether and how the current player can prevent this.

Chapter 7

Simple Java with Object Models

Before we are going to discuss testing in the next section, you need a certain intuition how the methods you will test look. Therefore, we now implement the first pieces of functionality for our Study-Right University example.

If you are an experienced programmer used to dealing with object models, you may skip this section. If you are not used to programming with object models, this section will be good training to get started.

In Chapter 6 we have developed a pseudo code algorithm for doing assignments in some room. This algorithm shall now be coded in Java using the implementation of our object model. Let us first revisit the class diagram we have derived from the object diagrams used in storyboards in Chapter 5, cf. Figure 7.1.

As discussed in Chapter 4 this class diagram is implemented in Java by creating Java classes with fields for the attributes of the classes. For example we implement or generate a Java class Student with a field credits of type int and with methods getCredits() and setCredits(int value) to control the access to this field, cf. Listing 7.1. The other attributes of class Student and the attributes of the other classes are implemented, similarly.

In addition, the lower half of Listing 7.1 shows the implementation of the Student part of the pos association between classes Student and Room, cf. Chapter 4. Similar code implements the opposite direction of this association in class Room. The done and the room association of Figure 7.1 are implemented in the same way. These class implementations are the basis for the implementation of our doAssignments method.

The first step in implementing the doAssignments method is to add its declaration to the Java code of class Student, cf. Listing 7.2 (we have omitted the attribute and association implementation parts).

```
1    package study_right;
2    public class Student
3    {
4        private int credits;
5
6        public void setCredits(int value)
7        {
8            this.credits = value;
9        }
10
11       public int getCredits ()
12       {
13           return this.credits;
14       }
15           . . .
16       private Room pos;
17
18       public void setPos (Room value)
19       {
20           if (this.pos != value)
21           {
22               Room oldValue = this.pos;
23               if (this.pos != null)
24               {
25                   this.pos = null;
26                   oldValue.removeFromStudents (this);
27               }
28               this.pos = value;
29               if (value != null)
30               {
31                   value.addToStudents (this);
32               }
33           }
34       }
35
36       public Room getPos ()
37       {
38           return this.pos;
39       }
40           . . .
41   }
```

Listing 7.1: Java code for class Student derived from the class diagram (excerpt)

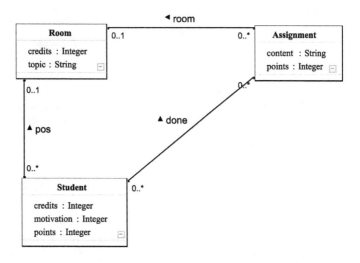

Figure 7.1: Class diagram for the "Karli does math assignments" storyboard

```
1   package study_right;
2   public class Student
3   {
4       . . .
5       public void doAssignments ()
6       {
7       }
8       . . .
9   }
```
Listing 7.2: Java code for method doAssignments, the declaration

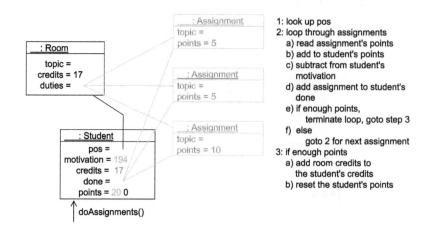

Figure 7.2: Earning the credits

Now we revisit the object diagram and the pseudo code algorithm for method doAssignments from Chapter 6, cf. Figure 7.2.

Action 1 of the algorithm requires us to look up the room where our student is positioned. As you see, this information is stored in the pos field of the Java class Student. To access this field we have to use the getPos method. The result may be stored in a variable currentRoom of type Room, cf. line 8 of Listing 7.3. Note, we use the text from the pseudo code as comment in method doAssignments. Thereby, we connect our implementation to this design step.

Action 2 of our algorithm in Figure 7.2 requires to loop through the assignments of the currentRoom. As we know from the implementation of the associations, the assignments of a room are stored in a LinkedHashSet in the assignments field of Java class Room and this LinkedHashSet instance may be retrieved by method getAssignments. To iterate through a collection of objects, Java provides a special for loop, cf. lines 10 through 14 in Listing 7.4. This for loop uses a loop variable, in our case nextAssignment, that is assigned each element of the collection, one after the other. The collection to be iterated through is given after a colon, in our case by currentRoom.getAssignments().

Action 2.a) and 2.b) of our pseudo code algorithm read the assignment's points, cf. line 14 of Listing 7.5 and add these points to the student's points. As we are not allowed to assign new values to the points field of our student, directly, we have to use the setPoints method, cf. line 17. Similarly, in line 20 we use method setMotivation to subtract the points from the student's motivation. This achieves action 2.c) of our pseudo code algorithm. Finally, we add the

```
1  package study_right;
2  public class Student
3  {
4       . . .
5      public void doAssignments ()
6      {
7          // look up pos
8          Room currentRoom = this.getPos();
9      }
10      . . .
11 }
```

Listing 7.3: Java code for method doAssignments(), getPos()

```
1  package study_right;
2  public class Student
3  {
4       . . .
5      public void doAssignments ()
6      {
7          // look up pos
8          Room currentRoom = this.getPos();
9
10         // loop through assignments
11         for (Assignment nextAssignment :
               currentRoom.getAssignments())
12         {
13
14         }
15     }
16      . . .
17 }
```

Listing 7.4: Java code for method doAssignments, loop

completed assignment to the done association of the student, cf. line 23.

As outlined in actions 2.e) and 2.f) of our pseudo code algorithm, we shall terminate the loop as soon as we have collected enough points. Enough points means, more points than credits of the current room. Thus, we use an if-statement comparing the student's points with currentRoom.getCredits and we use a break command to leave the loop, if we have enough points, cf. line 26 through 29 of Listing 7.6.

Our loop may terminate for two reasons: we have earned enough points or we run out of assignments. Thus, as outlined in action 3 of our pseudo code algorithm, after the loop we check again whether our student's points suffice to earn the room's credits, cf. line 33 of Listing 7.7. If we have enough points, line 36 adds the room's credits to our student's credits and then we reset the student's points as required in action 3.b of our pseudo code algorithm.

Now we are almost done.

Actually, we have now implemented our pseudo code algorithm. However, the pseudo code algorithm is not complete. Deriving it, we have not considered what happens when we visit a room a second time. In this case, the student shall not do the old assignments a second time but shall do the new assignments. To achieve this, we store the assignments that have been completed in the student's done association. But, we do not yet use this information to avoid double usage of the same assignment. Thus, we need to extend our algorithm to handle second visits. We should derive this extension for our algorithm by going through an extended model exploration as described in Chapter 6. This would reveal that at the beginning of our loop we should check, whether our student has already done this assignment and it should be skipped accordingly. In Java we might then implement this case distinction as shown in lines 15 through 17 of Listing 7.8. Here we use a Java continue statement to skip the current assignment. Alternatively, we might have wrapped the old loop body in an if-statement with an inverse condition.

We still need to handle yet another exceptional case: our student may run out of motivation. If the student's motivation does not suffice to do an assignment, we might skip that assignment and hope for an easier one. In our Java code this is achieved by lines 21 through 23 of Listing 7.8.

Well, do we have all cases now? So far we have identified missing situations by going through more alternative scenarios in our model exploration approach to algorithm design. While this works well in the beginning, it is pretty hard to really cover all cases by example situations. Therefore, an additional way to identify missing cases is to go through the code you are writing. For each statement you ask yourself: will this work in any situation? Is there a situation where this line might break?

Let us do this for the code in Listing 7.7. The code in line 8 finds currentRoom by invoking this.getPos(). Will this work in all cases? No:

```
1   package study_right;
2   public class Student
3   {
4       . . .
5       public void doAssignments ()
6       {
7           // look up pos
8           Room currentRoom = this.getPos();
9
10          // loop through assignments
11          for (Assignment nextAssignment :
                currentRoom.getAssignments())
12          {
13              // read assignment's points
14              int assignmentPoints = nextAssignment
                    .getPoints();
15
16              // add to student's points
17              this.setPoints(this.getPoints() +
                    assignmentPoints);
18
19              // subtract from student's motivation
20              this.setMotivation(this.getMotivation
                    () - assignmentPoints);
21
22              // add assignment to student's done
23              this.addToDone(nextAssignment);
24          }
25      }
26      . . .
27  }
```

Listing 7.5: Java code for method doAssignments(), handle one assignment

```
1   package study_right;
2   public class Student
3   {
4           . . .
5       public void doAssignments ()
6       {
7           // look up pos
8           Room currentRoom = this.getPos ();
9
10          // loop through assignments
11          for (Assignment nextAssignment :
                currentRoom.getAssignments ())
12          {
13              // read assignment's points
14              int assignmentPoints = nextAssignment
                    .getPoints ();
15
16              // add to student's points
17              this.setPoints (this.getPoints () +
                    assignmentPoints);
18
19              // subtract from student's motivation
20              this.setMotivation (this.getMotivation
                    () - assignmentPoints);
21
22              // add assignment to student's done
23              this.addToDone (nextAssignment);
24
25              // if enough points, terminate loop
26              if (this.getPoints () >= currentRoom.
                    getCredits ())
27              {
28                  break;
29              }
30          }
31      }
32          . . .
33  }
```

Listing 7.6: Java code for method doAssignments(), loop termination

```
1    package study_right;
2    public class Student
3    {
4        . . .
5        public void doAssignments ()
6        {
7            // look up pos
8            Room currentRoom = this.getPos ();
9
10           // loop through assignments
11           for (Assignment nextAssignment : currentRoom.
                 getAssignments ())
12           {
13               // read assignment's points
14               int assignmentPoints = nextAssignment.getPoints ();
15
16               // add to student's points
17               this.setPoints (this.getPoints () + assignmentPoints
                     );
18
19               // subtract from student's motivation
20               this.setMotivation (this.getMotivation () -
                     assignmentPoints );
21
22               // add assignment to student's done
23               this.addToDone (nextAssignment );
24
25               // if enough points, terminate loop
26               if (this.getPoints () >= currentRoom.getCredits ())
27
28                   {
29                       break;
30                   }
31           }
32
33           // if enough points
34           if (this.getPoints () >= currentRoom.getCredits ())
35           {
36               // add room credits to student's credits
37               this.setCredits (this.getCredits () + currentRoom.
                     getCredits ());
38
39               // reset the student's points
40               this.setPoints (0);
41           }
42       }
43       . . .
44   }
```

Listing 7.7: Java code for method doAssignments(), earn credits the student may be outside of the Study-Right University. Well, if the student is outside the university, why should anyone call doAssignments on him or her? Here we hit a very delicate case: Generally, on writing method doAssignments we might validly assume that it is used only for students who are in a room. This is somehow a precondition or consistency assumption of our method. Thus, if doAssignments is called on a student without a room, we consider this as an error. So, how shall we handle this error? We might use a Java assert statement to check this precondition during testing and to disable this test in the productive code, cf. line 9 of Listing 7.8. The authors of this book strongly recommend NOT to use Java assert. Java assertions might be turned off for the productive code and thus the error is not handled when it occurs after deployment of the program. This means, the error is not handled when the customer uses your program with real data. Bizarre!

On the other extreme, we might handle the error with an if-statement as in line 10 of Listing 7.8. In this if-statement we just terminate the current method. This is again NOT recommended. Terminating silently means that the error remains unreported and actually unhandled. Thus, the caller of your method will wonder why it does not work. Actually, the user will just see that something does not work and get no idea where to look for the cause of this. To actively report the error, the authors of this book strongly recommend to use Java exceptions. Raising an exception reports the position in code where the problem occurs. The error will not sneak out silently. And Java provides means for exception handling that enables you to catch the exception and do some rescue steps to keep your application alive in case it is already productive. Thus, we recommend to do nothing about the error in our method doAssignments but just let the NullPointerException occur. Still, your overall application needs to ensure that this will not happen and it should do exception handling somewhere above your method to handle the error. This should probably be done close to the user interface. Someone might get the idea to add a throws XYException to the declaration of our method to ensure that the user will not forget to take care of this error case. However, such throws declarations force to handle the exception at each point where our method is used. Probably we want to handle the error only once on a higher level closer to the user interface. When the user just adds the same throws declaration to his method, all users of this method get the same problem. At the end almost all methods have to be extended by throws declarations. This is just too tedious. Leave it unchecked. Make a note to handle it close to the user interface (and do not forget this note).

Let us continue to check the Java code of Listing 7.7 for alternative cases. Line 11 contains our for loop. Might this fail? Yes: getAssignments() might return null and cause the loop to throw an exception. As discussed above, we might just let this exception occur. However, it is also easy to ensure that the assignments field of the Java class Room is always initialized with an empty set. Then we are safe. [1]

Line 14 does not raise an exceptional case. The for loop guarantees that nextAssignment cannot be null.[2] Therefore, points might be negative (or NaN). However, this should be avoided elsewhere. Therefore, it is not a todo for us. The same is true for the setPos command in the next line.

Line 20 does not throw any exception but it actually reveals an important situation that is not yet addressed: the assignmentPoints may be greater than the student's motivation. While this safely computes to a negative motivation value for our student, our application example says that students get expelled from the university when they run out of motivation. This case has not been addressed in our algorithm design in Chapter 6 and thus our pseudo code algorithm does not cover it. By going through our code we have now detected this case. Whenever you detect such an important missing case, you need to identify how to handle it. It is a common software developer failure to do this on your own like "need to finish this, let's do that". Such cases need to be discussed with your customer. You as a developer usually do not know what your customer expects in how the system should behave in the new situation you have just identified. If you are lucky, the scenarios and storyboards you have discussed with your customer already covers this case, and it has just not yet been regarded in algorithm design. Therefore, try to look up the desired behavior and implement it. If the scenarios do not help, you need to create a new one in order to discuss the problem with your customer. With the help of the new scenario your customer will easily understand the problem and with the help of using the customer's domain knowledge it will be easy to determine how this case is supposed to be handled. This can then be used to extend your algorithm and to handle the new case in your code correctly. In our example, the scenarios already tell that student motivation should not become negative but the student shall be expelled from the StudyRight University. However, when we revisit this case with our customer, the customer may point to an example situation where the first assignment is really tricky and thus has e.g. 42 points while the next assignment is pretty easy and has e.g. only 5 points. If the student has a motivation of 23 left, this motivation does not suffice for the first assignment but it is still enough for the second. Accordingly, students should not be expelled on the first assignment they do not master, but we should go on visiting other assignments. In Listing 7.8 we achieve this by

---

[1]Caveat: in practice, a large fraction of the collection fields of your objects remain empty through the whole runtime of your application. Thus, if you initialize all collection fields of all your objects with empty sets you waste a substantial amount of memory. It is better to use a single empty set instance to initialize all collection fields. When the first object is added to a collection field, you create an individual set for that field containing the objects. The Fujaba code generator provides you with code that handles collections in such a way.

[2]Caveat: if you might manage to add null to your collection and thereby get null assigned to your loop variable. In our case the addToAssignments method handles null and does not add it to the collection.

the if-statement in lines 21 through 23. This if-statement uses a Java `continue` statement to go to the next iteration of our `for` loop.

Let us look at the next line 23 of Listing 7.7. This line may hardly raise an exception as neither `this` nor `nextAssignment` can easily be `null`. If you are very smart, this line may raise your interest as `nextAssignment` may already be contained in the student's assignment set. While this will not raise an exception, the students should not earn the assignment's points again, if they have already done this assignment. Thus, we need to avoid redoing assignments that students have already completed e.g. on an earlier visit. To be honest, it is very hard to spot this problem by reading the code. More likely you identify it through scenario elaboration with your customer. Anyway, our code needs to handle this case: we again use an `if`-statement this time at the beginning of our loop in lines 15 through 17 of Listing 7.8 that uses a `continue` command to skip already completed assignments.

The `if`-statement on line 26 of Listing 7.7 raises no new problems. Similarly, the if-statement in line 33 looks fine as well as line 36. In line 36 the student's credits may increase greater than the required total amount of credits that the student need to get the exam and in the Study-Right University having too many credits will also expel you from the university. However, this case will be dealt with in the exam room, nothing to be done here.

The next tricky line of code is line 39 of Listing 7.8. Actually, we should have spotted this problem already on line 14. Line 39 safely resets the students' points before they leave the current room to do assignments in another room. However, if the student did not earn enough points to achieve the credits, line 39 will not be executed at all and thus the achieved points will not be reset. We might fix this problem by moving the `setPoints(0)` statement behind the if-statement in order to guarantee that it is always executed. Doing this, we would still have to worry about "if problem then return" statements within the methods that could leave it without resetting the points. Thus, an experienced programmer would intuitively reset the points at the beginning of method `doAssignments`, cf. line 5 of Listing 7.8. It is just more secure to clean up the workspace yourself instead of relying on the assertion that others will leave the place tidy.

OK, this was a lengthy and detailed discussion and you might have got the impression that coding with objects is not easy at all. Honestly, doing the actual Java code is a challenging task requiring some training and experience. Still, if you compare our initial algorithm and our respective Java code, you have to admit that there is a close correspondence. As soon as you are used to the accessor operations that implement our object model, it becomes straightforward to realize the different steps of an algorithm. This is especially true if the algorithm is sufficiently detailed, or more precisely, if the algorithm is close enough to the object model. If it is hard to implement an algorithm step, usually such a step contains hidden complexity, and you may consider to refine this step into a more

```
1   package study_right;        public class Student {
2       public void doAssignments ()
3       {
4           // reset student's points
5           this.setPoints(0);
6           // look up pos
7           Room currentRoom = this.getPos ();
8           // no room, terminate
9           // assert currentRoom != null;
10          // if (currentRoom == null) { return; }
11          // loop through assignments
12          for (Assignment nextAssignment : currentRoom.
                getAssignments())
13          {
14              // if assignment has already been done
15              if (this.getDone().contains(nextAssignment)) {
16                  continue;
17              }
18              // read assignment's points
19              int assignmentPoints = nextAssignment.getPoints();
20              // if not enough motivation
21              if (this.getMotivation() < assignmentPoints) {

22                  continue;
23              }
24              // add to student's points
25              this.setPoints(this.getPoints() + assignmentPoints
                    );
26              // subtract from student's motivation
27              this.setMotivation(this.getMotivation() -
                    assignmentPoints);
28              // add assignment to student's done
29              this.addToDone(nextAssignment);
30              // if enough points, terminate loop
31              if (this.getPoints() >= currentRoom.getCredits())
                    {
32                  break;
33              }
34          }
35          // if enough points
36          if (this.getPoints() >= currentRoom.getCredits())
37          {
38              // add room credits to student's credits
39      this.setCredits(this.getCredits()+currentRoom.getCredits()
            );
40              // reset the student's points
41              this.setPoints(0);
42      }   }
43      . . .
44  }
```

Listing 7.8: Java code for method doAssignments, more conditions detailed description that is closer to the object model. Similarly, the identification of missing cases is a matter of experience. However, as we tried to show, there are some systematic checks you might go through that may already help you to identify missing cases. Any time you succeed in spotting such a missing case by just discussing scenarios with your customer or by checking your code line by line will save you hours and hours of debugging and bug fixing and will make your customer and manager happy.

When we go on with programming with the help of object models, we will introduce a graphical language for programming with object patterns, the so-called *story diagrams*. Story diagrams facilitate to cover complex cases more easily. Story diagrams will be introduced systematically in Chapter 9. As an example, we will give a story diagram for our example operation doAssignments Section 10.2, cf. Figure 10.11. Once you are able to read story diagrams, you may come back and compare the Java solution in Listing 7.8 with the story diagram in Figure 10.11.

7.1 Exercises

7.1.1 Mau Mau

Take the pseudo code algorithms of our Mau Mau example from Section 6.3.1 and implement these algorithms as Java methods.

- You may test your methods by invoking them in various situations created e.g. in the storyboard implementation done for Exercise 5.1.1.

- You may analyze the effects of your methods by inspecting the result (or intermediate states) with the help of eDOBS and the Eclipse debugger.

7.1.2 Battleships

Take the pseudo code algorithms of our Battleships example from Section 6.3.2 and implement these algorithms as Java methods.

- You may test your methods by invoking them in various situations created e.g. in the storyboard implementation done for Exercise 5.1.2.

- You may analyze the effects of your methods by inspecting the result (or intermediate states) with the help of eDOBS and the Eclipse debugger.

7.1.3 Mancala

Take the pseudo code algorithm of our Mancala example from Section 6.3.3 and implement this algorithm as Java method.

- You may test your method by invoking it in various situations created e.g. in the storyboard implementation done for Exercise 5.1.3.

- You may analyze the effects of your method by inspecting the result (or intermediate states) with the help of eDOBS and the Eclipse debugger.

7.1.4 Mensch Ärgere Dich Nicht

Take the pseudo code algorithms of our Mensch Ärgere Dich Nicht example from Section 6.3.4 and implement these algorithms as Java methods.

- You may test your methods by invoking them in various situations created e.g. in the storyboard implementation done for Exercise 5.1.4.

- You may analyze the effects of your methods by inspecting the result (or intermediate states) with the help of eDOBS and the Eclipse debugger.

7.1.5 Towers of Hanoi

Take the pseudo code algorithms of our Towers of Hanoi example from Section 6.3.5 and implement these algorithms as Java methods.

- You may test your methods by invoking them in various situations created e.g. in the storyboard implementation done for Exercise 5.1.5.

- You may analyze the effects of your methods by inspecting the result (or intermediate states) with the help of eDOBS and the Eclipse debugger.

7.1.6 ATM Money Withdrawal

Take the pseudo code algorithms of our ATM Money Withdrawal example from Section 6.3.6 and implement these algorithms as Java methods.

- You may test your methods by invoking them in various situations created e.g. in the storyboard implementation done for Exercise 5.1.6.

- You may analyze the effects of your methods by inspecting the result (or intermediate states) with the help of eDOBS and the Eclipse debugger.

7.1.7 Borrowing Electronic Books from Library

Take the pseudo code algorithms of our Library example from Section 6.3.7 and implement these algorithms as Java methods.

- You may test your methods by invoking them in various situations created e.g. in the storyboard implementation done for Exercise 5.1.7.

- You may analyze the effects of your methods by inspecting the result (or intermediate states) with the help of eDOBS and the Eclipse debugger.

7.1.8   Trouble Ticket System

Take the pseudo code algorithms of our Trouble Ticket System example from Section 6.3.8 and implement these algorithms as Java methods.

- You may test your methods by invoking them in various situations created e.g. in the storyboard implementation done for Exercise 5.1.8.

- You may analyze the effects of your methods by inspecting the result (or intermediate states) with the help of eDOBS and the Eclipse debugger.

7.1.9   Webshop

Take the pseudo code algorithms of our Webshop example from Section 6.3.9 and implement these algorithms as Java methods.

- You may test your methods by invoking them in various situations created e.g. in the storyboard implementation done for Exercise 5.1.9.

- You may analyze the effects of your methods by inspecting the result (or intermediate states) with the help of eDOBS and the Eclipse debugger.

7.1.10   Connect Four Game

Take the pseudo code algorithms of our Connect Four Game example from Section 6.3.10 and implement these algorithms as Java methods.

- You may test your methods by invoking them in various situations created e.g. in the storyboard implementation done for Exercise 5.1.10.

- You may analyze the effects of your methods by inspecting the result (or intermediate states) with the help of eDOBS and the Eclipse debugger.

Chapter 8

Testing

"Did you test your code?" - asks the Boss the programmer. Of course, you implemented some code, fired up the program and tried out the new functionality once – it works fine! However, this is not a test, this is a try-once-with-one-value verification. What if the program crashes on too large or negative user input values? What if you use it differently somehow? What if the functionality fails after being run once? To guard against these types of failures, we want to use software tests.

Testing our object structures at runtime has one major drawback: it requires many manual steps to produce a certain object structure when starting from scratch with an empty object heap in the runtime environment. A solution to that problem can be methods, which contain some story diagrams or code to produce the desired object structure, but we still have to inspect the structure manually, maybe after performing some manual modifications, whether it is still correct. The solution to that problem are software tests, which feature the following properties:

- A test is *fully programmatic*, meaning it can be executed without any user interaction required.

- If our test does not utilize any (truly) random data, it always produces the same result, so tests are *reproducible*.

- Instead of human inspection after running a test, it should look at the result itself, so tests are *self evaluating*.

As we are doing here Story Driven Modeling, testing is of course also an integral part of this software development method. We especially like to write tests first before we implement the corresponding program logic. If you have done programming before you will have seen similarities between our scenarios and storyboards. Also tests are very concrete and have a start situation and verify some part of the system against a desired end situation. The beauty of our scenarios is that you can translate them easily step by step into tests. We can even write the tests before we have our class diagram. As an example, we will take again a look at the scenario presented in Chapter 5. Take another look at Figure 5.1 for the start situation and Figure 5.1 for the scenario and Figures 5.2-5.4 for the storyboard. We will create a new project and in it a new test case, best named something like TestKarliMath. Then we will copy the scenario text into the test class and comment it out. Referring to the first object diagram storyboard and the start situation we will now implement the start situation. Implementing the first step, will result in the following code:

```
 1  // 1.  Karli  enters  the  Study-Right  University  in
         the  math  room.
 2  //       Karli  has  no  credits  yet  and  still  a
         motivation  of  214.
 3  Room r1 = new Room()
 4         .withTopic("math")
 5         .withCredits(17);
 6  Assignment a1 = new Assignment()
 7         .withContent("Matrix_Multiplication")
 8         .withPoints(5)
 9         .withRoom(r1);
10  Assignment a2 = new Assignment()
11         .withContent("Series")
12         .withPoints(6)
13         .withRoom(r1);
14  Assignment a3 = new Assignment()
15         .withContent("Integrals")
16         .withPoints(8)
17         .withRoom(r1);
18  Student karli = new Student()
19         .withName("Karli")
20         .withCredits(0)
21         .withPoints(0)
22         .withMotivation(214)
23         .withPos(r1);
```

If the classes have not yet been generated, you can quickly implement them as described in Chapter 4 (also refer to the explanation of the fluent Interface/with-based coding style there) using the quickfix-function of your IDE now. In step 2 Karli does assignment a1. Therefore, we can now implement the first method. The test code will look like the following:

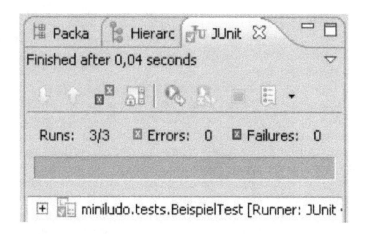

Figure 8.1: JUnit-Runner Screenshot

```
1  // 2. Karli does assignment a1 on Matrix
       Multiplication and earns 5 points
2  // (general rule: the student earns always full
       points for doing an assignment).
3  // Karli's motivation is reduced by 5 points to
       now 209.
4  karli.doAssignments(a1);
5  assertEquals("Karli has wrong amount of points.",
       5, karli.getPoints());
6  assertEquals("Karli has wrong amount of
       motivation.", 209, karli.getMotivation());
```

`assertEquals(..)` is used to check, if some value has the right value after executing a method. Here we are checking if the points have been added and deducted correctly. This is the basic working principle of software tests.

8.1   Testing in Java with JUnit

Software tests in Java is usually done with the JUnit library, developed by Kent Beck & Erich Gamma [15, 25].

The authors propose the test-first principle, which means that you write your tests before writing any productive code. That helps you a lot to stay on the concrete level when implementing. There is a concrete situation under test. When designing the test, you are forced to design a clean (public) interface of your objects under test. By adding more tests, and therefore different situations, we can make sure that we have chosen the right level of abstraction if our interface can cover these. There should be tests for failure situations, which forces the developer to think of them early, and to really execute the corresponding failure detection at some point.

JUnit features a Test Runner, which is probably also integrated into your favorite IDE. Figure 8.1 shows a JUnit Runner within the Eclipse IDE. A Test Runner takes one or more tests and executes them in a clean runtime environment. During that, a green progress bar is progressing for each executed test. A test can report a failure, for example in its self-evaluation, by throwing a certain exception, which gets caught by the Runner. As soon as there is at least one failure, the progress bar turns red. Therefore, a green JUnit result bar means all tests were successful, this is what the developer should aim for. A red bar means one or more tests failed, which usually means that the business logic implementation handles the test situation incorrectly, assuming that the test itself is correct. Tests are always concrete: They test, starting from a certain situation, that concrete values are met, as shown in the code examples above.

Some properties of your program are easy to test, luckily the important ones are:

- business logic - for example, when Alice has 150 EUR on her account and Bob 33 EUR, does the bank account transfer of 100 EUR from Alice' to Bob's account really result in Alice having in the end 50 EUR on her account and Bob having 133 EUR on his?

- calculations - for example, do the credit points of the rooms Karli visited with the pathfinder algorithm in the Study Right University really sum up to 214?

Other properties are difficult to test, especially Graphical User interfaces - is the "login" button really shown at pixel position 150, 100 and does the password dialog pop really up when clicking on it? Also difficult to test is when your program somehow interacts with the environment or certain operation conditions - does our database never deadlock when we have multiple low-bandwidth connections with reconnections?

8.2   Creating our First Test

In Java, software tests get organized in a so-called test case. A test case is nothing more than just a collection of individual test methods, each representing a different, independent test. Therefore, we create a test by writing a method, that follows the following structure:

1. A test creates a certain, concrete object structure, either by instantiating objects itself, linking them and assigning attributes, or, by calling API functions which do the work for us.

2. Then the test performs operations on the initial structure, for example by calling a method. It is calling your productive code (*business logic*), so some behavioral code implementing a certain functionality. It is important to call the actual productive code here, preferably with a single method call, and not doing the work a business logic method *would* do (by duplicating code).

3. Finally, the result of the method call or the resulting object structure is programmatically inspected and compared to the expected values or structures, which is again a concrete situation. The expected values can be obtained from the program specification. Comparing actual to excepted values is done with so-called assertion-methods.

Example: The object under test is an adder with the following interface:

```
class Adder
{
    int add(int a, int b) { ... }
}
```

The corresponding test method might look like this:

```
@Test
void testAdderSituation1 ()
{
    // build the initial situation
    Adder add = new Adder();
    int a = 5; int b = 3;

    // perform operation under test
    int result = adder.add(a, b);

    // evaluate result
    assertEquals(8, result);
}
```

The annotation @*Test* (from org.junit.Test) tells the JUnit framework that this is a test method, which can be run in a JUnit Test Runner. In this test method, we first create a new adder object, which is our object under test. We want to test that it summarizes the numbers 3 and 5 correctly. The assertion method used here is assertEquals(...), which compares any (primitive) expected value with the actual one (variable result).

As we learned before, a test class might contain multiple test methods. If these methods share a lot of the initial situation building, this can be collected in a separate setup method, which the JUnit Runner calls before executing each single test method. Such a method must carry the @Before annotation.

```java
@Before
public void setup()
{
    Bank b = new Bank();
    Customer alice = new Customer("Alice");
    Customer bob = new Customer("Bob");
    aliceAccount = new Account(b, "32442545").
        withOwner(alice);
    bobAccount = new Account(b, "44543214").
        withOwner(bob);
    aliceAccount.deposit(10000);
    bobAccount.deposit(10000);
}


@Test
public void transferOK()
{
    aliceAccount.transfer(5000, bobAccount);
    assertEquals(5000, aliceAccount.getBalance())
        ;
    assertEquals(15000, bobAccount.getBalance());
}

@Test
public void transferSilentlyDenied()
{
    bobAccount.transfer(15000, aliceAccount);
    assertEquals(10000, aliceAccount.getBalance()
        );
    assertEquals(10000, bobAccount.getBalance());
}
```

So, why do we have the balance of 10000 for each account finally at the end of the test? First of all, JUnit doesn't necessarily execute the test methods in the given order - transferSilentlyDenied might be executed first. However, if it would be executed with the balance of 15000 for Bob and 5000 for Alice as we have after the first test transferOK, we would accept the transfer to be OK, right? JUnit ensures that each test method finds the same preconditions. That is done by invoking the @Before method before *each* individual test method. So, then `transferSilentlyDenied` starts, we again have the balances of 10000 each, as `setup` has been just called. The test denies the transfer silently, because Bob's balance is only 10000 compared to the requested 15000. Generally, it's a good idea to have individual test methods as independent as possible. Group them in one class when they use the same preconditions (the object structure built by the `setup` method in this case), use different classes for different test environments. Your IDE will even help you in organizing tests in packages or test runners to run multiple test classes at once.

8.3 JUnit Assertions

There exist various assertion methods in JUnit for comparing all primitive values as well as objects:

- `assertEquals(Object expected, Object actual)` calls `Object.equals()`. Overriding this method in your model classes simplifies comparison if you do not want to just test for object identity.

- `assertEquals(boolean | byte | short | int | long expected, boolean | byte | short | int | long actual)` does the same for comparing primitive Java types.

- `assertEquals(float | double expected, float | double actual, float | double epsilon)` does so for floating-point numbers. Because floating-point numbers cannot precisely represent all real numbers, this method accepts an epsilon parameter that specifies the range in which both numbers are considered to be equal. E.g. 0.1 will be represented as 0.100000001490116119384765625[1] in single precision, so you'd need an epsilon of at least 10^{-8} to compare such numbers.

- `assertTrue( boolean )` most basic assertion - but beware of using `assertTrue( a. getBalance() == 10000)` as you lose descriptive JUnit error messages.

- `assertFalse( boolean )` is just the opposite, helpful to improve readability of double-negations. `assertFalse( script. hasSyntax-Errors())` reads better than `assertTrue(!script.hasSyntax-Errors())`, as the exclamation mark can be easily missed.

- `assert[Not]Null(Object)` is the simpler and more descriptive assertion compared to `assertTrue(room. getParent() == null))`.

---

[1] try it: `System.out.println(new java.math.BigDecimal(0.1f));`

- assert[Not]Same(obj1, obj2) - in contrast to assertEquals(..) this method does not call Object.equals() but enforces the same object identity - which is simply done by a obj1 == obj2 expression[2]. Objects can be equal (that definition is up to the programmer, usually specified with the equals()-method), but here we ask if different references to one object really point to the same object in heap memory.

- fail() will be explained in the next section - it can be used to enforce a assertion error and often makes sense in combination with some control flow and code blocks which shouldn't be reached when the test runs as intended.

We suggest to do a static import to the Assert class, so all assertion methods are available in the local namespace: You don't have to write Assert.assertSomething(), but can simply write assertSomething(..).

On a failed assertion or explicit call of fail() JUnit will throw a junit.-framework.AssertionFailedError, which is usually not caught by any try/-catch block in the code under test because it is derived from java.lang.Error. It will be caught by the JUnit framework and tells it that the test has failed, which will lead to the red bar, if only a single error occurs.

All assertion methods are also available with a ,String message' as first parameter. The parameter is optional, this message will be passed through JUnit when an assertion fails and be visible on the error report. That message might help to understand what went wrong, especially when the assertions are more complex. On a failed assertion, JUnit will pass this string to the AssertionFailedError and therefore it will be displayed in the resulting error view. Example:

```
public void testByteOverflow ()
{
  byte value = 100;
  value *= 2;
  assertEquals("value_should_double", value, 200);
}
```

This code will produce an overflow of the byte variable value, as its range is only from -128 to 127. JUnit will show the error message *Value should be double*. One way to fix this test would be to declare value as int.

---

[2]Remember when you learned, as Java beginner, that (someString == "Hello World!") did not work but s.equals("Foo") did the job?

8.4 Testing for Errors

A test method might throw any exception (checked exceptions just have to be declared). If thrown, the JUnit Runner denotes this method as failed. For example, if your business logic code throws a `NullPointerException`, the test will fail with such a message. However, good tests evoke exceptions: We should test that our code reacts correctly to erroneous situations, and that should be done with exceptions. Let us have a look at an example that tests for such a case:

```
public void testOverdrawFailure()
{
    Account ac = new Account(100);
    try
    {
        ac.withdraw(200);
        fail();
    } catch (NoDepositException e)
    {
        // you may use assert to check the
        // exception details
    }
}
```

...with the following implementation...[3]:

```
public void withdraw(int amount) throws
    NoDepositException
{
    if (balance - amount < 0)
    {
        throw new NoDepositException();
    }
    balance -= amount;
}
```

A complete test for testing depositing into our bank account, testing a positive withdrawal, and a overdraw, looks like this:

```
import static org.junit.Assert.assertEquals;
```

---

[3]We use a checked exception here to create this JUnit example : `NoDepositException` derives from `java.lang.Exception`, thus it must be declared to be thrown which enforces the programmer to add a try/catch-Block or re-throw the exception in the calling code. We strongly discourage the use of checked exceptions as it bloats the code and is a common pitfall for beginners (when it's unclear how and where to handle the exception). Use runtime exceptions instead, document them well of course.

```java
import static org.junit.Assert.fail;

public class BankTest
{

    Account ac = new Account(100);

    @Test
    public void testWithdrawal() throws
        NoDepositException
    {
        ac.withdraw(100);
        assertEquals(0, ac.getBalance());
    }

    @Test
    public void testOverdrawFailure()
    {
        try
        {
            ac.withdraw(200);
            fail();
        } catch (NoDepositException e)
        {
            // you may use assert to check the
            exception details
        }
        assertEquals(100, ac.getBalance());
    }
}
```

In both tests, we check that the final deposit is still correct.

A good practice is to keep your production code completely free from JUnit dependencies. Therefore, different source folders for test and production code within our project help a lot. Later on, you can decide to distribute only the production code. But you can use the same package names, that way access to package-local declared members is possible within test classes.

Another thing you need when writing more complex tests are mock-ups and test drivers. This is especially true for distributed applications: running a test should not rely on the external (production) database system, should not rely on real-world PayPal payment system to test for example shopping workflows. Therefore, you need to mock-up a coupled system or datasource or network resource to be able to let your test run, and to be able to rollback its changes after-

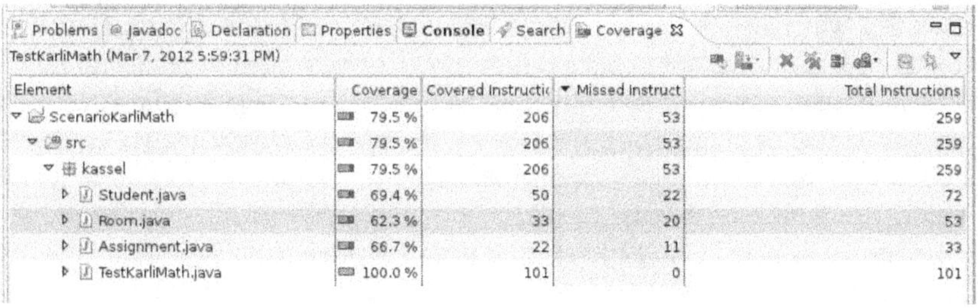

Element	Coverage	Covered Instructic	Missed Instruct	Total Instructions
ScenarioKarliMath	79.5 %	206	53	259
src	79.5 %	206	53	259
kassel	79.5 %	206	53	259
Student.java	69.4 %	50	22	72
Room.java	62.3 %	33	20	53
Assignment.java	66.7 %	22	11	33
TestKarliMath.java	100.0 %	101	0	101

Figure 8.2: Test Coverage Statistics

wards. Keep that in mind when designing the interfaces to those. A test driver is a component that helps you to control the environment of your test run, for example a mocked up generator for generating asynchronous user input events, which your code under test has to handle.

Tests introduced so far are just a single method call within the JUnit framework, so the test is single-threaded. When having a more complex, concurrent application (see Chapter 12), your application might split the work into multiple threads and you cannot tell easily whether the operation of your productive code has been finished and the test code can check its assertions or the operation is still running. Adding synchronization possibilities should be preferred instead of just waiting X seconds in your test.

8.5 Test Coverage

Apart from testing functionality, we can also test which parts of the code are actually executed. If you find code which is not covered by your tests (which you actually constructed from your scenarios or storyboards), you have most likely found some code which deals with some kind of exceptional case, which has not been discussed with the client or potential user. It might be a good idea to initiate this discussion now and adapt the scenarios correspondingly. What should happen if Karli's motivation drops under zero, will he be thrown out of the university, go (how long) on vacation, or is there an entity where he can get new motivation? You do not want the developers to make this decision on their own, the client has to approve.

To do coverage testing in Eclipse, there is an excellent plugin, called *eclEmma*[3]. If we run our initially described test with this plugin, we get statistics like in Figure 8.2.

eclEmma will also color all lines of codes it covered in green, all lines of code it did not cover in red, and partially covered lines (like only partially executed `if`-conditions) in yellow. Therefore, our interest goes to the red and yellow lines, which can be easily found, if we look at the file listed in the statistics. However, it is normal not to have full coverage of generated code. There might be a lot of methods generated which are not needed in the particular context of the system you develop. For Fujaba-based models, we have usually a coverage around 70% due to various support methods and due to the fact that only the minority of generated accessor methods are used (however, they can be proven to be correct as being auto generated all from the same template). Manually developed code should have a coverage of close to, but not exactly 100%. To reach 100% you would have to throw each checked exception so its corresponding catch block gets covered, and therefore you need lots of error-prone code like `if (testMode) { throw IOException("Just testing!"); }` in productive code, this is a bad idea. Remember, the aim of testing and coverage is to improve your code, quality, and maintainability!

8.6   Exercises

8.6.1   Mau Mau

Take the storyboard implementation for our Mau Mau example from section 5.1.1 and turn it into a JUnit test:

- Add calls to the methods developed in exercise 6.3.1 in appropriate places.

- After each method call, add assert statements to ensure that the methods achieve the desired effects.

- Run your test and get a green JUnit result bar.

- Validate that your test finds bugs by introducing some bugs to your methods (you may e.g. comment some lines of code) and rerun your test. This should result in red JUnit result bars.

- Check the test coverage achieved by your (successful) tests using e.g. eclEmma. Try to improve your test coverage by extending your tests.

8.6.2   Battleships

Take the storyboard implementation for our Battleships example from section 5.1.2 and turn it into a JUnit test:

- Add calls to the methods developed in exercise 6.3.2 in appropriate places.

- After each method call, add assert statements to ensure that the methods achieve the desired effects.

- Run your test and get a green JUnit result bar.

- Validate that your test finds bugs by introducing some bugs to your methods (you may e.g. comment some lines of code) and rerun your test. This should result in red JUnit result bars.

- Check the test coverage achieved by your (successful) tests using e.g. eclEmma. Try to improve your test coverage by extending your tests.

8.6.3 Mancala

Take the storyboard implementation for our Mancala example from section 5.1.3 and turn it into a JUnit test:

- Add calls to the methods developed in exercise 6.3.3 in appropriate places.

- After each method call, add assert statements to ensure that the methods achieve the desired effects.

- Run your test and get a green JUnit result bar.

- Validate that your test finds bugs by introducing some bugs to your methods (you may e.g. comment some lines of code) and rerun your test. This should result in red JUnit result bars.

- Check the test coverage achieved by your (successful) tests using e.g. eclEmma. Try to improve your test coverage by extending your tests.

8.6.4 Mensch Ärgere Dich Nicht

Take the storyboard implementation for our Mensch Ärgere Dich Nicht example from section 5.1.4 and turn it into a JUnit test:

- Add calls to the methods developed in exercise 6.3.4 in appropriate places.

- After each method call, add assert statements to ensure that the methods achieve the desired effects.

- Run your test and get a green JUnit result bar.

- Validate that your test finds bugs by introducing some bugs to your methods (you may e.g. comment some lines of code) and rerun your test. This should result in red JUnit result bars.

- Check the test coverage achieved by your (successful) tests using e.g. eclEmma. Try to improve your test coverage by extending your tests.

8.6.5   Towers of Hanoi

Take the storyboard implementation for our Towers of Hanoi example from section 5.1.5 and turn it into a JUnit test:

- Add calls to the methods developed in exercise 6.3.5 in appropriate places.

- After each method call, add assert statements to ensure that the methods achieve the desired effects.

- Run your test and get a green JUnit result bar.

- Validate that your test finds bugs by introducing some bugs to your methods (you may e.g. comment some lines of code) and rerun your test. This should result in red JUnit result bars.

- Check the test coverage achieved by your (successful) tests using e.g. eclEmma. Try to improve your test coverage by extending your tests.

8.6.6   ATM Money Withdrawal

Take the storyboard implementation for our ATM Money Withdrawal example from section 5.1.6 and turn it into a JUnit test:

- Add calls to the methods developed in exercise 6.3.6 in appropriate places.

- After each method call, add assert statements to ensure that the methods achieve the desired effects.

- Run your test and get a green JUnit result bar.

- Validate that your test finds bugs by introducing some bugs to your methods (you may e.g. comment some lines of code) and rerun your test. This should result in red JUnit result bars.

- Check the test coverage achieved by your (successful) tests using e.g. eclEmma. Try to improve your test coverage by extending your tests.

8.6.7   Borrowing Electronic Books from Library

Take the storyboard implementation for our Library example from section 5.1.7 and turn it into a JUnit test:

- Add calls to the methods developed in exercise 6.3.7 in appropriate places.

- After each method call, add assert statements to ensure that the methods achieve the desired effects.

- Run your test and get a green JUnit result bar.

- Validate that your test finds bugs by introducing some bugs to your methods (you may e.g. comment some lines of code) and rerun your test. This should result in red JUnit result bars.

- Check the test coverage achieved by your (successful) tests using e.g. eclEmma. Try to improve your test coverage by extending your tests.

8.6.8 Trouble Ticket System

Take the storyboard implementation for our Trouble Ticket System example from section 5.1.8 and turn it into a JUnit test:

- Add calls to the methods developed in exercise 6.3.8 in appropriate places.

- After each method call, add assert statements to ensure that the methods achieve the desired effects.

- Run your test and get a green JUnit result bar.

- Validate that your test finds bugs by introducing some bugs to your methods (you may e.g. comment some lines of code) and rerun your test. This should result in red JUnit result bars.

- Check the test coverage achieved by your (successful) tests using e.g. eclEmma. Try to improve your test coverage by extending your tests.

8.6.9 Webshop

Take the storyboard implementation for our Webshop example from section 5.1.9 and turn it into a JUnit test:

- Add calls to the methods developed in exercise 6.3.9 in appropriate places.

- After each method call, add assert statements to ensure that the methods achieve the desired effects.

- Run your test and get a green JUnit result bar.

- Validate that your test finds bugs by introducing some bugs to your methods (you may e.g. comment some lines of code) and rerun your test. This should result in red JUnit result bars.

- Check the test coverage achieved by your (successful) tests using e.g. eclEmma. Try to improve your test coverage by extending your tests.

8.6.10   Connect Four Game

Take the storyboard implementation for our Connect Four Game example from section 5.1.10 and turn it into a JUnit test:

- Add calls to the methods developed in exercise 6.3.10 in appropriate places.

- After each method call, add assert statements to ensure that the methods achieve the desired effects.

- Run your test and get a green JUnit result bar.

- Validate that your test finds bugs by introducing some bugs to your methods (you may e.g. comment some lines of code) and rerun your test. This should result in red JUnit result bars.

- Check the test coverage achieved by your (successful) tests using e.g. eclEmma. Try to improve your test coverage by extending your tests.

Chapter 9

Story Diagram Idioms

Story diagrams have proven to be a powerful language for programming the behavior part of complex object models. However, many beginners having backgrounds in textual object oriented languages have difficulties in expressing standard idioms like for-loops, switch case constructs, and recursion. Therefore, this chapter provides a systematic overview of the most important story diagram idioms. By listing all these story diagram idioms, this chapter is somewhat boring and eventually due to the lack of examples difficult to read. For examples, have a look at Chapter 10. Actually, we recommend to just browse through this chapter and then use it as a kind of dictionary to look-up certain idioms as you need them for your own story diagram.

To explain the execution of story diagrams we will use an abstract machine model, the *FAMous Fujaba Abstract Machine*. Therefore, for each example our figures show a split screen where the left panel shows the internal state of the Fujaba Abstract Machine while the right panel shows the story diagram under execution, cf. Figure 9.1. With the help of these two views we go through example scenarios and explain the execution semantics of our story diagram idioms step by step.

9.1 Story Diagram Control Flow Idioms

Let us start with control flow idioms.

9.1.1 Empty Story Diagram

Story diagrams consist of activities connected by transitions, cf. Figure 9.1, lower right part. Story diagrams are based on UML activity diagrams. In UML activity diagrams, the control flow always starts at a bullet. From there, transition

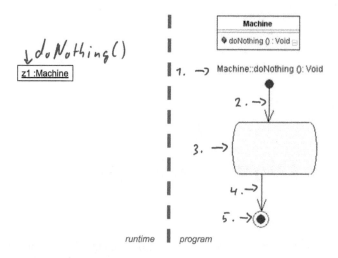

Figure 9.1: Executing an empty story diagram

arcs guide you to the first activity and then to the next activities until you reach a bull's eye, where execution terminates. Story diagrams use the same execution semantics. Thus each story diagram has a bullet representing its so-called *start activity* and a bull's eye called *stop activity*. The transitions of a story diagram form a control flow graph where all possible paths through a story diagram start at the start activity and eventually terminate at a stop activity.

In Figure 9.1, the control flow of the doNothing story diagram at the right is a straight sequence. This story diagram belongs to a class with name Machine shown above the story diagram. On the left of Figure 9.1 there is an instance z1 of class Machine. If we invoke operation doNothing on z1, the computer first looks-up the story diagram for this call, i.e. the doNothing story diagram and searches for its start activity. Second, the computer follows the only leaving transition arc leading it third to the empty activity. As there is nothing to do for an empty activity, in the fourth execution step the computer follows the only leaving transition and reaches in the fifth step the stop activity. At the stop activity, the method execution returns.

9.1.2   Java Statements in Story Diagrams

The simplest thing, a story diagram activity might contain, is a Java statement, cf. Figure 9.2. Actually, a story activity may contain any number of Java statements. As story diagram activities usually contain object diagrams, the Java statements are handled as diagram elements. This means, the Java statements may be placed

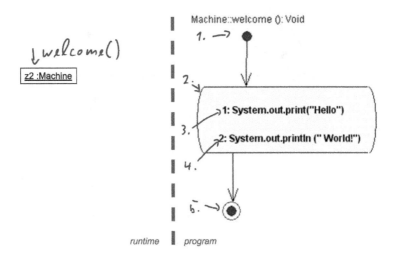

Figure 9.2: The must have "Hello World" story diagram

anywhere in the activity. Thus, we need running numbers to denote the order in which the Java statements shall be executed by the computer.

In our example, the execution of the welcome method would reach the story diagram activity with the Java statements in step 2. Due to the running numbers, the computer would in the third step execute the upper Java statement and print the word "Hello" on standard out. In step 4, the second Java statement is executed and the word "World" is printed. Then, in step 5 the stop activity is reached and the method terminates.

9.1.3 Sequences of activities

You may also have multiple activities within a story diagram, cf. Figure 9.3. As discussed, the computer starts the execution at the start activity and from there it will first visit the upper activity and execute the contained Java statement, i.e. it will print "first action". Then, the computer proceeds to the lower activity and prints "second action". In general, story diagrams may contain sequences of activities in arbitrary length.

9.1.4 If-Then-Else Control Flow

There are two different idioms for if-then-else control flow in story diagrams. Figure 9.4 uses a branch activity rendered as a diamond. This diamond stems

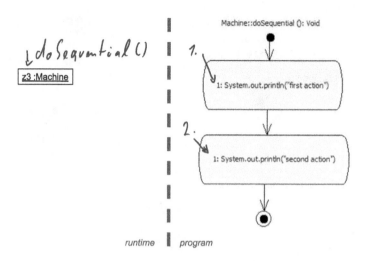

Figure 9.3: Sequence of activities

from old flow diagrams popular in the 70th. In flow diagrams you draw the condition within the diamond and you use `true` and `false` arcs to reach the `then` or the `else` activity, respectively. In UML activity diagrams and in story diagrams you attach the branch condition to the `then` arc and use a special `[else]` arc for the other case.

In UML activity diagrams, such a branch activity may have more than two leaving arcs. This allows to model if-then-else-if chains. However, in case of multiple arcs with condition expressions attached to them, it might happen that multiple conditions evaluate to true and then the computer would not know which one it should follow. To avoid such obstacles, story diagrams allow only one arc with a condition and the other arc has to be an `[else]` arc. Thus, an if-then-else-if chain would need multiple branch activities where the else arc of one branch activity leads to the next branch activity.

Actually, any story diagram activity may have an outgoing pair of condition and else arcs, cf. Figure 9.5. In Figure 9.5 we have just omitted the branch activity. Instead we have attached the branch condition to the left arc leaving the first activity and the [else] to the right arc. After executing the first Java statement, in the second step the computer examines the two leaving arcs and evaluates the condition arc. If `true`, as in our example, the computer follows this arc, otherwise it would have followed the `[else]` arc. Thus, in the third step of our example the computer reaches the lower activity, prints "2 is even" and terminates the method execution. As you see, omitting the branch activity results in more compact story diagrams and is therefore recommended.

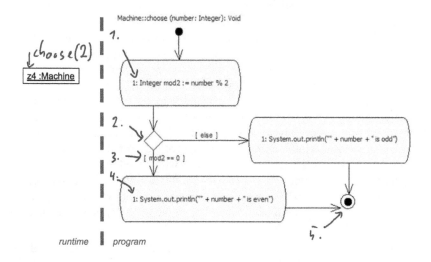

Figure 9.4: If-then-else control flow

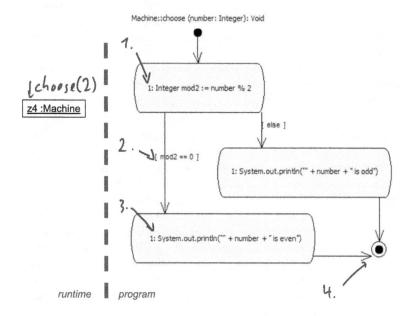

Figure 9.5: Omitting the branch activity

9.1.5   Loop Control Flow

Story diagrams provide various kinds of loop constructs. Well, for-loops are not directly supported by story diagrams. For-loops are merely used to iterate through arrays, and arrays are evil. Thus, story diagrams boycott for-loops. However, if you do not use an array but still need a for-loop, you may easily simulate the for-loop by for example a while-loop, cf. Figure 9.6. In Figure 9.6 the computer first initializes the loop variable i:=1. Note, during this example execution, variable i will be read several times and it will change its value several times. Thus, the computer needs to keep track of the current value of variable i. Therefore, the computer creates a sticky-note within the left panel of Figure 9.6 where its current memory state is shown. On this sticky-note the computer puts the names and values of the variables of the current method. Each time a variable is read, the computer looks-up the sticky-note. If the variable is written, the computer updates the sticky-note.

After storing the parameter number on the sticky-note and after initializing variable i, the computer evaluates the loop condition [i=number]. It looks-up i yielding a 1 and number yielding a 3 and thus the condition evaluates to true. Thus the computer reaches the lower activity and in the third step, it again looks-up i to print its value 1. In step 4, the computer has to increment variable i. Therefore, it looks-up variable i on the sticky-note, wipes out the old value 1 and stores the new value 2. After this, the loop body is done and the computer proceeds to the loop condition, again. This is repeated two more times until the loop condition fails and the method terminates. On method termination, the computer grabs the corresponding sticky-note and puts it into some virtual garbage bin. Maybe let us be a little bit more ecological: the computer collects the sticky-note, wipes it out and puts it on store for later reuse.

Note, understanding the concepts of variables and loops is a major obstacle for programming beginners. From the didactic point of view, this problem is well identified. A beginner reads a program top-down like a novel. During such a single walk through, the beginner is able to recognize variable assignments and to substitute later occurrences by the assigned values. However, a loop forces the beginners to jump back in their reading and read the same lines again. They think: "I have read this before. I know it." However, in a loop, the second time you go through the loop body, some variables may have changed their values and therefore, the meaning of the program text has changed. The program may even go through different branches of contained if-statements and thus this time the loop body has a totally different meaning. Strange. This never happened in school (outside the computer science course). To overcome this mental problem, the beginners need to add something like an abstract machine to their mental model. This abstract machine executes the program line by line and maintains a memory separate from the program code where variable values are stored. This

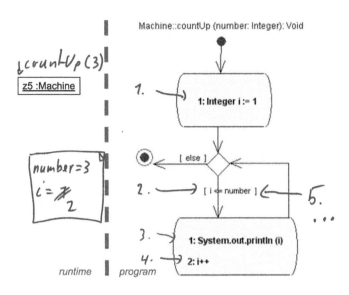

Figure 9.6: A standard loop

separate memory explains why on different runs the same line of code delivers different values for its variables and thus computes different results, causing for example different branching behavior. Note, the same problem occurs on recursive method execution: on the second visit / reading, the code in the method body has a different meaning / behavior. Therefore, recursion is another major obstacle for beginners. Again, a separate memory place, this time deploying a stack for variable values, helps to understand this phenomenon.

From a teaching point of view or from a textbook's point of view, this means, to explain the semantics of a programming language we need to provide an abstract machine that offers a separate memory space to maintain the different variable values during program execution. For teaching a language using object models, we actually need an abstract machine with separate memory space for variables and for the current object structure, i.e. we need the FAMous Fujaba Abstract Machine.

Story diagram activities may not only contain Java statements but also object diagram patterns. An activity containing an object diagram pattern is called a *story pattern* activity or short a story pattern. The systematic discussion of story pattern elements is done in Section 9.2. Here we just pick one story pattern element which is a boolean constraint rendered within curly braces, cf. the second activity of Figure 9.7. The semantics of a story pattern is to match it against

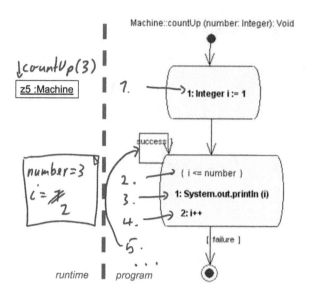

Figure 9.7: Looping without branch activity

the current object structure. You may also consider it as a kind of model query. When the computer tries to find a match for a story pattern, it might succeed or fail depending on the current situation. In a story diagram, you want to be able to react on success or failure of a story pattern. Therefore, story diagrams provide special [success] and [failure] arcs for story patterns that allow us to specify where the execution shall continue after success or failure of a story pattern matching. Of course the [success] arc does not need to lead back to the same node. It can lead to a different one and can be used to construct bigger and more complex loops. In addition, actions contained in the story pattern as e.g. Java statements are executed only if the matching was successful.

Overall, each story diagram activity is a small if-statement in itself. If the contained constraints are satisfied (the contained pattern matches), its actions are executed and the computer proceeds with the [success] arc, else the computer does not execute the actions and follows the [failure] arc. Using this feature usually results in more compact story diagrams and is thus recommended.

In Figure 9.7 we have moved the loop condition into a boolean constraint within the second activity. Thus, when the computer reaches the second activity it first evaluates the contained constraint. As stored in the sticky-note on the left panel of Figure 9.7 at this point variable i equals to 1 and variable number equals to 3. Thus the constraint evaluates to true and the two Java statements are

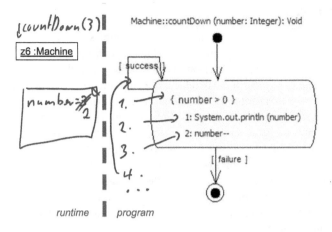

Figure 9.8: Looping without branch activity

executed. Since the constraint evaluation was successful, the computer follows the [success] arc leading it again to the second activity. Thus, the constraint is evaluated the second time, the Java statements are executed the second time and we follow the [success] arc a second time. Then, we repeat these steps a third time. On the fourth visit of the constraint, the value of variable i on the sticky-note has changed to 4 and thus the constraint is violated. Thus, the computer follows the [failure] arc, method execution terminates, the sticky-note is collected, wiped, and stored for reuse.

As discussed the use of a boolean constraint enabled us to get rid of a branch activity and to shorten the story diagram for our loop somewhat. Unfortunately, we cannot move the initialization of variable i into the loop body to get rid of the first activity, too. If we would initialize variable i within the loop body, it would be re-initialized on each iteration and thus never reach the termination condition. Thus, to get rid of the first activity we would need to get rid of variable i at all. We might do so by decrementing parameter number instead of incrementing a loop variable, cf. Figure 9.8. However, now it is no longer a countUp but merely a countDown.

9.1.6 Return Values

A story diagram may also have a return value. To return a value, you attach an expression to the stop activity. Note, a story diagram may have multiple stop activities (with different return expressions). With the help of return values, Figure 9.9 shows a story diagram computing the faculty of a number with recursive method invocations.

9.1.7   Recursion

On the initial invocation, the computer creates the blue[1] sticky-note and stores value 3 for parameter x. On execution step 1, the computer evaluates the branch condition to true and reaches the right stop activity. In step 2, the computer tries to evaluate the return expression. Therefore, the computer invokes the faculty method, recursively, this time with parameter value 2. For this new invocation, the computer creates another sticky-note. To simulate the procedure call stack, the computer glues this new sticky-note on top of the previous one. To distinguish the different sticky-notes, we draw them in different colors, this time we use green. On the new green sticky-note, we store value 2 for parameter x. In step 3 of our overall scenario we again evaluate the branch condition, it is again true. Thus, in step 4 the computer evaluates the return expression for the second time and invokes the faculty method now with parameter value 1. The computer creates another sticky-note, this time in red, and stores the parameter value on it. This time (overall step 5) the branch condition evaluates to false. Therefore, in step 6 the computer evaluates the return expression at the lower stop activity. This is just the constant 1. Thus, the red method execution terminates, the red sticky-note is collected and the return value is stored on the green sticky-note using a bull's eye as variable name. The green method execution is still evaluating the right return expression. Green x=2 multiplied by red return value 1 computes to 2. Thus, the green method execution terminates, the green sticky-note is collected and the green return value is stored on the blue sticky-note. The blue method invocation now multiplies blue x=3 by green return value 2 which results in 6. The blue method execution terminates and the blue return value is attached to the initial method invocation on object z7.

9.1.8   Exception Handling

Using Java methods and statements, sometimes you need exception handling, cf. Figure 9.10. In story diagrams, you may use a special [Exception e] arc. This creates a try-catch block with the corresponding catch-clause around the activity that is the source of the exception arc. In our example, the two Java statements in the first activity are surrounded by a try-catch block. Within the second activity, our example shows the body of our catch-clause. Of course, the body of the catch-clause might be more complex. However, at the end, the control flow of the catch-clause body should reach the same activity that is reached from the activity surrounded by the try-catch statement. In our case we need to reach the stop activity.

---

[1]For black and white printing, in Figure 9.9 we have marked the blue sticky-note and the first blue step number with a "b". The green and red elements are marked with "g" and "r", respectively.

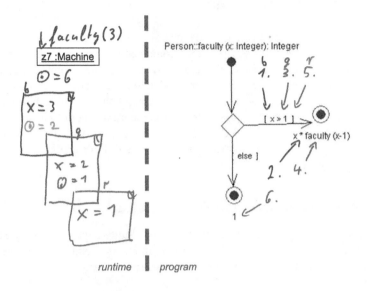

Figure 9.9: The other must have: a faculty function

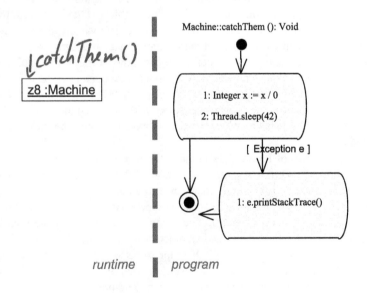

Figure 9.10: Exception handling

9.2   Story Pattern Elements

Story diagrams may contain activities that contain object diagram patterns. We call such activities *story patterns*. When the computer reaches a story pattern, it tries to match the contained object diagram pattern on the current runtime object structure. If this succeeds, the actions contained in the story pattern are executed and the computer proceeds with a [success] arc. If the matching fails, the computer proceeds with a [failure] arc. Object diagram patterns may contain various kinds of elements like objects and links to be matched and attribute value conditions and general boolean constraints to be fulfilled. Let's go through these elements step-by-step.

9.2.1   Pattern Variables and Pattern Objects

Figure 9.11 uses a slightly modified version of our Study-Right University example. This version uses explicit door objects to model the connection between different rooms. In Figure 9.11 we call method readEdgeSimple with parameter a3 on object s2.

As discussed in the previous section, to deal with loops and (recursive) method invocations, the computer needs to maintain the values of local variables separate from the program code / story diagram. In the previous section, we used colored sticky-notes to store plain numbers or string variables. To store the match of a story pattern, the computer introduces object valued variables for the objects that form the story patterns. Within these object valued variables the computer stores matching objects from the runtime object structure. In our object structure view, the computer maintains object valued variables by gluing a sticky-note with the variable's name onto the (upper right corner) of the runtime object currently contained in the variable. We also say *the variable is bound to an object*. If the variable value changes, its sticky-note is moved to the new content object. If the variable becomes null or the method terminates, the sticky-note is collected.

The story diagram of Figure 9.11 deploys three story patterns with overall nine pattern objects. Different pattern objects in different story patterns may share the same name. For example, there are three pattern objects with name this, one in each story pattern. There are two objects with name loc, one in the first and one in the third story pattern. The second and third story pattern each contain an object with name other and an object with name assign.

Pattern objects with the same name share the same variable. This means, we use one variable with name loc to store first the match of the loc object in the first story pattern and later to store the match for the loc object in the third story pattern. This way, we use the first story pattern to find a match for the loc object which is stored in the loc variable. When we reach the third story pattern, we

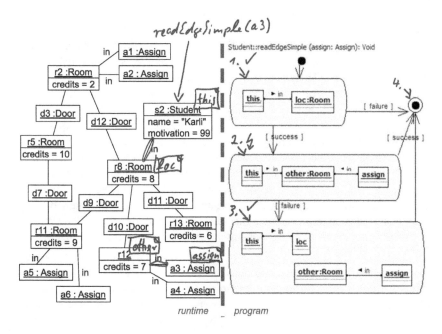

Figure 9.11: Simple story patterns

look-up the `loc` variable and reuse the contained object as match for the second `loc` object.

Overall, the story diagram of Figure 9.11 deploys four different variables `this`, `assign`, `loc`, and `other`. The `this` variable is an implicit variable that is bound to the method invocation target. In our example variable `this` is bound to object s2 as we invoke method `readEdgeSimple` on s2. See the sticky-note glued to object s2 in Figure 9.11. Variable `assign` represents the formal parameter of method `readEdgeSimple`. On method invocation, variable `assign` is bound to object a3 passed as actual parameter. Object a3 is shown in the lower right part of the object structure view of Figure 9.11 (just left of the vertical dashed line, second object from the bottom). Variables `loc` and `other` will be bound during the story pattern matching steps. Thus, the sticky-notes for `loc` and `other` are kept aside for later use. Note, if our current method calls another method, for the variables of this new method execution we use new sticky-notes with a different color. This way, the sticky-notes show us / and the computer at each time, which variable of which method execution refers to which runtime object.

9.2.2 Matching Objects and Links

In the first execution step of Figure 9.11, the computer tries to match the first story pattern. The first story pattern consists of two objects this and loc connected by an in link. The this object shows only the object name "this" while the loc object shows object name and type "loc:Room". Story pattern objects that show only their name tell the computer to look-up the value of the corresponding variable. We call such story pattern objects *bound pattern objects* or just *bound objects*. The runtime object contained in the variable corresponding to a bound pattern object is called the *runtime object matched by the bound pattern object* or short the *matched object*. Story pattern objects that show name and type tell the computer to ignore any existing content of the corresponding variable. Instead, the corresponding variable is set to null and a new binding shall be found such that all constraints of the story pattern are fulfilled. We call such story pattern objects *unbound pattern objects* or just *unbound objects*.

To execute the first story pattern of Figure 9.11 the computer shall look-up the binding / the sticky-note of variable this and find a new binding for variable loc. We also say, the computer has to *match pattern object* loc. Thus, the computer needs to match the unbound pattern object loc to a runtime object of type Room such that the objects matched by this and loc are connected by an in link. If we go through our runtime objects there are five candidates of type Room. From these five objects only object r8 has an in link connecting it to another object s2. Luckily, s2 is matched by this and thus s2 and r8 and the connecting in link are a perfect match for our story pattern. To record this, the computer binds variable loc to r8 and labels r8 with a loc sticky-note. Note, to match the loc object the computer actually does not need to go through the whole object structure to find candidates. As the this object is already matched, the computer may examine object s2 and look for neighbors reachable via in links. Actually, in this direction the in link is a to-one association and thus the computer may just look-up the corresponding attribute. In general, for matching an object diagram pattern, the computer will start from already bound objects and try to compute matches for the unbound objects by following neighbor links. This strategy usually results in efficient match computations.

In our example, the computer has successfully matched the first story pattern, thus it follows the [success] arc to the second story pattern. The second story pattern deploys three pattern objects. Two of these objects are bound, the this variable and the assign variable that represents the formal parameter of our method. The third pattern object with name other is unbound. This means, the computer needs to match pattern object other to a Room object that is connected to the match of the this object via an in link and in addition to the match of the assign object via another in link. As an exercise, you may now try to do the computer's job: use the sticky-notes to find the matches of this and assign in our example objects structure. Then try to match the other object. If you succeed you will have made a mistake. Unfortunately, none of the room objects in our example object structure has the required links. Room r8 is connected to s2, but not to a3. And room r12 is connected to a3 but not to s2. The other rooms have no connection to r8 or s2 at all. Thus, the computer fails to find a valid match for story pattern object other and thus the matching of the second story pattern fails.

As the matching of the second story pattern has failed, the computer now follows the [failure] arc to the third story pattern. The third story pattern contains three bound objects this, loc, and assign. Thus, the computer looks-up the corresponding matches and double checks whether the matches of this and loc are connected by an in link. For the match of the assign object, the computer looks-up the leaving in link. Thereby, object r12 is identified as match for pattern object other. Now, all pattern elements are matched or checked. Thus we have a match for the whole story pattern and the computer may proceed to the next step, i.e. to the stop activity.

Even if this was difficult until now, we now have laid the foundations of story pattern matching. Thus, the remaining elements are easier to explain.

9.2.3 Attribute Conditions

Sometimes, you want to ensure that the attributes of objects matched by a story pattern have certain values. For example you might search for a student with a certain name or for a room with less than 10 credits. In story patterns this is achieved using attribute conditions attached to pattern objects.

In Figure 9.12 we call method readAttribute on our student object s2. In the first story pattern, the this object shows an attribute condition "motivation>10". The this object is bound. Thus the computer looks-up the this variable and retrieves runtime object s2. Then the computer checks the attribute condition, i.e. it checks whether the motivation attribute of s2 is greater than 10. This holds. Next, the unbound loc object is considered. The loc object has an attribute condition "credits<10". Thus, the computer has to match loc to a runtime object with a credits attribute lower than 10. In addition, the desired match needs an in link coming from s2. In our example, only r8 has such an in link. Luckily, r8 has only 8 credits. Thus, r8 is a valid match and thus the story pattern succeeds. The violation of either the link or the attribute condition would have invalidated the match candidate. If no valid candidate is found, the story pattern fails.

So far we have used attribute conditions that are attached to single objects. Sometimes you want to compare the attribute values of two objects, e.g. the student's motivation should be higher than the room's credits. Well, you could e.g. use an attribute condition on the this object like

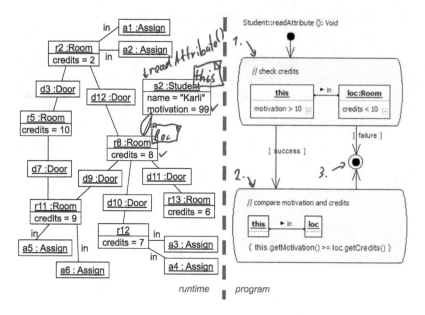

Figure 9.12: Attribute conditions

"motivation>loc.getCredit()". However, in principle this attribute condition is symmetric for the two objects. Thus you might feel uncomfortable to
be forced to attach the attribute condition to one of the objects. Therefore, story
patterns provide general attribute constraints denoted in curly braces.

In our example the second story pattern uses an attribute constraint to ensure
that the student's motivation is higher than the current room's credits. Both objects in the second story pattern are bound. Thus, the computer just looks-up the
corresponding variables, double-checks that the variables are not null, double
checks that the matched objects are connected by an in link, and double checks
the attribute constraint. In our case s2 and r8 are connected by an in link and
99 is higher than 8, thus the story pattern succeeds.

9.2.4   Java Statements in Story Patterns, a Complex Example
for the FAMous Fujaba Abstract Machine

In the previous section we have seen story diagrams using Java statements. Java
statements may also be used within story patterns. Such Java statements may
access story pattern objects and their attributes. In addition, such Java statements
may be used to invoke methods on objects. As example Figure 9.13 shows a

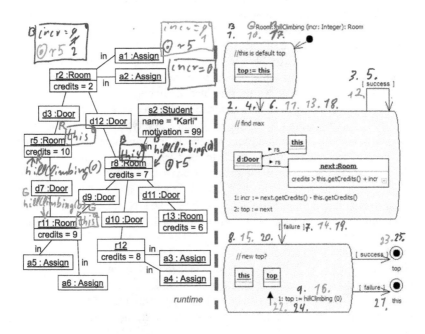

Figure 9.13: Story patterns with Java statements

slightly complex example using these features.[2]

The story diagram in Figure 9.13 specifies a little hill climbing algorithm. Starting on some room, it looks for the neighbor room with the maximal credits. If this credits are a step up the hill, method hillClimbing is called recursively. The top room is returned. Note, this example became slightly more complicated than necessary for illustrating Java statements in story pat-

---

[2]To go through this example in detail you might need some colored sticky-notes. You do not have some at hand? Copy these:

this	incr=0	(.)	top	d	next
this	incr=0	(.)	top	d	next
this	incr=0	(.)	top	d	next

terns. Well, to some extension, we (the authors) became tired of the artificial toy examples. In addition, this example allows us to dig somewhat deeper into the story pattern matching process as this example searches through a to-many association. The example also allows to discuss injective versus surjective story pattern matching which has some relevant practical effects.

Let's go through the first steps of the example in some more detail. If we call hillClimbing on room r8 (the one visited by our student), the computer marks r8 with a blue[3] this sticky-note and stores the value of the actual parameter incr=0 on an extra blue sticky-note shown in the upper left corner of Figure 9.13. The first story pattern shows a special pattern object top:=this. As discussed, the computer creates variables for all deployed pattern objects. For pattern objects showing only their name the computer looks-up the corresponding variable. For pattern objects showing name and type, the computer tries to find a new match. In addition, pattern objects with an assignment to its name may be used to assign a certain value to the corresponding variable. Thus, the first story pattern just assigns the match of this to variable top. Accordingly, we glue a blue top sticky-note on object r8 (in addition to the this sticky-note that is already there). Now variable top is bound and its value may be looked-up by a bound pattern object in a later story pattern. In our example this is used in the third story pattern.

The second story pattern has two unbound pattern objects d and next. Thus the computer searches for a Door object attached to r8 by an rs link and a Room object also attached to that door object by an rs link. In our example, e.g. objects d11 and r13 satisfy these constraints. Thus, you may mark d11 and r13 with blue d and next sticky-notes, respectively. However, the attribute condition of the next object requires that the credits of the matched object are greater than the credits of the object matched by this plus the current incr. Looking-up the sticky-notes, 6 credits are not greater than 7+0 credits. Thus, d11 and r13 do not match the attribute condition.

The computer might now try to use objects d11 and r8 as matches for d and next, respectively. Ups, r8 is also a match for pattern object this. Looks strange. Would the computer do this? The computer starts the pattern matching from r8 which is the match of pattern object this. The computer looks for an rs link to a Door object, thus it might bind d to d11, fine. Now, the computer looks for an rs link leaving d11. There are two of those. Thus, the computer might try the upper one leading back to r8. Object r8 is a Room so nothing wrong with it, the computer would bind it to pattern object next. Thus, the computer might easily get the idea to match pattern object next to the same object as pattern object this. In graph grammar theory, matchings where multiple pattern objects share a common target object are called non-injective matches. There are

---

[3]For black and white printing, in Figure 9.9 we have marked the blue sticky-notes and the first blue step number with a "B". The green and red elements are marked with "G" and "R", respectively.

many graph grammar types that use non-injective matchings as default. Actually, these graph grammars can do spectacular tricks with non-injective matches like cloning of objects. However, for most users non-injective matches are very contra-intuitive. Thus, story diagrams use injective matchings by default. Thus, on each matching step, the computer double-checks whether the candidate is already matched by a previous pattern object *of the same story pattern*. In such cases the candidate is rejected. For you, just stick to your intuition, this will work right.

As r8 is no valid match for pattern object next, the computer might try objects d10 and r12 as matches for d and next, respectively. Please move the sticky-notes for d and next. Objects d10 and r12 have the required links and r12 has 8 credits which fulfills the attribute condition. We have a match.

On a successful match, the story pattern actions are executed. In our case these are the two Java statements shown in the second story pattern. The first Java statement computes 1 as the new value of variable incr. Thus, we adjust the value of incr at the extra blue sticky-note on the top left of Figure 9.13. The second Java statement changes the value of variable top to the object matched by next. Thus, we move the blue top sticky-note to r12, too.

Note, the variables introduced for the story pattern objects are standard variables and may thus also used and modified within the Java statements as shown above. Be careful, such modifications interfere with the computer's handling of those variables. Still we use this trick quite often.

In our example, we have now executed the actions of the second story pattern and want to proceed to the next step. As the pattern matching was successful, step 3 of our example execution follows the [success] arc of the second story pattern. This directly brings us back to the second story pattern. Thus, in step 4 of our example execution, we again search for a match of the second story pattern.

On this second matching, the computer will most likely go through the same matches as in the first run. Thus, it starts with candidates d11, r13. Rejected. Then, d10, r12. This time r12 is no longer good enough for the attribute condition of the next object, because we have changed variable incr to 1 and 8 credits are not greater than 7 credits plus an increment of 1. Next candidates might be d9, r11. This works, 9 credits are greater than 7 credits plus an increment of 1. We have a match. Adjust the sticky-notes. Change incr to 2. Put the top sticky-note on r11.

In step 5, we follow the [success] arc the second time and in step 6 we reach the second story pattern the third time. We go through the candidate pairs again. This time, none of them fulfills the attribute condition. (Variable incr is now 2, 9 is not greater than 7+2)(d12, r2 has only 2 credits.) Thus, pattern matching fails. On failure, the actions in the Java statements are *not* executed. Thus, step 7 just follows the [failure] arc leading to the third story pattern.

In step 8 we execute the third story pattern. This story pattern uses only two bound objects and no other conditions. Thus, no matching but only variable look-up. Caution: for bound pattern objects the computer at least checks that the corresponding variables are not null. In addition, we require injective matches. Thus, the computer also checks that the two pattern objects match different run-time objects. This is exactly what the third story pattern shall do: In the first story pattern we assign the match of this to variable top. If the second story pattern fails directly, the value of top remains unchanged. In such a case, the third pattern would detect that top and this still refer to the same object and it would fail. In that case we would follow the [failure] arc leading to the lower stop-activity and our method would return the value of the this variable. Thus, the third story pattern checks, if the second story pattern was able to find a better room. If not, recursion terminates and the current room is returned.

In our example step 8, the second story pattern has succeeded in finding a bet-ter room. Thus this and top match different objects (r8 and r11, respectively, check the sticky-notes :). Thus, the story pattern matching succeeds and in step 9 the Java statement of the third story pattern is executed. This Java statement has a small arrow attached to it, pointing to pattern object top. This means that the method invocation contained within the Java statement is sent to the object matched by top. We use such an arrow as a kind of comment that improves the readability of Java statements. It just helps you to see that a method is invoked on some object.

As you know, each method execution deploys its own set of local variables. In step 9 of our scenario we have called method hillClimbing from within a first execution of that method. As discussed above, in case of multiple method invocations, we use sticky-notes of different colors to distinguish the variables of the different methods. Thus, our example uses now the green color for the steps and sticky-notes of the second execution of method hillClimbing. (Get your green sticky-notes ready.)

If you go through it, in this second call to method hillClimbing, the first execution of the second story pattern (step 11) will identify room r5 as an im-provement. A second try in step 13 will not be able to improve r5 again, we reach the third story pattern and call method hillClimbing a third time now on object r5.

For the third run of method hillClimbing we use red steps and sticky-notes. In the third run, the second story pattern fails to find an improvement for room r5. Thus, in step 20 the third story pattern fails and step 21 returns r5 as method result. We record this on the green sticky-note of the calling method execution as the content of the bull's eye variable, cf. upper right corner of the object structure view of Figure 9.13.

The green method has initiated the red method execution in the Java state-ment in the third story pattern. Thus, on termination of the red method, the green method continues with the execution of that Java statement and step 22 assigns the returned object r5 to variable top. (Please adjust the green sticky-note for top accordingly.)

Now the green method execution terminates returning r5. We record this on the blue sticky-note. The blue method is still executing the Java statement in the third story pattern. Thus in step 24 the blue method execution assigns r5 to its copy of variable top (move the blue sticky-note) and then the blue method execution terminates with return value r5. Eventually, this is recorded with a bull's eye below the initial call to method hillClimbing on object r8 and we are done.

Congratulations. You managed another lengthy section. Still, we think it is worth to go through this to get a feeling for the story pattern matching mechanism and for the handling of variables by the Fujaba Abstract Machine.

9.2.5 Attribute Assignments, Object and Link Creation and Deletion

Let us go for something simpler. We now go through the story pattern features used for object structure modifications. First, attribute assignments. Figure 9.14 shows a simple story diagram with two pattern objects. On each pattern object you may specify multiple attribute conditions and in addition multiple attribute assignments of the form "attrname:=value". The value is computed by an arbitrary Java expression. Note, for the value expression the visibility rules of Java apply. Thus, in the this object, the value expression may access the attributes credits and motivation, directly. However, the value expression within the r object needs to call r.getCredits(). Note, the story diagram specifies the body of a method of class Student. If the attribute assignment of r would just write "credits:=credits+1" the "credits" of the value expression part would refer to the credits attribute of class Student i.e. to the credits of the this object. If we write "credits:=r.credits+1", the code in class Student tries to access attribute credits in class Room. According to our code generation concepts, the attribute itself is private and you need to use the public getCredits() method to read it.

After matching, a story pattern may also modify matched links. This is achieved by adding «destroy» or «create» markers to the links to be destroyed or created, respectively, cf. Figure 9.15.

Similarly, we use «destroy» or «create» markers to destroy or create objects, cf. Figure 9.16. (Note, Figure 9.16 omits objects d11, r13, a3, and a4 from the previous figures just to give room for the new objects d14, r15, and d16.) Note, deletions and creations are executed only after a successful match. And, in order to delete something you first have to find / match it. Thus, the computer first searches for unmarked elements and for elements marked with a «destroy»

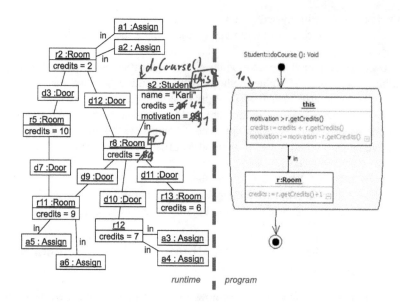

Figure 9.14: Attribute assignments

and only on success, the «destroy» elements are actually destroyed. Objects to be destroyed may carry attribute conditions, however attribute assignments make little sense.

Well, how are objects destroyed? Actually, Java does not allow you to destroy objects actively. This is done by the garbage collector. Thus, all you can do is to remove all links that are attached to an object and thereby offer it to the garbage collector. In our model implementation, this is achieved by the removeYou method provided for all model classes. Thus, a «destroy» marker on a story pattern object advices the computer to call removeYou on the matched object. After calling removeYou you may safely access the object as long as you have a grip on it. Thus, you might still assign new values to its attributes. Until you loose the reference and it becomes garbage collected.

As we have seen that it is OK to execute the assignment after the deletion, we can assume the following simple execution strategy:

1. the pattern is matched,

2. deletions are executed,

3. creations are executed,

4. attribute assignments are executed,

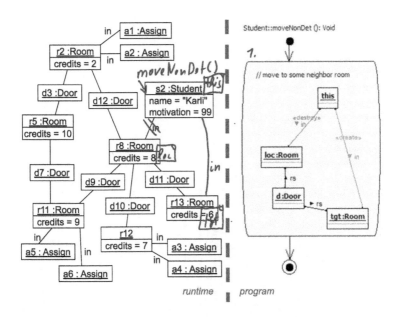

Figure 9.15: Deleting and Adding links

5. Java statements are executed.

In our example this means, first the story pattern of Figure 9.16 is matched onto objects r8, d10, and r12. Then, object d10 and its links are removed. Note, since the removal of object d10 already removes all adjacent links, explicit «destroy» markers on the story pattern links are not mandatory. Still, we recommend to mark such links in the story pattern, too, for readability.

Note, if a runtime object has more links attached to it than the pattern object has attached to it in the story pattern, this is no problem for pattern matching and no problem for removing the runtime object. In graph grammar terms this means, story patterns are able to destroy objects in unknown contexts. In graph grammar theory there are many approaches that do not allow us to destroy elements in unknown contexts. This is called the dangling edge condition. If you require that destroyed objects must not leave dangling edges, dangling edges become part of the pattern matching process. A runtime object that shall be destroyed matches to a pattern object only, if all adjacent links are matched by the pattern, too. Otherwise the dangling edge condition is violated and the runtime object is no valid match. From a software engineering point of view the dangling edge

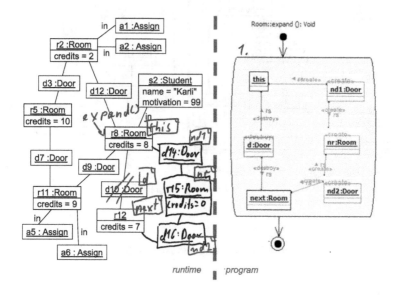

Figure 9.16: Deleting and adding objects

condition is evil: if a program is extended and e.g. a new association is added, all story diagrams that destroy an object of an participating type would become invalid. Small extensions that invalidate large program parts would create an unbearable maintenance problem. Therefore, story diagrams do *not* employ the dangling edge condition but story diagrams allow to destroy objects with unknown contexts. However, this comes for a price. Deploying the dangling edge condition allows to revert the direction of graph rewrite rules. Thus rules with dangling edge condition may be executed in both directions which allows for nice algebraic term transformations on sequences of rules. While this is nice, small extensions invalidating large programs are evil and thus story diagrams allow deletion in unknown contexts.

Runtime objects that are created by a story pattern do not exist before the pattern is executed. Bound pattern objects signal that they are already matched to some runtime object. Thus bound pattern objects with «create» markers are a contradiction in itself. Similarly, attribute conditions on created objects make no sense since attribute conditions are evaluated before story pattern actions are executed and thus before the corresponding objects are created.

9.2.6 Using Marker Nodes as Collections

Now for something completely different. In programming with large object models (many objects and links) you frequently want to search through the object structure and collect certain elements. In our example, we might want to identify all rooms that have assignments / that do not have assignments or all rooms that require less than 8 credits, we want to find the room with minimal / maximal credits, or something else. In Figure 9.13 we tried to find a room with maximal credits using a recursive method. This is a bit tedious and error prone. Actually, the hillClimbing method of Figure 9.13 may get caught in a local optimum and fail to find the overall optimum. To solve such problems, we propose to use *marker objects* or short *markers*. As shown in Figure 9.17 markers just have a to-many association c (for contains) to other objects of any type, i.e. of type java.lang.Object. To be able to declare the c association in the class diagram, you add class java.lang.Object to it. To avoid that Fujaba now generates code for the just added class java.lang.Object from your class diagram into your ./generated folder, you mark the class with the stereotype «reference».[4]

Next, for some stupid technical reasons, you need to tell the code generator *explicitly* that all your own classes inherit (directly or indirectly) from java.lang.Object. Otherwise, the Fujaba editor will not allow you to attach c links to your objects in story patterns.[5]

The Marker class uses a unidirectional association to class java.lang.Object. This is just because we are not able to add the attribute for the reverse direction to class java.lang.Object. Actually, markers are usually used as temporary values or intermediate results. Thus, you may not want to have attribute fields in your (permanent) model elements that store such temporary elements. A unidirectional association serves this intention.

Finally, you sometimes write methods that shall return more than one marker. Unfortunately, Java allows only one return value for a method. To circumvent this limitations, you might use a marker that contains multiple markers. If you do so, it is handy to name markers. The receiver may then easily search in the

---

[4]Caution: Fujaba tends to loose this stereotype on store and new load. Then it generates code for java.lang.Object and then the Java compiler complains that Classes now inheriting from your version of java.lang.Object do not provide operations like equals or hash. This is a nasty bug, someone should fix it. You?

[5]Again, someone should fix this. You?

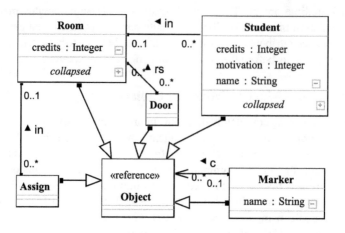

Figure 9.17: Marker objects

set of markers e.g. for a "todo" marker or an "error" marker. We will use this technique, below.

Note, the class diagram of Figure 9.17 proposes very general markers that are usable in all contexts. In easier cases you may introduce a marker that e.g. contains only Room objects. Then you may have a simple association to class Room and avoid dealing with java.lang.Object.

Figure 9.18 shows a typical use of our markers.

Execution of the first story pattern creates runtime object marker m1 and attaches room r8 to it. The second story pattern uses a new pattern element, a *negative link*. A negative link is rendered with a big cross over the link name, cf. the upper link between pattern objects allRooms and next in Figure 9.18. A valid match for a story pattern with a negative element must not contain a match for that negative element. Thus, the runtime objects matched by the pattern objects allRooms and next must not be connected by a c link. In other words, next must not be contained in allRooms (already).

Thus, step 2 of the execution matches the pattern object r of the second story pattern to runtime object r8 and pattern object d e.g. to d10 and accordingly pattern object next to r12. (Please get some sticky-notes and attach them accordingly.)[6] As r12 is not yet contained in / attached to m1 the negative link constrained is not violated and thus this match is valid. The execution of the

---
6

Copy template for sticky-notes:

| this | loc | allRooms | r | d | next | (.) |

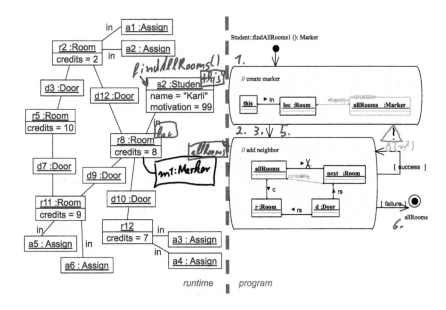

Figure 9.18: Finding all rooms with a marker

pattern actions creates a new c link connecting m1 and r12. Please take a pencil and add this link to Figure 9.18. As r12 is now contained in m1, another attempt to match pattern object next to r12 will now fail because it would violate the negative link constraint. Therefore, we may safely execute story pattern 2 in a loop using a [success] arc. On each execution, a new room object is added to the marker and already marked rooms cannot be matched by next again. Thus, the loop will eventually terminate / the story pattern will eventually fail and the execution terminates. On termination, there is no more room outside the marked set that may be reached from inside the marked set. Thus all rooms of our object model or at least all rooms of the connected component containing the start object are marked.

Note, while the negative link together with the link creation safely guarantees termination of our story pattern and while the result contains all expected rooms, the loop construction in Figure 9.18 has an efficiency problem. On each iteration, the computer starts a new matching for the second story pattern. To compute a matching for the second story pattern, the computer looks-up the allRooms variable and then the c link of the matched marker object. After some executions, the marker will contain $O(n)$ rooms (a number proportional to the total number of rooms). Now the computer goes through this set in order to find one that has a neighbor that is not yet contained in our marker. The container classes used by

Fujaba deliver their elements always in insertion order. Thus, looping through the set of already marked rooms starts with r8, the initial room, and continues with the neighbors of r8 and then with the neighbors of these neighbors. When we have already added all neighbors of half of the rooms, i.e. for $O(n)$ rooms, we will go through all these rooms only to find out that they still have no unmatched neighbors. We do this again after each addition of a new room, i.e. $O(n)$ times. Thus, above story diagram has a runtime complexity of $O(n^2)$, which is unnecessary high.

To overcome this efficiency problem, Figure 9.19 shows a variant of method findAllRooms that uses a second todo marker. The todo marker contains rooms where the neighbors still need to be investigated. Thus, the second story pattern of Figure 9.19 removes the first entry from the todo list and, on success, it jumps to the third story pattern. If we are out of todo entries the method terminates. The third story pattern looks-up neighbors of the current todo entry that are not yet contained in the all marker. Such neighbors are added to the all marker and to the todo marker. If we run out of new neighbors for the current todo item, we jump back to the second story pattern and look-up the next todo entry. You might get yourself sticky-notes and go through the steps of this scenario in detail[7].

9.2.7   Handling Multiple Matches: For-Each Activities

The story diagram in Figure 9.19 is already quite efficient as we consider the neighborhood of each room only once. However, the loop with the third story pattern still suffers from the problem that each time we re-enter that pattern we first loop through the elements we have already visited before we reach new elements.

Actually, there hides a deeper problem behind this efficiency problem. As story patterns are patterns by nature, we have to distinguish three cases: First, the pattern matching may fail. Second there might exist exactly one possible match. Or third, there might be multiple possible matches. The first and the second case have a clear semantics and in a given situation we can predict the effect of executing the story pattern, exactly.

In case of multiple possible matches, the semantics of story patterns do not specify, which match will be found by the computer. Actually, the semantics description says it is a non-deterministic choice. This means, any valid match may be chosen. Depending on the match the actions of the story pattern will be executed on different objects. We will end up with a different end situation.

---

[7]

Copy template for sticky-notes:

| this | loc | all | todo | r | d | n | (.) |

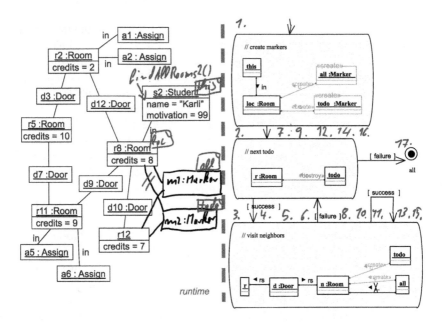

Figure 9.19: Finding all rooms with two markers

This means, in case of multiple matches, given an example situation and a story pattern, you cannot tell where the computer will match the pattern and what will be the outcome.

In principle, this non-determinism is undesired. As software engineers we would like to be able to predict the behavior of our programs. On a closer look, this non-determinism is not the fault of the story pattern matching approach but it is the fault of the problem: usually, you have a set of candidates and you just do not know in which order they are visited. However, if you have a set of candidates, usually you do not want to visit just one of it but you want to deal with all of them. As this is a quite frequent case, story diagrams provide a special language feature to deal with multiple matches efficiently, the for-each story pattern.

Figure 9.20 computes all rooms of our example using a *for-each story pattern*. A for-each story pattern is rendered using two stacked story pattern shapes. As the name says, a for-each story pattern does not just the first match but it tries to do all matches. In practice, the computer starts the story pattern matching as usual. However, on the first match, the actions are executed and then the computer just continues its search. Thereby, the other matches are found and handled, too.

Again the first story pattern creates a marker for the current room. The computer starts the execution of the for-each pattern by looking-up the marker and then by searching for leaving c links. Initially, there is just the one c link created by the first story pattern. Thus, we match pattern object r to runtime object r8. Then, we may as usual match d to d10 and n to r12. Match found. You may get yourself some sticky-notes and record this.[8] We add r12 to our marker.

The for-each story pattern may have an [each-time] arc leading to something like a loop body. Each time the for-each pattern has found a match, it tries to follow an [each-time] arc. If there is such a a loop body, the reached story pattern is executed and its leaving arcs are followed maybe to even more loop-body story pattern. Eventually, execution should reach the for-each pattern again, to continue its matching. In Figure 9.20 our for-each pattern has such a loop body just for the sake of demonstration. For our example, this loop body may be omitted.

Our example execution has just found its first match and added room r12 to the marker. It jumps to the third story pattern and does the println. A usual story pattern would stop now. The for-each pattern just continues its search. In our example, the computer was searching for neighbors of r8 and has just found r12. Thus, we continue with the next neighbor of r8, e.g. r11. Match, add it to the marker. Do println. Next neighbor of r8 is r2. Add it. println. Do not forget the sticky-notes. No more neighbor of r2. Hm. Do we have another candidate for pattern object r? Yes, meanwhile our marker has three new rooms attached to it. Thus, the for-each pattern continues with the next element of our marker. Recall, after r8 the next room added was r12. Thus we continue by matching pattern object r to r12. We search for neighbors of r12. Yes, there is one (r8) but that one is already marked and thus the negative link constraint is violated. Ok, next match for r, this time r11. (Do not forget the sticky-notes.) Neighbors for r11? Yes, r8 and r5. Object r8 is already matched, but r5 results in a new match. Add and print. Go on by matching r to r2 and then to r5 and then we are done.

For very experienced Java programmers, it might come as a surprise that the search for elements attached to our marker finds elements that are added after the search has begun, too. Usually, a search is done by doing a loop through a set of candidates. In Java sets are implemented by container classes like java.util.HashSet. To loop through such a set, you use an iterator. In general, HashSet iterators do not play well with the fact that you add or remove elements to a set while you loop through it. Recall from your data structures lecture: hash tables might reorganize themselves e.g. if they become over-

---

8

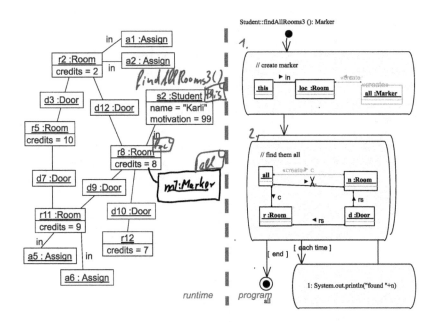

Figure 9.20: For each room

full. An iterator that uses an index to the internal hash table would be invalidated by such a reorganization. Therefore, usual Java iterators tend to throw a ConcurrentModificationException. Thus, the first thing a Java programmer learns is: do not modify the set you are looping through. To circumvent this problem, you might copy the set and then iterate through the copy. Either way, you will never get grip on elements added within the loop. Well, Fujaba uses its own container classes that deal with concurrent modifications. Thus we can do it :). In addition, the Fujaba container classes guarantee a stable order of elements. This means, you always loop through the elements in the order in which they have been inserted. For our non-deterministic pattern matching this gives a little predictability. However, meanwhile there are Java container classes with similar properties. In addition, some new young Fujaba developers may at some time switch to some other container classes with properties we cannot yet predict. So do not rely on this too much.

9.2.8   Some Special Pattern Elements: Type Casts

To be able to illustrate dynamic casting, we introduce a base class Person with subclasses Student and Professor, cf. Figure 9.21.

In Figure 9.13 we have used a Java statement 2:   top := next to assign a

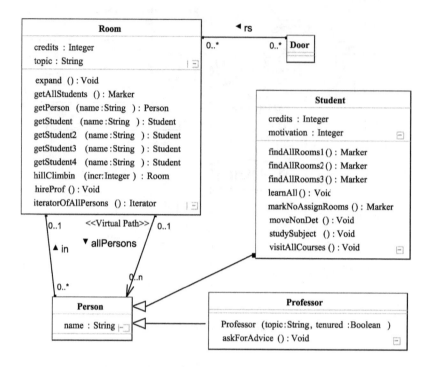

Figure 9.21: Simple inheritance structure

new value to a story pattern variable. Similarly, the first story pattern uses a pattern object top := this to assign a new value to story variable top. Pattern objects (and Java statements) allow also for (more) complex expressions to initialize a story variable. As an example, in the upper story diagram of Figure 9.22 we call method getPerson(name) to initialize pattern object stud. Figure 9.22 also uses a type cast to convert the result of getPerson(name) from Person to Student. In our example, we call method getStudent on runtime object r8 with actual parameter "Karla". This actual parameter is passed to the invocation of method getPerson within our pattern object initialization. Thus, method getPerson will deliver runtime object p3 of type Professor instead of the expected Student object. Thus, the type cast within the pattern object will fail. In Java this would cause a ClassCastException.

In story diagrams, we often do type casts implicitly. For example, the lower story diagram in Figure 9.22 searches for a Student object connected to the Room this via an in link. As the class diagram in Figure 9.21 shows, the in association connects class Room with class Person. Thus, when the computer

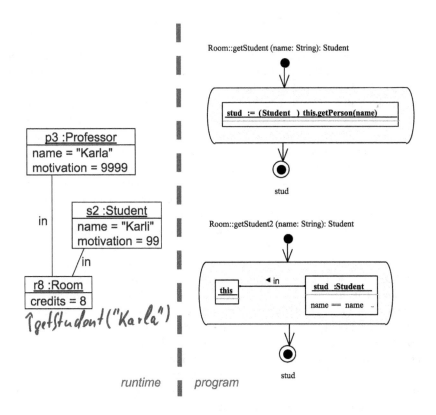

Figure 9.22: Complex pattern object assignment

follows an in link from the current room it iterates through a set of Person objects. In our case this set will contain a Professor object (p3) and a Student object s2. However, the type of the pattern object stud is Student. Thus, only a Student object is allowed as a valid match. In such cases, story diagrams use implicit instanceof conditions to ensure the desired runtime type for the matching object. If the condition holds, story diagrams use implicit type casts to assign the matching result to the corresponding story diagram variable.

Accordingly, a complex pattern object initialization that uses a type cast is translated to an instanceof condition checking the runtime type of the computed object and doing the type cast only if the condition holds. Thus, in our example, we do not throw a ClassCastException but an instanceof check recognizes that runtime object p3 is not of type Student and thus, p3 is not a valid match for pattern object stud. The matching fails but no ClassCastException is thrown.

9.2.9   Some Special Pattern Elements: Paths

Sometimes one needs a more complex computation or navigation to find a certain object in the current runtime model. One solution for this is to write a method like getStudentXY that does the complex computation and then you use e.g. a complex pattern object initialization to invoke that method and to assign the result to a story variable. Because complex navigations are such a frequent problem, story diagrams provide special *path expressions* for them. The same dialog, that is used for link creation allows in its lower part to enter a path expression. A path expression consists of role names and the operators ".", "or", and "*" and brackets. In Figure 9.23 the path expression "doors.rooms" navigates from the starting room to the attached doors and from there to the reachable rooms. In our example, we start at room r5. For room r5 the path "doors" reaches doors d3 and d7. Thus, for room r5 the path expression "doors.rooms" reaches all rooms attached to d3 and d7, i.e. from d3 rooms r2 and r5 and from door d7 rooms r5 and r11. If we collect these rooms in a set, r2, r5, and r11 are reached. The "*" operator builds the transitive closure of the contained path expression. This means, the contained expression is applied to the result set as long as new elements are added to it. The starting set is also contained in the result. Thus, in our example, the path expression "(doors.rooms)*" starts with room r5. After the first iteration rooms r2, r5, and r11 are added to the result set, i.e. we have r2, r5, r11. In the next iteration, all neighbors of r2 (i.e. r2, r5, r8) and all neighbors of r11 (i.e. r5, r8) are added resulting in r2, r5, r8, and r11. The third iteration adds all neighbors of r8 (i.e. r11, r12, r13) and the final iteration adds the neighbors of r12 and r13. Thus, the path expression "(doors.rooms)*" collects all rooms of our example. Applying ".persons" to the set of all rooms results in the set of all persons reachable from the rooms via an in link against its direction (persons is the role name for the reverse direction of the in link, cf. Figure 9.21). In our example, only room r8 has a person attached to it, thus the whole path expression computes the set {s2} as a result. Thus, in the story diagram of Figure 9.23 the path expression binds pattern object stud to s2.

Path expressions offer a pretty handy mechanism for complex navigation in our object model. However, compared e.g. to OCL expressions, story diagram path expressions have only very limited features. For example, path expressions do not allow to check attribute values of visited objects. There is no "not". There is no "and". Etc. Well, we (the authors) think that OCL expresssions are pretty clumsy and hard to read and write. Thus, we propose to use graphical story pattern features instead. We show the usage of story diagrams for paths via so-called virtual paths below. After all path expressions are handy as they allow to compute on sets of objects. For this purpose concatenation and transitive closure have turned out to be the most important features that are thus supported.

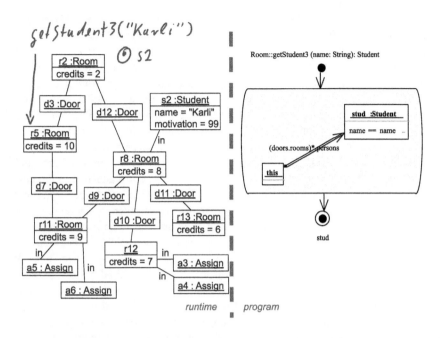

Figure 9.23: Complex navigation with path expressions

In Fujaba, path expressions are translated into calls to a library class Path that accepts a path expression as string argument and provides methods to compute the set of result objects from a given (set of) start objects. Unfortunately, Fujaba does not yet provide any type checking for path expressions. Thus any typo in the path expression may result in runtime failures which silently result in empty result sets. Similarly, our "*" operator requires that results of one iteration may serve as valid inputs for the next iteration. In our example the path expression "doors.rooms" leads from rooms to rooms. Thus, transitive closure works fine. However "(doors.rooms.persons)*" applied to r5 would have delivered the set containing only the start node (just no person attached to r2 or r11). And "(doors.rooms.persons)*" applied to e.g. r2 would create the set {r2, s2} (the starting node and the person object reached via room r8). Applying the path expression doors.rooms.persons to s2 in the second iteration of our "*" operator makes no sense since s2 is no room and thus cannot have a doors link. This could be checked statically. Someone should add such runtime checks to Fujaba. We are open for volunteers.

As announced, for more complex navigations that e.g. may include attribute checks or recursion. Story diagrams provide so-called *virtual paths*. A virtual path consists of a declaration in the class diagram and a number of methods implementing it. As example, in Figure 9.21 we declare a virtual path `allPersons`. A virtual path is just a usual association with a stereotype `Virtual Path` attached to it. This stereotype tells the Fujaba code generator *not* to generate *any* implementation for this association. Still you are allowed to use links of this type in your story patterns, cf. the upper story diagram of Figure 9.24. As the Fujaba code generator does not implement the association, you may / have to do this instead. Depending on the usage of the corresponding links, you have to provide appropriate setter and getter methods. In our case, we use the `allPersons` link attached to a bound pattern object `this` and an unbound pattern object `stud`. Thus, the code generation for story diagram `getStudent4` generates code that iterates through the set of `allPersons` attached to the current room. This is done using an `Iterator` retrieved by calling the getter method `iteratorOfAllPersons`. Thus, we have to provide our own implementation of method `iteratorOfAllPersons`. This method may easily be implemented using a story diagram, cf. the lower story diagram in Figure 9.24. This method is declared as a usual method in class Room, cf. Figure 9.21. You just need to stick to the naming and coding conventions of Fujaba. This method has to return an `Iterator`. We do so by computing a set of result objects and then we retrieve an `Iterator` for that set. The set of result values is collected using a `Marker` persons. Again we want to collect people from all rooms. Thus, we use another `Marker` todo to collect rooms and a for-each story pattern to look-up all neighbors of rooms from the todo list. Note, our for-each story pattern iterates through all matches of neighbor rooms and through all matches of persons attached to a room. If a room has e.g. 3 neighbor rooms and 4 persons attached to it, this results in 12 matches for the different combinations of neighbor rooms and persons. Thereby, each person is added 3 times to the `Marker persons` and each neighbor room is added 4 times to the `Marker todo`. This could be optimized by using two for-each patterns, one that deals with persons and one that deals with neighbor rooms. While this is the better modeling, it would have required more space in Figure 9.24 ... Feel free to take some sticky-notes and to walk through the execution of our example.

Our virtual path implementation method `iteratorOfAllPersons` does not yet use any attribute checks. However, it is straight forward to extend our example e.g. with a boolean attribute flagging locked doors and to extend our story diagram for `iteratorOfAllPersons` with an attribute condition for pattern object d that allows to go through open doors only. Similarly arbitrary complex conditions are possible and one may call helper methods. Thus, virtual paths allow for complex navigation operations. This comes for the price of slightly cumbersome declarations in the class diagrams, and you need to know Fujaba's naming and coding conventions by heart. For different usages of a to-many association you may need to implement many access methods yourself. Thus, in simple cases, we still recommend to use path expressions, instead.

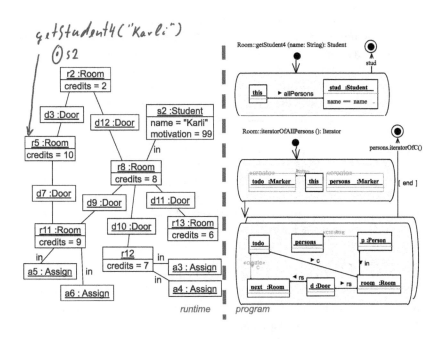

Figure 9.24: Complex navigation with a virtual path

9.2.10 Handling Multiple Matches: Set Valued Pattern Objects

As discussed, many story patterns may have multiple matches. The standard way to deal with this are for-each patterns. However, in simple cases, one may also use *set valued pattern objects*. The story diagram in Figure 9.25 uses a set valued pattern object studs rendered as two stacked dashed boxes. A set valued pattern object matches not just one runtime object but it may match a set of runtime objects. In our example, we use a path expression to compute the set of all persons within the current building. Unfortunately, our runtime object structure contains only one person, i.e. our Student s2. However, in general we may retrieve multiple persons. As our set valued pattern object studs is of type Student, an instanceof check is used to restrict the set of all persons to the set of reachable Student objects. Set valued pattern objects may also contain attribute conditions to further restrict the contained elements. Next, set valued pattern objects may contain attribute assignments. Such assignments are applied to each element of the set. Set valued pattern objects may contain a Marker destroy, destroying all matched runtime objects. And, links attached to a set valued pattern object may carry Marker destroy or Marker create. A

Marker destroy on a link attached to a set valued pattern object would destroy all corresponding runtime links. A link with a marker create results in the creation of a corresponding runtime link for each matched runtime object. Thus, in our example, we would create c links from the new Marker results to each element of the studs set.

In our example, method getAllStudents returns a Marker object that points to all found students. Instead of the explicit Marker object, we might have returned variable studs directly. This means, method getAllStudents would have result type java.util.Set. While this is more elegant for the story diagram within method getAllStudents, the usage of method getAllStudents becomes more complicated. Actually, story diagrams have no means to deal with objects of type java.util.Set, directly. Yes, we might use a bound set valued pattern object for this, but the Fujaba code generator does not deal with it correctly. Some students have tweaked the code generator to allow for to-many associations with empty role names. In that case, the code generator does not use an iteratorOf method but a plain iterator method. Applied to a pattern object of type java.util.Set this allows you to use a link with some name to some neighbors and thereby to iterate through the java.util.Set content. However, this is cumbersome, tricky, and still some features for sets are missing. For example the computation of the intersection or union of two sets or the restriction to elements matching certain constrains is not well supported.

After all, story diagrams consider container objects as internal helpers for the implementation of to-many associations. Thus, container objects are no first level entities and therefore story diagrams do not provide appropriate means to model with container objects. The recommended way to deal with sets of objects is the usage of Marker objects. Marker objects work exactly like container objects while Marker objects are well supported first level entities within story diagrams. Using set valued pattern objects, it is easy to model how the intersection or union of two markers is marked by a third Marker object. It is easy to restrict the set of elements marked by a Marker object to objects that match certain constrains. And, all this fits well into the existing story pattern language. This comes for the price of explicit creation and management of Marker objects. Yes, set valued pattern objects actually create the temptation to compute with java.util.Set objects directly. Our fault. However, be strong, resist this temptation, use Marker objects. They are the better deal.

9.2.11 Important Pattern Elements We Did Not Yet Use: Optional Objects, Negative Objects, Complex Constructors

For some reasons, our example did not yet make use of some pattern elements that still are very important. First of all, story pattern provide optional pattern

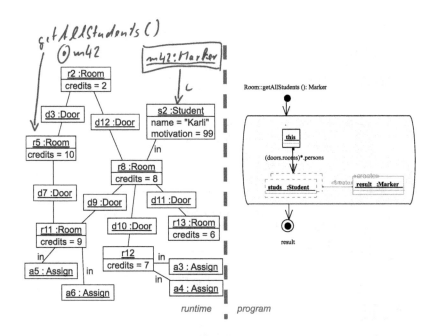

Figure 9.25: Handling multiple matches with set valued pattern objects

objects. Optional pattern objects help to handle runtime objects that might be attached to some core structure or that might be missing. The upper story diagram in Figure 9.26 uses an optional pattern object p:Professor rendered by a dashed box. First, the pattern matching is done without considering the optional elements. Thus, if we call studySubject() on runtime object s2, we match pattern object r to runtime object r8. Once a match for the core elements has been found, we try to extend this match by matches for the optional elements. In case of our Student "Karli", we find Professor "Karla" and thus, the optional pattern object p is matched to runtime object p3. If we call method studySubject() on Student "Mira" / runtime object s3, there is no Professor in Room r9 and thus, no match for pattern object p is found. Still, the core pattern has a match and thus the story pattern execution is successful, in both cases.

Optional pattern objects may show destroy markers, attribute assignments, links with create or destroy markers and may be target of Java statements. Such actions are executed only, if the optional pattern element has a match, otherwise these actions are ignored. Thus, in our example the call on Student "Karli" will modify the credits attribute *and* execute the Java statement giveAdvice() on the matched professor while the call on Student "Mira"

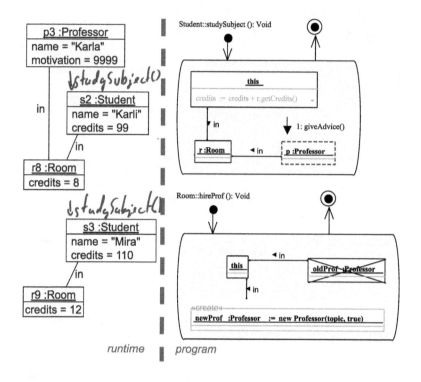

Figure 9.26: Optional or negative objects and complex constructors

will modify the `credits` attribute only.

Without optional nodes, we would need two story patterns to express the same behavior. Thus, optional nodes allow to write two story patterns within one. Well, we might have used a set valued pattern object to achieve the same effect. However, for a set valued object, we expect a potentially large number of matching runtime objects. Thus, it feels strange to use it if you expect one or zero objects.

Story diagrams provide not only negative links but also *negative pattern objects*. Like negative links, negative pattern objects must not have a match in the current runtime object structure. The lower story diagram of Figure 9.26 show a negative pattern object `oldProf` rendered by a box that is crossed out. If we call method `hireProf()` on runtime Room r8, we find a match for pattern object `oldProf` and thus the pattern matching fails and no action is executed. If we call method `hireProf()` on runtime Room r9, there is no `Professor` and thus matching is successful.

The lower story diagram of Figure 9.26 also shows the creation of an object with a *complex constructor* call. The action for usual pattern objects that carry a `create` marker result in calls to the default constructor of the corresponding class. However, some classes may only provide constructors that require parameters and some classes may require the usage of a factory method. To be able to deal with such cases, story diagrams allow for additional constructor expressions within objects with create markers. In our case we call a `Professor` constructor with two parameters.

Note, in principle, we might have used an object with a complex initialization, cf. section 9.2.8. However, complex initializations are executed before or during pattern matching. Thus, a complex initialization that creates a new object may be executed although the pattern matching fails later on. Contrarily, complex constructor expressions are part of the actions of a pattern that are executed only if the pattern matching is successful. In addition, a complex constructor expression may e.g. safely access attributes of other pattern objects. Contrarily, a complex initialization is executed at the beginning of during pattern matching and if we try to access an attribute of some other pattern object, this might raise a `NullPointerException`, because the pattern object might not have been matched yet.

9.3 Exercises

9.3.1 Mau Mau

Implement the methods for our Mau Mau example from Section 7.1.1 again, now using story diagrams. Test the new implementation with the JUnit tests developed in Section 8.6.1.

You may do the story diagrams either with Fujaba or with SDMLib. In case of Fujaba you may do the JUnit tests with Fujaba storyboards, too. Alternatively, generate the story diagram code in another folder than the manual test code and add the folder with the generated code to Eclipse's source path. Your test may then need to create an action object in order to invoke the story diagram method.

9.3.2 Battleships

Implement the methods for our Battleships example from Section 7.1.2 again now using story diagrams. Test the new implementation with the JUnit tests developed in Section 8.6.2.

You may do the story diagrams either with Fujaba or with SDMLib. In case of Fujaba you may do the JUnit tests with Fujaba storyboards, too. Alternatively, generate the story diagram code in another folder than the manual test code and add the folder with the generated code to Eclipse's source path. Your test may then need to create an action object in order to invoke the story diagram method.

9.3.3   Mancala

Implement the methods for our Mancala example from Section 7.1.3 again now using story diagrams. Test the new implementation with the JUnit tests developed in Section 8.6.3.

You may do the story diagrams either with Fujaba or with SDMLib. In case of Fujaba you may do the JUnit tests with Fujaba storyboards, too. Alternatively, generate the story diagram code in another folder than the manual test code and add the folder with the generated code to Eclipse's source path. Your test may then need to create an action object in order to invoke the story diagram method.

9.3.4   Mensch Ärgere Dich Nicht

Implement the methods for our Mensch Ärgere Dich Nicht example from Section 7.1.4 again now using story diagrams. Test the new implementation with the JUnit tests developed in Section 8.6.4.

You may do the story diagrams either with Fujaba or with SDMLib. In case of Fujaba you may do the JUnit tests with Fujaba storyboards, too. Alternatively, generate the story diagram code in another folder than the manual test code and add the folder with the generated code to Eclipse's source path. Your test may then need to create an action object in order to invoke the story diagram method.

9.3.5   Towers of Hanoi

Implement the methods for our Towers of Hanoi example from Section 7.1.5 again now using story diagrams. Test the new implementation with the JUnit tests developed in Section 8.6.5.

You may do the story diagrams either with Fujaba or with SDMLib. In case of Fujaba you may do the JUnit tests with Fujaba storyboards, too. Alternatively, generate the story diagram code in another folder than the manual test code and add the folder with the generated code to Eclipse's source path. Your test may then need to create an action object in order to invoke the story diagram method.

9.3.6   ATM Money Withdrawal

Implement the methods for our ATM Money Withdrawal example from Section 7.1.6 again now using story diagrams. Test the new implementation with the JUnit tests developed in Section 8.6.6.

You may do the story diagrams either with Fujaba or with SDMLib. In case of Fujaba you may do the JUnit tests with Fujaba storyboards, too. Alternatively, generate the story diagram code in another folder than the manual test code and add the folder with the generated code to Eclipse's source path. Your test may then need to create an action object in order to invoke the story diagram method.

9.3.7 Borrowing Electronic Books from Library

Implement the methods for our Library example from Section 7.1.7 again now using story diagrams. Test the new implementation with the JUnit tests developed in Section 8.6.7.

You may do the story diagrams either with Fujaba or with SDMLib. In case of Fujaba you may do the JUnit tests with Fujaba storyboards, too. Alternatively, generate the story diagram code in another folder than the manual test code and add the folder with the generated code to Eclipse's source path. Your test may then need to create an action object in order to invoke the story diagram method.

9.3.8 Trouble Ticket System

Implement the methods for our Trouble Ticket System example from Section 7.1.8 again now using story diagrams. Test the new implementation with the JUnit tests developed in Section 8.6.8.

You may do the story diagrams either with Fujaba or with SDMLib. In case of Fujaba you may do the JUnit tests with Fujaba storyboards, too. Alternatively, generate the story diagram code in another folder than the manual test code and add the folder with the generated code to Eclipse's source path. Your test may then need to create an action object in order to invoke the story diagram method.

9.3.9 Webshop

Implement the methods for our Webshop example from Section 7.1.9 again now using story diagrams. Test the new implementation with the JUnit tests developed in Section 8.6.9.

You may do the story diagrams either with Fujaba or with SDMLib. In case of Fujaba you may do the JUnit tests with Fujaba storyboards, too. Alternatively, generate the story diagram code in another folder than the manual test code and add the folder with the generated code to Eclipse's source path. Your test may then need to create an action object in order to invoke the story diagram method.

9.3.10 Connect Four Game

Implement the methods for our Connect Four Game example from Section 7.1.10 again now using story diagrams. Test the new implementation with the JUnit tests developed in Section 8.6.10.

You may do the story diagrams either with Fujaba or with SDMLib. In case of Fujaba you may do the JUnit tests with Fujaba storyboards, too. Alternatively, generate the story diagram code in another folder than the manual test code and add the folder with the generated code to Eclipse's source path. Your test may then need to create an action object in order to invoke the story diagram method.

Chapter 10

Simple Story Driven Modeling

You have now mastered the ideas of modeling and programming with objects and you are familiar with story diagrams (well, at least you get an idea what they might do, when you see one). So, in this section we revisit some of our examples and exemplify how we realize them completely on the model level with storyboards and story diagrams. The idea is, that you learn Story Driven Modeling not by looking at the outcome of this process but by watching the process of story diagram creation.

10.1   The Study-Right University doAssignments

The Study-Right University has served us as example for modeling object structures and deriving class structures for an application. Unfortunately, the problem provides little dynamics, i.e. most of the time we just visit our object structures but we do not do major reconstructions e.g. on our floor plan. However, in Chapter 7 we developed the method doAssignments in Java exploiting the object structures developed in the earlier parts of this book. While we claim that the development of the Java code for doAssignments already benefits a lot from our modeling with objects approach, we also claim that modeling and implementing the behavior of doAssignments with story diagrams again facilitates this task, significantly. Let us have a look.

   In Chapter 5 we have already developed a storyboard for the doAssignments functionality, cf. Figures 5.2, 5.3, and 5.4. From this story we have derived a pseudo code algorithm in Chapter 6. Figure 10.1 shows the result of this step, again.

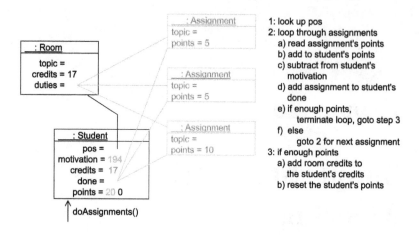

Figure 10.1: Earning the `credits` (copy of 6.11)

Now we try to turn our pseudo code algorithm into a story diagram. First we add method `doAssignments` to the class `Student` and ask Fujaba to create a basic story diagram for this method. At first this basic story diagram contains only the start activity. We ask Fujaba to append a "story pattern with this" (pop menu successor) and then to append a stop activity, cf. Figure 10.2. This corresponds to Listing 7.2 of Chapter 7.

Action 1 of our pseudo code algorithm requires to look up the current position. Recall that we use a `pos` link to store in which room a student is located. Thus, we add a `currentRoom` object to our story diagram activity and link it to the `this` object representing the current student, cf. Figure 10.3. (We added `currentRoom` above the `this` object to match the layout of our object diagram in Figure 10.1.)

Action 2 of our algorithm requires to loop through the assignments of `currentRoom`. Thus we add a `nextAssignment` object, link it to the `currentRoom` and turn the activity in a `for-each` activity, cf. Figure 10.4 (compare also Listing 7.4).

Action 2.a) and 2.b) of our pseudo code algorithm require to add the assignment's points to our student's `points`. We do so by adding an attribute constraint to the `this` object, cf. Figure 10.5. Similarly, we subtract the assignment `points` from the student's `motivation`. This achieves action 2.c) of our pseudo code algorithm. To mark `nextAssignment` as done, we add a `done` link with a create stereotype. Please compare Figure 10.5 with Listing 7.5.

As outlined in actions 2.e) and 2.f) of our pseudo code algorithm, our loop shall terminate when we have collected enough points, i.e. more points than the

Student::doAssignments (): Void

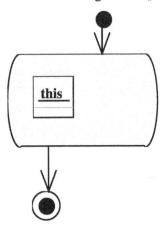

Figure 10.2: Story diagram for doAssignments, declaration

Student::doAssignments (): Void

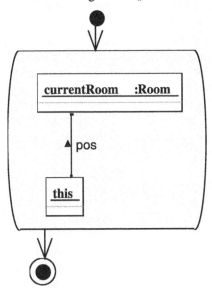

Figure 10.3: Story diagram for doAssignments, look up pos

Student::doAssignments (): Void

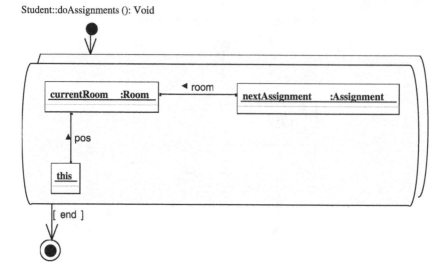

Figure 10.4: Story diagram for doAssignments, loop through assignments

room has credits. To achieve this, we just add an attribute condition to the this object, cf. Figure 10.6, see also Listing 7.6.

Our loop may terminate for two reasons: we have earned enough points or we run out of assignments. Thus, as outlined in action 3 of our pseudo code algorithm, after the loop we check again whether our student's points suffice to earn the room's credits. In Figure 10.7 we do so by a new story pattern and an attribute constraint for the this object. If we have enough points, another attribute constraint adds the room's credits to our student's credits and then we reset the student's points as required in action 3.b) of our pseudo code algorithm. See also Listing 7.7

We are almost done now. We have achieved the functionality outlined by our pseudo code algorithm. This story diagram may now be tested with the storyboard from Chapter 5. This should work fine as this storyboard cover only a simple case and as this storyboard has served as input for the design of our pseudo code algorithm. However, as discussed in Chapter 7, there are a number of additional cases that are not yet covered. As discussed, we might analyze more scenarios and storyboards to detect the missing cases. In addition and alternatively, we should go through our story diagram element by element and try to ask ourselves whether this will work in all cases or whether there are hidden cases where this story diagram element will not work properly. Let's try this.

Student::doAssignments (): Void

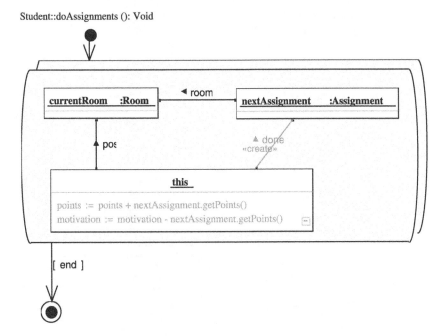

Figure 10.5: Story diagram for doAssignments, handle assignments

For the first story pattern in Figure 10.7 we ask ourselves may it fail to identify appropriate assignments? Matching the this object never fails. Matching the currentRoom may actually fail. In this case the loop would terminate. We would go to the second story pattern, directly. There we use an attribute condition that looks up the credits of the currentRoom. This will cause a NullPointerException. Exactly what we want. Nothing to do here.

Next, the room may have no assignments. Loop terminates. Correct. The computation of the student's points do not contain a problem, too. However, the computation of the new motivation may trigger your interest. The motivation shall not become negative. In our story diagram, this is not guaranteed. As discussed in Chapter 7 we need to discuss this case with our customer. Therefore, we build a new scenario and storyboard that addresses this case, cf. Figure 10.9. We will analyze this new storyboard below. The discussion with our customer reveals that in case of insufficient motivation, we shall skip the hard assignment and look for an easier one. In our story diagram this is achieved by just adding a new attribute constraint ensuring sufficient points to the this object of the for-each story pattern, cf. Figure 10.8.

As discussed, our for-each pattern adds completed assignments to the stu-

Student::doAssignments (): Void

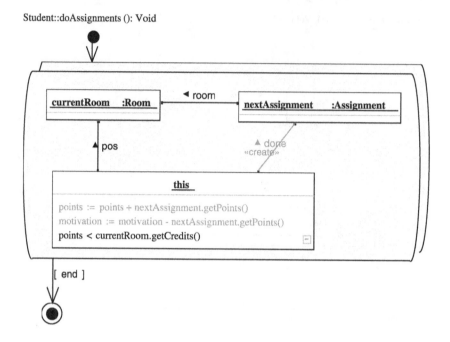

Figure 10.6: Story diagram for doAssignments, loop termination

dent's done list. As discussed in Chapter 7, if you are very smart you may spot a problem here: why do we store this information if we do not use it? If students do a second visit to a room, they should not do the already completed assignments, again. Thus, we need to exclude assignments that have already been done. In our story diagram we achieve this with a negative link between this and nextAssignment, cf. Figure 10.8.

Let us go on checking Figure 10.7. The remaining elements of our for-each activity look fine. The second activity is more interesting. First of all, the for-each activity may fail on the first iteration without matching a thing. Thus, we should check, whether we use any object of the for-each activity that may not have been bound. Yes, we do so, our attribute constraints access the currentRoom. This case has already been discussed above, no problem here. Increasing the credits looks fine, too. Resetting the points look fine either. Stop. There is an attribute condition on our this object that may prevent the reset operation from being executed. Already in the for-each activity, we increase the points attribute without initializing it properly. As discussed in Chapter 7 we should initialize the points attribute at the beginning of our story diagram, cf. Figure 10.8.

Student::doAssignments (): Void

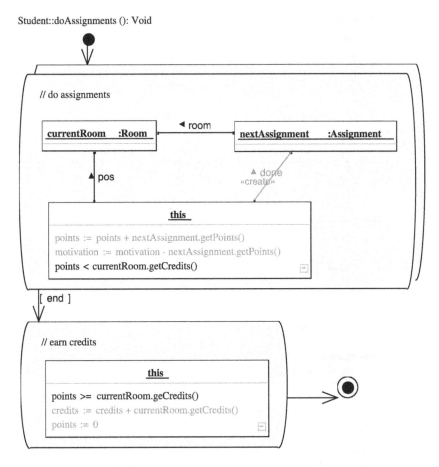

Figure 10.7: Story diagram for doAssignments, earn credits

OK, this was again a lengthy and detailed discussion and you might have got the impression that Story Driven Modeling is not simple at all. Honestly, doing the actual story diagrams remains a challenging task requiring some training and experience. Still, if you compare our initial algorithm and the Java code that we have created in Chapter 7 and now the story diagram we have just created: what do you like more the direct Java coding or the story diagram? We claim that the story diagrams are on a somewhat higher level of abstraction. At least you avoid some tricky details in dealing with loops and pointers. We also claim that the visual notation for story diagrams make them easier to recognize. This holds at least if you do a presentation to a larger audience, this works much better with story diagrams as with code snippets. Similarly, for us (the authors)

Student::doAssignments (): Void

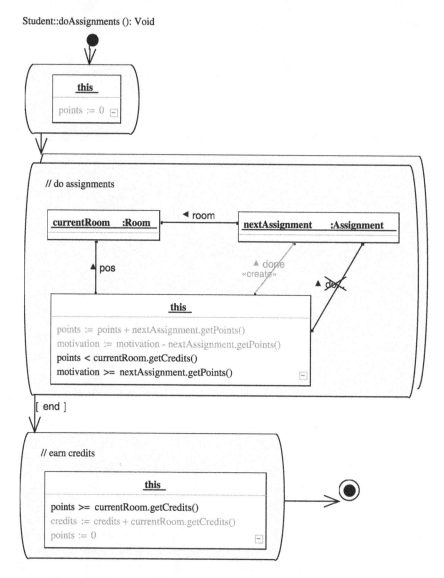

Figure 10.8: Story diagram for doAssignments, more conditions

it is much easier to spot potential problems and missing cases in story diagrams than in Java code. (Well we all grade programming exercises and are trained in this.) Note, story diagrams are appropriate for problems dealing with complex object structures and complex conditions on these structures. If your application deals with simple structures only or you do e.g. only number crunching or GUI programming, stay with plain Java. Another rule of thumb is: if all your story patterns contain less than 3 objects, your cases are simple and may be handled in Java easily. On the reverse, if your Java code employs nested if- and loop-statements on objects you might consider story diagrams.

To complete our example, Figure 10.9 shows a storyboard for a more complicated scenario that covers the more special cases of the doAssignments methods. Karli is in the math room with a motivation of only 42. There are five assignments with different points. Karli shall first do the vector assignment[1] earn 20 points which already suffices to earn the 17 math credits, Karli's motivation drops to 22, and the first visit is done, cf. storyboard step 2. To trigger these actions, the first storyboard step calls method doAssignments on the karli object. If the execution of our doAssignments story diagrams starts by matching the vector assignment, we earn 20 points in the first iteration of our for-each loop. This suffices to pass the math course. Thus, the for-each activity terminates and the lower story pattern is executed, i.e. we earn the credits. Altogether, we expect that in the second storyboard step karli has done the vector assignment, karli has 22 motivation left, karli has 0 points, and karli has 17 credits, cf. step 2 of the storyboard in Figure 10.9. If we have achieved this, the second storyboard step calls doAssignments the second time on the same room (formally we should do another room in between). On this second run our for-each activity will probably first match the vector assignment again. However, this should be rejected as karli has already done it. Next the for-each activity may visit the circles assignment with 30 points. As karli's motivation has dropped to 22, karli should skip this one, too. Next, the roots assignment should work, karli gains 10 points and motivation goes down to 12. As 10 points do not suffice for the math credits, karli next does polynomes, gains another 10 points and motivation goes down to 2. Now karli has sufficient points and the for-each activity terminates without doing the adding assignment. In the lower story pattern, karli earns another 17 credits and points are resetted. Thus, in the third step of our storyboard, we expect that karli has done vector, roots, and polynomes,

---

[1]Recall, the assignments of a room are organized in a LinkedHashSet. When you iterate through a LinkedHashSet e.g. with a for-each activity, the assignments are visited in the order in which they have been added to the set. The test code that is generated from the storyboard step contains a sequence of statements that add the assignments to the math room. These statements are generated from the first storyboard step by iterating through the elements of that step. As you might expect, the elements of a step are stored in a LinkedHashSet again. This LinkedHashSet is filled while you draw the storyboard. This means, the assignments will appear in the order in which you have added them to the first storyboard step. This order stays valid in code generation and similarly in test execution. Thus, Karli visits the assignments in the same order in which you (well we) have added them to the first storyboard step. This is a hidden feature of storyboards. Stable ordering of sets is important for reproducible test runs and should therefore be guaranteed even by future versions of our code generation.

`karli`'s motivation is 2, the `points` are 0 and the `credits` are 34.

This storyboard thus covers many of the cases we have spotted above and ensure that our implementation now works and it may be used to verify with the customer that we have achieved the desired behavior.

10.2   The Study-Right University findPath

As we started this book with the demand for a solver for our Study-Right University, we finally deliver such a solver here. Figure 10.10 shows a storyboard that models the floor plan of our Study-Right University. In addition, we call method `findPath(214, "")` on the `math` room. This is the result of a model exploration step that we used to derive the pseudo code algorithm given in Listing 10.1.

For the model exploration we started by visiting the `math` room. We decided to have an extra sticky-note to write down the path of rooms that we have already visited. Thus, step 2 of our algorithm adds the name of the current room to that path. Next we use another sticky-note to keep track of the motivation that is left. Thus, step 3 reduces this motivation. Now we need to distinguish several cases. If our motivation is 0 and we are in the `exam` room, we print the path we have found, cf. step 4 and 4.a) of our algorithm. If there is still motivation left, we visit all neighbor rooms, cf. step 5 and 5.a). This one is tricky. In our model exploration we soon identified that in each room we are doing the same thing, until our motivation is gone. Then, we go back to another neighbor of a room we have visited earlier. For example, if we start in the `math` room with only 37 motivation, the `math` room reduces the motivation to 20. If we now go to the `algebra` room, the path extends to `"math algebra"` and the motivation becomes negative. We stop. We go back to the `math` room and e.g. now visit the `calc` room. However if we go from the math to the `calc` room we want to restart with path `"math"` and with a motivation of 20. In this situation we decided to use a new copy of our sticky-notes for the path and for the motivation each time we visit a new room. This means, we decided to do a procedure call and pass a copy of the current path and the current motivation as parameters. With this idea it was obvious that we were designing an recursive method. With this knowledge in mind, it became clear that step 6 of our algorithm just means to trigger backtracking, i.e. to return without doing anything else.

Figure 10.11 shows the story diagram that we have derived from our pseudo code algorithm. We use a method `findPath` with an `int` parameter for the current `motivation` and an `String` parameter for the `path` of already visited rooms. Note, on each (recursive) method call, the `int` parameter value will be copied. The `String` parameter is passed by reference (as pointer), but when we append a new name to this `String`, a new `String` is constructed and the

```
findPath  algorithm :
        1:  visit  room
        2:  extend  current  path
        3:  reduce  motivation  by  credits
        4:  if  motivation  equals  0  and  we  are  in
            the  exam  room
                    − print  path
        5:  if  motivation  is  greater  than  0
                    − visit  all  neighbor  rooms
        6:  if  motivation  is  less  than  0
                    − proceed  another  alternative
```

Listing 10.1: Pseudo code algorithm for findPath

old String (still used by the caller) remains unmodified. Overall, we get new copies for our sticky-notes on each method call.

The first activity of our story diagram in Figure 10.10 just computes the new motivation and the new path as outlined in step 2 and 3 of our pseudo code algorithm. The second activity checks whether we are in the exam room with motivation 0 and prints the current path in that case, cf. steps 4 and 4.a) of our algorithm. The third activity is a for-each activity that visits all neighbor rooms, if we still have motivation left, cf. steps 5 and 5.a). As discussed, step 6 of our algorithm requires no implementation. That's it.

You have doubts? Listing 10.2 shows the console output produced by executing our storyboard test.

10.3 Exercises

This section addresses story diagrams again. Thus, as exercise just do the exercises of Section 9.3 that you have not done yet.

```
 1   found:  math  calculus  math  calculus  math  calculus
         math  calculus  math  calculus  modeling  exam
 2   found:  math  algebra  math  modeling  exam  modeling
         exam  modeling  exam  modeling  exam  modeling  exam
 3   found:  math  algebra  philosophy  algebra  math
         calculus  modeling  exam  modeling  exam
 4   found:  math  algebra  philosophy  algebra  math
         modeling  calculus  modeling  exam
 5   found:  math  algebra  philosophy  modern  arts
         philosophy  algebra  math  modeling  exam
 6   found:  math  modeling  stochastic  modeling  exam
         modeling  exam  modeling  exam  modeling  exam
         modeling  exam
 7   found:  math  modeling  exam  modeling  stochastic
         modeling  exam  modeling  exam  modeling  exam
         modeling  exam
 8   found:  math  modeling  exam  modeling  exam  modeling
         stochastic  modeling  exam  modeling  exam
         modeling  exam
 9   found:  math  modeling  exam  modeling  exam  modeling
         exam  modeling  stochastic  modeling  exam
         modeling  exam
10   found:  math  modeling  exam  modeling  exam  modeling
         exam  modeling  exam  modeling  stochastic
         modeling  exam
```

Listing 10.2: Console output

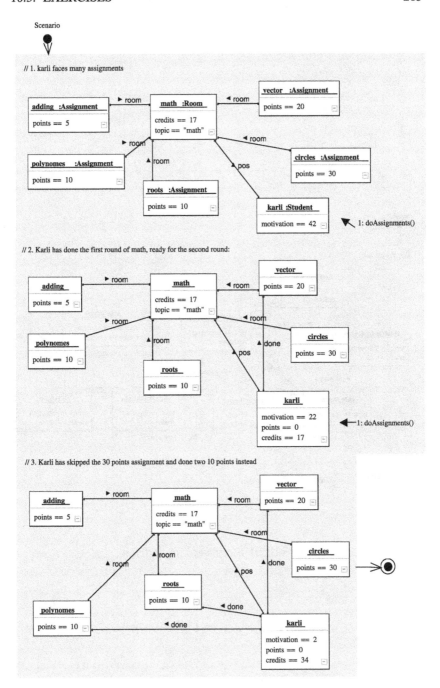

Figure 10.9: Storyboard for doAssignments twice

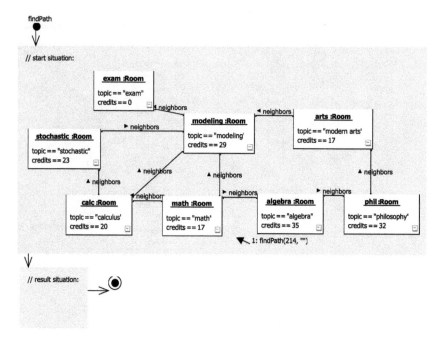

Figure 10.10: Storyboard for findPath

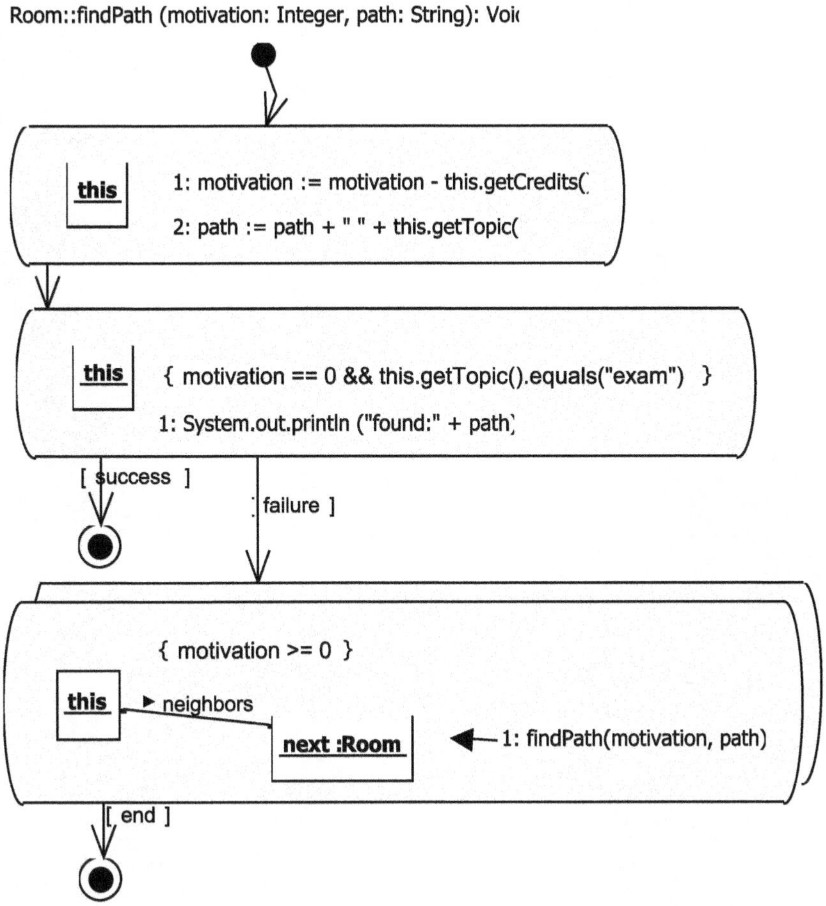

Room::findPath (motivation: Integer, path: String): Voi
this
1: motivation := motivation - this.getCredits(
2: path := path + " " + this.getTopic(
this
{ motivation == 0 && this.getTopic().equals("exam") }
1: System.out.println ("found:" + path)
[success]
failure]
{ motivation >= 0 }
this
neighbors
next :Room
1: findPath(motivation, path)
[end]

Figure 10.11: Story diagram for `doAssignments`

Chapter 11

SDM of GUI Applications

So far we have learned how to model the behavior of an application designed in a story driven manner. Most of the behavior was focused on model transformations. In this chapter, we will learn how Story Driven Modeling based development integrates with graphical user interfaces and user interface design. Also here, we will use a simple example scenario to outline the concepts:

The Group Register

Or: How to support going dutch in a pot luck barbecue.

If you ever have visited Germany and have been out with Germans, you might have discovered a small cultural peculiarity. If it comes down to paying for going out or paying for a party, we[1] like to split the bill very exactly (often much to the annoyance of people from cultures not used to this habit) – this behavior is strangely referred to as "going dutch" in English. As German software developers or software developers attending a German party, we therefore urgently need an application helping us with doing the respective (and usually due to the number of participants and items brought tedious) math. Usually one person takes on the task of creating a register of all stuff brought, how much people spent on it, and computing and re-distributing the money to even it out. Therefore, we will call our application the Group Register.

A sample scenario for this application would be the following:

1. Karli, Bobby, and Olga agree on having a pot luck barbecue, but want to share the cost evenly. On the day of the barbecue, Karli brings his notebook running the Group Register application. He assumes that Bobby and

---

[1]The initial authors are all German, so we assume being politically correct referring to this.

Olga will bring enough for them all, so he does not bring any food items. After starting the application it shows the initial screen of the application with no entries.

2. Karli adds himself, Bobby, and Olga to the list of participants.

3. Bobby shows up and brings some beer for 12 EUR. Karli enters that Bobby brought beer for 12 EUR into the system. Olga brings bread for 4.50 EUR and salad for 3.00 EUR. Karli enters the items for Olga and Karli to the system.

4. The food items sum up to 19.50 EUR. Therefore, the share of each participant equals to 6.50 EUR. As Karli has not spent any money for food items, he has to pay the full share of 6.50 EUR. As Bobby has already spent 12 EUR, he has to receive back 5.50 EUR. Olga has spent 7.50, so she has to receive 1 EUR back.

Such a scenario is similar to an initial version which might have been discussed with a customer. As such a program will usually have a graphical user interface, a discussion about the user interface can be used to refine the scenario. There are several possibilities to carry out and facilitate such a user interface discussion. A frequent approach is the use of wireframes (or sometimes also called mock-ups). These are manual or electronic sketches of parts of a potential user interface. There exist several commercial programs to support the creation of wireframes. However, it is also possible to use any vector graphics editor. There are several templates of widgets freely available in the Internet. We provide one of these templates here in the book (see Figure 11.1) Most commonly wireframes are still prepared interactively and manually on paper with pen, on white- or blackboards, or with paper snippets cut out of templates and scotch tape. If you use a GUI editor for designing wireframes, be aware that it can become easily very confusing for a customer, because it will be not clear which elements on the screen belong to the GUI builder and which belong to the wireframe. For demonstration purposes we use here some hand drawn wireframes. We assume furthermore that we do these wireframes interactively together with a potential customer. In other situations, there might be some time and preparation between the initial scenario design and the first wireframe GUI discussion. In this case the discussion with the customer, which we are outlining here, happens just in the head of the GUI designer.

We will now go step by step through the scenario and discuss its implications:

1. *Karli, Bobby, and Olga agree to have a pot luck barbecue, but want to share the cost evenly. On the day of the barbecue, Karli brings his notebook running the Group Register application. He assumes that Bobby and Olga will bring enough for them all, so he does not bring any food items.*

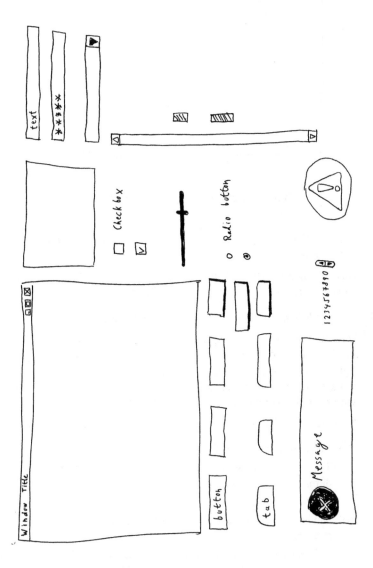

Figure 11.1: Wireframe template. Copy or print, cut in pieces with scissors, take some glue, sticky tape, pencils and build your GUI!

Figure 11.2: Empty application wireframe

After starting the application it shows the initial screen of the application with no entries.

This step mentions that we have an application with an initial screen. This leads us to an initial wireframe like in Figure 11.2.

2. *Karli adds himself, Bobby, and Olga to the list of participants.*

   This step mentions a *list of participants*. Therefore, we need a list showing the names of the participants. A possible wireframe is depicted in Figure 11.3. Looking at this wireframe will make us question, how we will actually get the participants into the list. Initially, we will have just a window with an empty list of participants as shown in Figure 11.4.

   With the empty list, we have now several options to add participants:

   (a) Just editing the table (Figure 11.5).

   This requires however some pretty complex handling of a single dummy line at the end of the table and might pose some difficulties in programming.

   (b) Having some fields and an add button underneath to enter one person at a time (Figure 11.6).

   This is easy to implement and we assume for now that we agree with the customer on this idea.

   (c) An add button on top which creates an empty line, which is editable (Figure 11.7).

   This is a combined idea from (a) and (b) and removes some of the complexity from (a). We will still stick with (b) here.

Figure 11.3: Application wireframe with one list and the participants

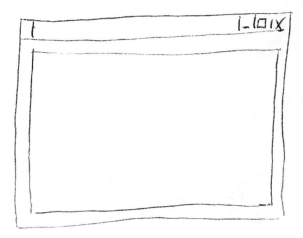

Figure 11.4: Application wireframe with one list and no participants

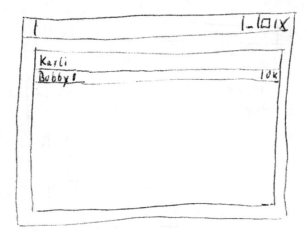

Figure 11.5: Application wireframe, with table and edit field, name edited in place and typed in

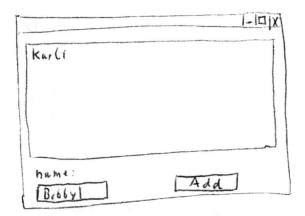

Figure 11.6: Application wireframe, with table and name field and add button (below list)

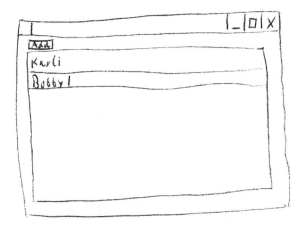

Figure 11.7: Application wireframe, with table and add button on top list, edit in place

3. *Bobby shows up and brings some beer for 12 EUR. Karli enters that Bobby brought beer for 12 EUR into the system. Olga brings bread for 4.50 EUR and salad for 3.00 EUR. Karli enters the items for Bobby and Karli to the system.*

   From this step, we can derive that we need something to store bought items, the person who bought it, and the price of each. This also suggests to use some kind of table with the columns person name, item description, and price. Also here, we could discuss different options to fill in the values like in the last step, but also here we will settle on the option of adding some entry fields and an add button. This could be done in a different window, but we will put it in the same to make all information visible at all times. A wireframe of this is shown in Figure 11.8. Having decided for two tables leads to the idea that we should be able to show different proportions of these tables. Therefore, we add a split bar, which can be dragged to resize the proportions (Figure 11.9). To test how it looks, we add one item (Figure 11.10). This leads to the question, how can we make sure to only add persons, which were already added as participants on the left hand side. Therefore, we transfer the item name field into a pull-down-list (Figure 11.11).

4. *The food items sum up to 19.50 EUR. Therefore, the share of each participant equals to 6.50 EUR. As Karli has not spent any money for food items, he has to pay the full share of 6.50 EUR. As Bobby has already spent 12 EUR, he has to receive back 5.50 EUR. Olga has spent 7.50, so she has to*

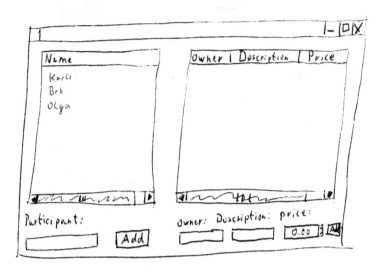

Figure 11.8: Application wireframe with two lists

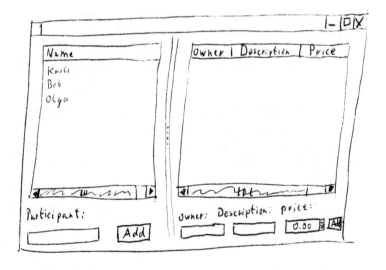

Figure 11.9: Split bar added.

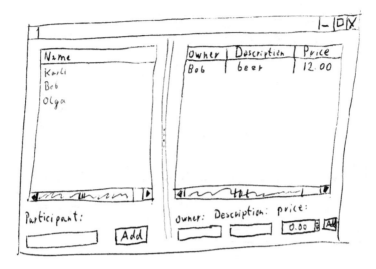

Figure 11.10: One food item added.

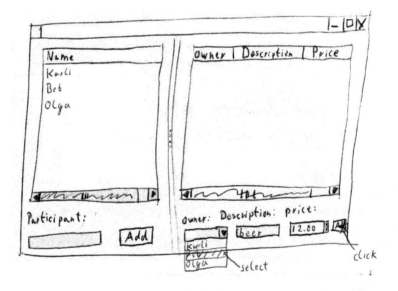

Figure 11.11: Application wireframe with two lists and pull-down menu for owners of food items

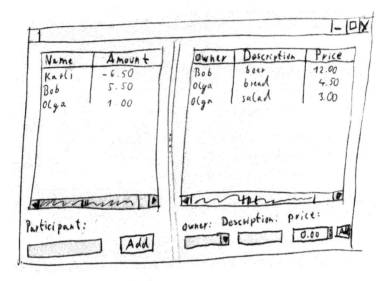

Figure 11.12: Amount column with balance values added.

receive 1 EUR back.

So far, we have not taken into account that we want also to see the amounts of the balance each participant has to pay to the register. We could now either add a button to compute the balance and show a different window with the results or we could also show the balance all the time in the participants list. Let us assume that our potential customer prefers the version showing the balance all the time. We therefore add a column Amounts. We show the result of the current step in Figure 11.12. We also want to see the current values all the time. It should update after each item we add. So if we had only one item, we would see something like in Figure 11.13.

The final empty wireframe is shown in Figure 11.14. Further discussion and playing with these wireframes might lead to some further requirements and ideas. Possible questions would be: Is it possible to remove items from the list or will it be possible to edit the names of the participants? You might have discovered that we used here the names Bob and Bobby for the same person in different wireframes, so we might want to be able to change this. We also might want to adjust the price of the food items. Figure 11.15 shows some in-place editing for these requirements and a delete button to remove items.

The discussion carried out in the initial graphical user interface design leads to several new ideas refining the initial scenario.

1. We are working with two different table-like lists.

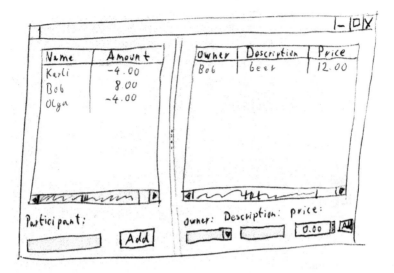

Figure 11.13: Balances directly after adding one food item.

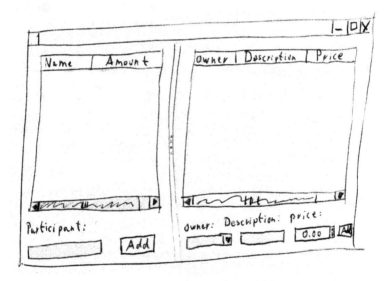

Figure 11.14: Final empty wireframe

Figure 11.15: Further requests: edit participant name, edit price, delete button for shopping items

2. The participants list always shows the balances.

3. For the food items, a participant must have been added in advance and must be selected from a pull-down menu.

4. We add items to the list one by one always triggering directly an update of the whole content.

In an ideal world these extra requirements should now be reflected in a refined scenario/user story. Furthermore, the wireframes we selected should be linked in this user story and amended due to changes implied in the user story. This means for better explanations some more wireframes can and should be added. The refined user story would look like the following:

1. Karli, Bobby, and Olga are agreeing to have a pot luck barbecue, but want to share the cost evenly. On the day of the barbecue, Karli brings his notebook running the Group Register application. He assumes that Bobby and Olga will bring enough for them all, so he does not bring any food items. After starting the application it shows a screen with two lists: one for participants, and one for brought food items and their prices. Both lists are empty (Figure 11.14).

2. Karli adds himself to the list of participants. (Figure 11.16)

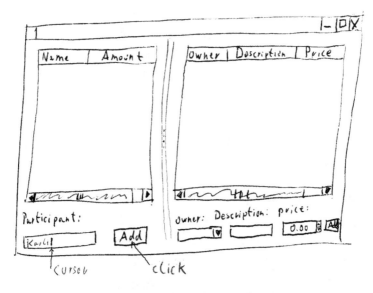

Figure 11.16: Karli adds himself to the list of participants.

3. His name as well as an amount of 0.00 he has to pay to the register show up. (Figure 11.17)

4. He also adds Bobby and Olga as participants. He writes as Bobby's name just Bob, just for his random convenience. He intends to change the name later, if Bobby should not like it. The program lists initially their names and the amount of 0.00 for each of them within the Amount column. (Figure 11.18)

5. A little later Bobby shows up and brings a couple of bottles of beer for 12 EUR. Karli selects Bobby from the list of participants and adds that Bobby brought the item with the description beer for a price of 12.00. (Figure 11.19)

6. The program now shows one entry in the items list: the item's owner is Bob, the description is beer, and and the price is 12.00. In the list of participants it shows as amount to pay to the register for Karli -4.00, for Bob 8.00, and for Olga -4.00. This means that at this point Karli and Olga have to pay 4 EUR each to the register and Bobby would receive 8 EUR. (Figure 11.13)

7. Olga brings bread for 4.50 EUR and salad for 3.00 EUR. Karli adds to the program two items brought by Olga: bread with price of 4.50 and salad

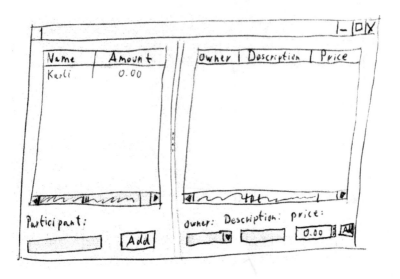

Figure 11.17: Karli added as participant

Figure 11.18: All participants added.

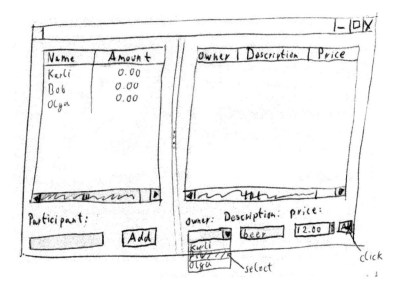

Figure 11.19: Adding beer for Bob.

with price of 3.00.

8. After adding these two items the list of participants shows for Karli -6.50, Bob 5.50, and Olga 1.00. (Figure 11.12)

9. Optional extension would be to allow Karli to delete the salad entry from the list of food items,

10. change the entry Bob to Bobby,

11. and change Olga's bread price to 7.50. (Figure 11.15 and Figure 11.20)

There are also several tools which allow to do such wireframes electronically but look more like hand drawn wireframes (cf. Figure 11.21). However, here is still the danger that this looks too professional and makes the potential customer think that the GUI and the underlying functionality has already been implemented.

After designing your wireframes, it is a good idea to play through them. Therefore, you should make several copies of them and eventually glue scotch tape on fields which could have text in them (and bring pens to write on the tape and erase it again), or bring lots of small paper slips and paper clips to temporarily glue into your wireframes. It is not wise to play through wireframes inside a program as this will give the impression that some part of the GUI have been already implemented, so print outs are usually better. Also redrawing the GUI onto a whiteboard in front of the customer can be a reasonable approach

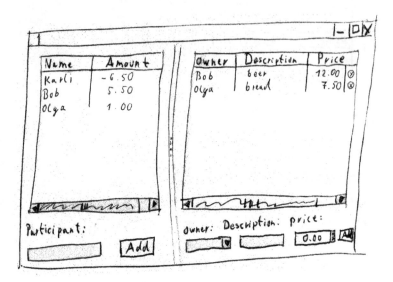

Figure 11.20: Applied further changes.

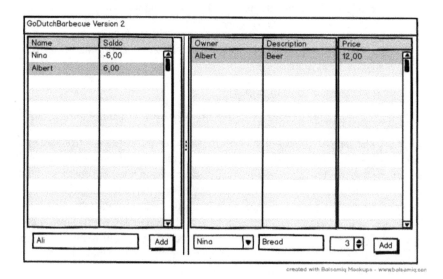

Figure 11.21: Alternative wireframe in Balsamiq mock-up [2]

as entering and removing text is easily simulated. Then you take the scenarios again and go step by step through them and let a potential customer enter text, press buttons, and show corresponding changes in the respective GUI elements. We also call this playing through the *User Game*. Players are usually one or several users and customers, a backend person, and an observer and interviewer. The backend person builds and updates the GUI in each step after actions (like button presses or text entries) have been performed, therefore this person simulates the program. The observer or interviewer will watch closely for problems in the simulated program user interaction and later the observer will interview the participating users or customers. This is usually a very good base for finding the points in the simulated GUI where things are missing or hard to find (like a hidden menu entry).

It stays the question, when in the Story Driven Modeling process do we use the technique on GUI-based modeling. Do we first build scenarios and storyboards and do then the GUI design or do we even use the GUI modeling to help us building the scenarios. As usually, this depends highly on the project and also on the persons carrying it out. A more detailed discussion about this can be found in the beginning of Chapter 13.

11.1 Storyboard and Behavior Modeling

After designing the scenario(s) and the GUI, we can build the corresponding storyboard and derive the class diagram. Therefore, we take another look at the with wireframes amended scenario and add object diagrams to respective steps where the runtime object structure changes. Explanations for the chosen object diagram will be in the storyboard.

1. *Karli, Bobby, and Olga are agreeing to have a pot luck barbecue, but want to share the cost evenly. On the day of the barbecue, Karli brings his notebook running the Group Register application. He assumes that Bobby and Olga will bring enough for them all, so he does not bring any food items. After starting the application it shows a screen with two lists: one for participants, and one for brought food items and their prices. Both lists are empty.*

   Object Diagram:

gr: GroupRegister

Gui:

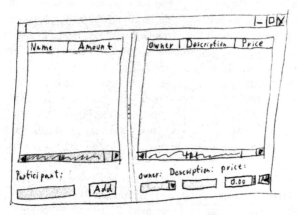

At this point we only have the just initialized system. Therefore, we only show this system as one object.

2. *Karli adds himself to the list of participants.*

   Object Diagram:

   GUI:

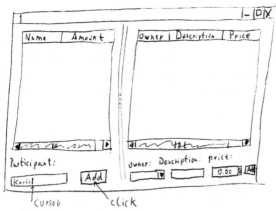

As written in the scenario we need an object for Karli and need to add it to the system. As we are creating this object and the association to the system, we color the new object and association green and label them with a <<create>>-label.

3. *His name as well as an amount of 0.00 he has to pay to the register show up.*

No object diagram changes
GUI:

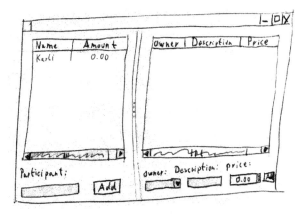

The "showing up" part is GUI specific and here not relevant in the object diagram. However the mentioning of the amount reminds of a calculation of the amount which has to be done. This hints at a method which recalculates the amounts which have to be paid. It seems like there is some algorithm, we have to execute after we add persons.

4. *He also adds Bobby and Olga as participants. He writes as Bobby's name just Bob, just for his random convenience. He intends to change the name later, if Bobby should not like it. The program lists initially their names and the amount of 0.00 for each of them within the Amount column.*

Object diagram:

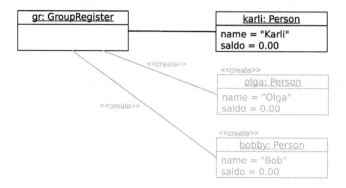

GUI:

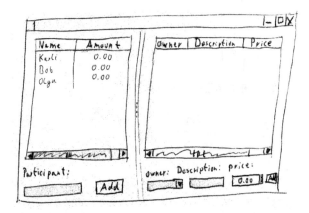

Like in step 2, we add two new persons and mark them and their associations with green and the <<create>>-label.

5. *A little later Bobby shows up and brings a couple of bottles of beer for 12 EUR. Karli selects Bobby from the list of participants and adds that he brought the item with the description beer for a price of 12.00.*

Object diagram:

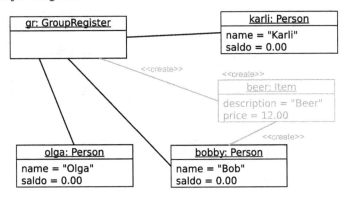

GUI:

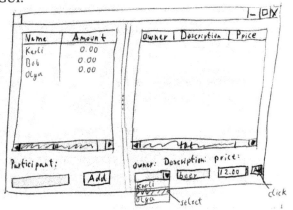

We need to show here the set of items Bobby brought. Therefore, we add now an object beer with the respective price value to our object diagram and associate it with the system and with Bobby to remember that he brought it.

6. *The program now shows one entry in the list of items brought. It shows Bob as the owner, beer as the description, and 12.00 as the price. In the list of participants it shows as amount to pay to the register for Karli -4.00, for Bob 8.00, and for Olga -4.00. This means that at this point Karli and Olga had to pay at this time 4 EUR each to the register and Bobby would receive 8 EUR.*

Object diagram:

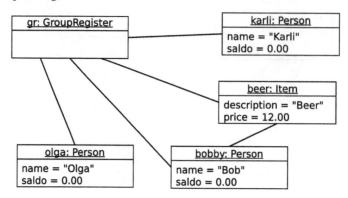

GUI:

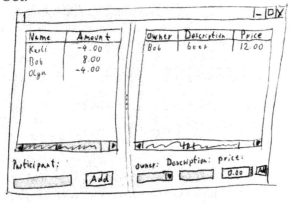

Here is the obvious hint that we call a method which re-calculates values. We will call them (as already done before, but here we learn what they really are) saldos. They show how much money each person has to pay back to the register or receives from it. We will call this method updateSaldos and remember it when we derive its functionality. We can already here see that this method needs to take a look at all participants and all their items, count their absolute value, divide this by the number of participants and subtracts this from the amount of the sum of all items the participants brought.

7. *Olga brings bread for 4.50 EUR and salad for 3.00 EUR. Karli adds to the program two items brought by Olga: bread with price of 4.50 and salad with price of 3.00.*

Object diagram:

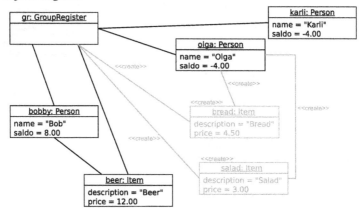

No visible change in GUI at this point.

Here happens basically the same as in step 6 just for two items of one person. It has the same implications.

8. *After adding these two items the list of participants shows for Karli -6.50, Bob 5.50, and Olga 1.00.*

Object diagram:

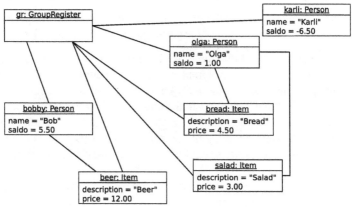

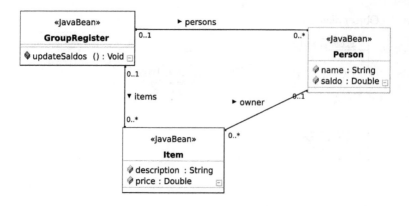

Figure 11.22: Group register class diagram

GUI:

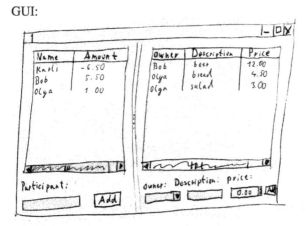

Also, here the recalculation of the saldos has to be triggered, which changes the saldo values of the participants. This step is analogue to step 6.

Due to the various object diagrams, we have now, we can derive the class diagram. We see, that we have different Persons, a GroupRegister (as the "system") and different Items. We already know that we need one method (we called updateSaldos). We will add this to the GroupRegister class as all objects are associated to the corresponding system object. The class diagram is depicted in Figure 11.22. As we are talking in the scenario list of participants and a list of items the system handles, we select here 1-to-many cardinalities for both associations.

As we have now a very extensive storyboard and a class diagram, we can now derive the algorithmic part with any method discussed in Chapter 6. We should especially look for this at the steps 6 to 8. A generalization discussion should yield here that we have to compute the total of all items bought by all participants. This can be easily done in going over all items connected to the Group Register system object and adding them up. Then we can compute the total share for each person in dividing the total by the number of participants. From this shared total we need now to subtract for each person the items they have bought to compute how much money they will get back (negative) or have to give (positive). For this we have to loop through all persons and through all the items they brought.

Therefore, we will amend steps 6 to 8 with the following pseudocode in the storyboard:

```
Loop over all items brought to the BBQ:
     sum up prices to a total

Divide this total by number of persons and save
     it as shared total

Loop over all persons:
     Loop over all items connected to the
     person:
               sum up the values of the items
                    they bought
               and substract them from the
                    shared total
     Save this difference as the saldo of the
     person
```

Now we can implement the code. The result might look like Listing 11.1. This behavior can also be modeled like depicted in Figure 11.23. As we see here, the effort for writing code in Java or modeling the story diagram might be sometimes in favor of writing Java code. However, depending on the audience sometimes the story diagram might be easier to understand. For an open discussion, our experience shows that story diagrams are usually easier. However, we leave this decision to the reader.

11.2 Using a GUI Construction Toolkit

If you need a graphical user interface in your application, there are in general two possibilities to create it: (1) code it manually or (2) use a GUI Construction Toolkit or GUI Editor.

As the second is usually visual and should be intuitive, in this book we are focusing on the latter as it can be seen as the modeling tool for user interfaces. The question, we want to answer in this section, is, how do we integrate the

```
 1  public void updateSaldos(GroupRegister gr)
 2  {
 3          double total = 0.0;
 4
 5          // Get total spent
 6          for (Item item: gr.getItems()) {
 7                  total += item.getPrice();
 8          }
 9
10          // turn total in total per person
11          total /= gr.getPersons().size();
12
13          for (Person p : gr.getPersons()) {
14                  double saldo = total;
15
16                  for (Item item : p.getItems()) {
17                          saldo -= item.getPrice();
                                // subtract items
                                bought
18                  }
19                  p.setSaldo(saldo); // compute
                        total the person has spent
20          }
21  }
```

Listing 11.1: Code to update the saldos.

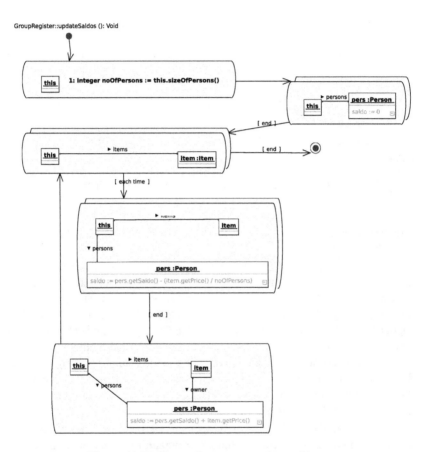

Figure 11.23: Story diagram to update saldos.

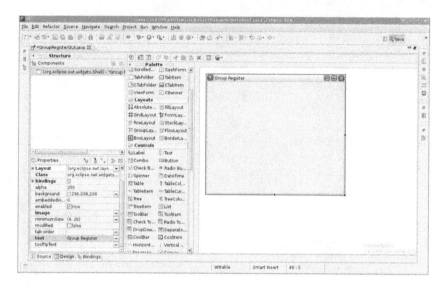

Figure 11.24: Start designing in Windowbuilder

usage or a GUI Construction Toolkit with the Story Driven Modeling approach
of code development.

There are several GUI Construction Toolkits: Visual Studio has a very powerful Kit, Windowbuilder is becoming currently the de-facto standard for Java
(Swing and SWT) and for the Google Web Toolkit (GWT). There are also QT
Designer for QT, Glade for GTK, and wxGlade for the wx toolkit, Android Designer for Android, or Cocoa (touch) for Mac OSX (and iPhone OS), which are
in active use today. They all work very similar, but Visual Studio and Windowbuilder support simultaneous editing of code and the graphical editing of the user
interface. As most of the tools discussed in this work are Java-based, we will use
Windowbuilder here as an example. The described process is though easy to
transfer to other GUI editors.

In the beginning of the time of Widget and GUI editors, layouts were often
absolute, and different screen resolutions or default font sizes often made GUIs
look strange or even unusable. Today's editors usually use relative layouts and
can deal with these differences. However, the technique of layout managers
usually takes some practice and a while of getting used to produce reasonably
looking results.

When creating a new SWT class, the screen will look like described in Figure 11.24. For our BBQ-example we will first select a Composite Sash Form to
enable the divided structure into users on the left and bought goods on the right.
As layout, we advise to use a Gridlayout even if Filllayout would have

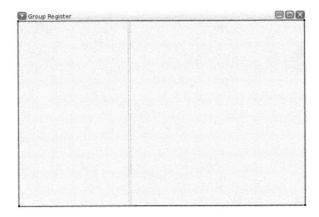

Figure 11.25: Composite Sash in Windowbuilder

worked here too. (Our experience shows that all usual relative layout options apart layering can usually be covered with grid layouts.) We will see something like Figure 11.25.

To scale the sash in horizontal and vertical direction to maximum dimensions of the enclosing window, we set both grabExcessHorizontalSpace and grabExcessVerticalSpace to true and horizontal and vertical alignment to Fill. As a next step we will add composites for the left and right tables and buttons. In these go the tables for users and food items, respectively, with the headers we have defined in the analysis phase. Figure 11.26 shows the current state of the GUI.

Under the tables the buttons and pull-downs corresponding to our mock-ups have to be added and the result is shown in Figure 11.27.

After drawing the GUI, we can define listeners to react to events in the GUI. Therefore, we select a GUI element like the add button, right click on it, select add event handler, and will for a button usually select selection – Widget Selected. After this, we should switch to the source code view and will discover that Windowbuilder created an anonymous method to be registered to the listener like the following:

```
1  addPersonButton . addSelectionListener (new
       SelectionAdapter () {
2      @Override
3      public void widgetSelected ( SelectionEvent e)
           {
4      }
5  });
```

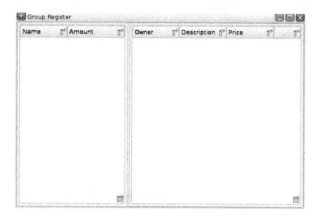

Figure 11.26: Two tables in Windowbuilder

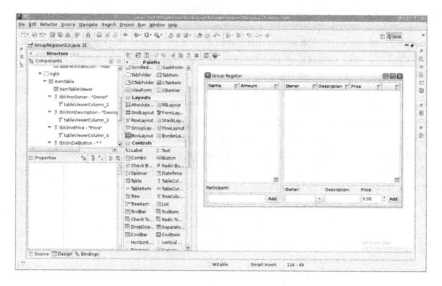

Figure 11.27: Final GUI in Windowbuilder

As you would expect, when having it made so far in our book, we consider this evil coding. Fortunately, we can quickly use an Eclipse refactor[2] method and turn this first into a nested inner class and directly continue to turn it into a real class in its own file. We considered the first version evil as it violates separation of concern. As the GUI changes very rapidly, it makes sense to have this code at a different point in the project. For developing an application with a GUI it is also good practice to separate model, view, and controller parts (cf. Model-View-Controller (MVC) pattern in [26]). The model we have created already pretty well with our Story Driven Modeling approach, this part here belongs into the controller.

A controller could look like this:

```
1  public class GroupRegisterControl {
2      public static void main(String args[])
3      {
4          GroupRegister root = new GroupRegister();
5          root.addPropertyChangeListener(new
               UpdateSaldoListener(root));
6          GroupRegisterGUI.root = root;
7          GroupRegisterGUI.main(args);
8      }
9  }
```

The main problem of splitting the system by introducing a controller module is making the model known to the view (GUI). The available GUI editors usually do not support a plain MVC pattern. In the case of Windowbuilder we need to add a static `root` variable to the class and set it as just described in the code.

To easily fill the tables with data from the model, we can define databindings. For this, we switch the GUI to the binding tab. As we have added the root variable to it, this is now visible. We select it, the person table view and the persons-container as shown in Figure 11.28.

In Figure 11.29, we conclude the binding in selecting class `Person` and from this the `name` and the `saldo`. Analog, we add for the right table the item `description`, item `owner` name, and the `price` (cf. Figure 11.30).

To be able to edit a field in the table, we need to select a `ViewerColumn` and double click on `editSupport` in the properties which creates again an inner edit class for us. This can be turned in a stand alone class by two more calls to refactoring functions provided by Eclipse as discussed before. In the class the methods `setValue` and `getValue` have to be adapted so that they set or return the corresponding elements from our model like described in the following code snippet:

---

[2]As a very brief explanation: refactoring means an editor (here usually Eclipse) supported change to the code in multiple places. It is usually done to increase code quality.

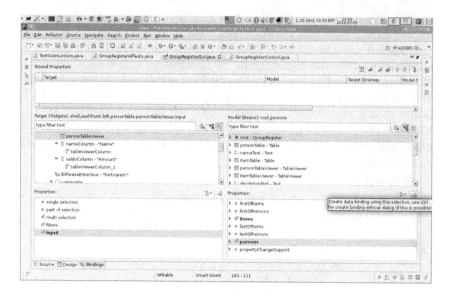

Figure 11.28: Windowbuilder binding tab for adding persons to table

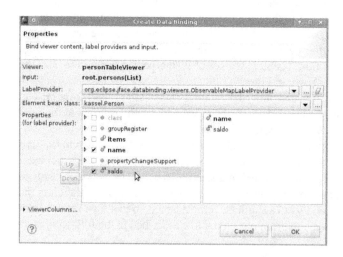

Figure 11.29: Windowbuilder binding dialogue for adding persons to table

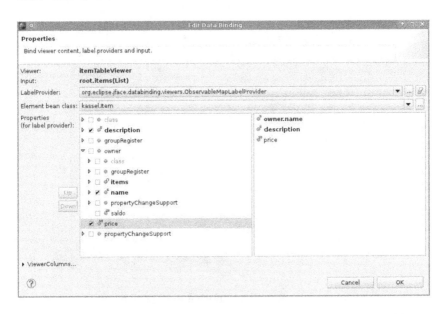

Figure 11.30: Windowbuilder binding dialogue for adding items to table

```
1  protected Object getValue(Object element) {
2      return ((Person)element).getName();
3  }
4
5  protected void setValue(Object element, Object
       value) {
6      ((Person)element).setName((String)value);
7  }
```

11.3 Testing Graphical User Interfaces

As described in Chapter 8, testing is an integral part of software development. However, testing GUIs can be very cumbersome as they are designed to be the interface to the user. Therefore, the natural approach to testing GUIs would be to use human testers working through test protocols or scenarios and verifying a specific functionality or flow of events. However, our experience shows that humans adapt really quickly to quirks in user interfaces and start overlooking problems and peculiarities already after several hours. Therefore, this might work for a rough initial testing to find major flaws, but plenty of minor flaws might be overlooked. Experienced developers might have observed that in de-

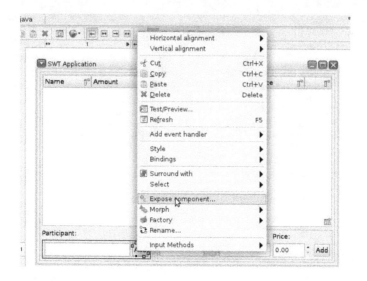

Figure 11.31: Expose component in Windowbuilder

bugging processes with user interfaces, doing the same steps over and over again
to come to a point where a potential mistake might arise is itself error prone and
some time for automating these initial setup steps might be well worth the effort
in comparison to all the manual work of setting up the situation.

To avoid human testers, we can go just one step lower in the abstraction and
fill some of the GUI elements programmatically and create the events, which
usually are fired by user interaction, manually and send them out. For this
we need access to the elements of the user interface frame or window. In the
MVC-based approach with Windowbuilder we just described, this means we
need to get access to the window object initialized in the static main method of
our GUI. Therefore, we have to make the local window object static and public. As the main GUI thread is protected against interaction with the GUI elements from outside its thread, we need to build a testHook. Therefore, we
add first a **static** Runnable testHook; to our other two static variables and we
call the run method of this testHook in the open-method of the GUI just after the main layout call. Then we exchange in our main method of our GUI
the e. printStackTrace () ; with **throw new** RuntimeException(e); to be able to
receive exceptions later in our unit testing framework. We have now three extra static variables: root (a reference to our model), window, testHook, the
method call of the hook, and the passing on of caught exceptions. To access the
elements, we also need to expose (with the expose component function as shown
in Figure 11.31) the elements defined by Windowbuilder.

To test for example the add person functionality, we can use the following code, which we will put into an inner class:

```
1   private class TestHook implements Runnable {
2       @Override
3       public void run() {
4           GroupRegisterGUI window =
                  GroupRegisterGUI.window;
5           window.getNameText().setText("Abu");
6           while (Display.getDefault().
                  readAndDispatch()) {}
7           Button addPersonButton = window.
                  getAddPersonButton();
8           addPersonButton.notifyListeners(SWT.
                  Selection, null);
9           // select Abu in newItemsPanel
10          Combo combo = window.getOwnerCombo();
11          combo.notifyListeners(SWT.FocusIn, null);
12          Assert.assertTrue("not_enough_names_in_
                  combo:_" + combo.getItemCount(), combo
                  .getItemCount() >= 1);
13      }
14  }
```

First, we read the static `window` variable to be able to access and interact with the GUI elements. Then, we add the name `Abu` to the `name` field. Afterwards, we simulate a button press on the `addPersonButton` in notifying the respective listeners. We then notify the combo that it got a focus event to update its content and finally check, if the just added person is available in the combo. The test method itself will look like the following:

```
1   @Test
2   public void testGroupRegisterGui()
3   {
4       GroupRegister root = new GroupRegister();
5       root.addPropertyChangeListener(new
                  UpdateSaldoListener(root));
6       GroupRegisterGUI.root = root;
7       GroupRegisterGUI.testHook = new TestHook();
8       GroupRegisterGUI.main(null);
9   }
```

The first lines are the same lines used in the controller to initialize the model and start the GUI. We add an `TestHook` object to our GUI and run the `main` thread, which calls itself the method we defined before in `TestHook`.

If we also wanted to test if the food items can be added correctly, we can amend our test code with the following lines:

```
1   combo . select (0) ;
2   window . getDescriptionText () . setText ("Chicken") ;
3   window . getPriceSpinner () . setSelection (1200) ;
4   Button addItemButton = window . getAddItemButton () ;
5   addItemButton . notifyListeners (SWT. Selection , null
        ) ;
6   TableViewer tv = window . getItemTableViewer () ;
7   ObservableListContentProvider cp = (
        ObservableListContentProvider ) tv .
        getContentProvider () ;
8   IObservableSet dos = cp . getKnownElements () ;
9   Item it = (Item ) dos . iterator () . next () ;
10  Assert . assertEquals ("No chicken in item list or
        wrong price in item . ", it . getDescription () , "
        Chicken") ;
11  Assert . assertEquals ( it . getPrice () ,12.00, 0.1) ;
```

11.4 Exercises

11.4.1 Mau Mau

Build a graphical user interface for our Mau Mau example. In this version all players shall sit in front of one computer and share mouse and keyboard.

- Extend the Mau Mau storyboards with wireframe GUI models. (Yes, wireframe models for each step.)

- Discuss your wireframe models and scenarios with friends and try to resolve usability issues.

- Construct the modeled GUI with the help of a GUI Construction Toolkit (e.g. Windowbuilder).

- Bind the GUI to the Mau Mau implementation we have developed in the previous sections. Add Listener and Handler classes where necessary.

- Change the JUnit tests we have developed into GUI tests.

- Play the game with some friends and have fun.

11.4.2 Battleships

Follow the steps of the Mau Mau Exercise 11.4.1 for our Battleships example.

11.4.3 Mancala

Follow the steps of the Mau Mau Exercise 11.4.1 for our Mancala example.

11.4.4 Mensch Ärgere Dich Nicht

Follow the steps of the Mau Mau Exercise 11.4.1 for our Mensch Ärgere Dich Nicht example.

11.4.5 Towers of Hanoi

Follow the steps of the Mau Mau Exercise 11.4.1 for our Towers of Hanoi example.

11.4.6 ATM Money Withdrawal

Follow the steps of the Mau Mau Exercise 11.4.1 for our ATM Money Withdrawal example. (Well, the "have fun" step might be a little bit tough.)

11.4.7 Borrowing Electronic Books from Library

Follow the steps of the Mau Mau Exercise 11.4.1 for our Library example.

11.4.8 Trouble Ticket System

Follow the steps of the Mau Mau Exercise 11.4.1 for our Trouble Ticket System example.

11.4.9 Webshop

Follow the steps of the Mau Mau Exercise 11.4.1 for our Webshop example.

11.4.10 Connect Four Game

Follow the steps of the Mau Mau Exercise 11.4.1 for our Connect Four Game example.

Part III

Scaling Up

Chapter 12

SDM for concurrent applications

Up to now we have only dealt with single-threaded programs. We carefully avoided concurrency and parallel programming. We did so for good reasons: concurrency is extremely difficult and error prone. Concurrency is one of the mainly unsolved problems in software engineering. We strongly advice you to avoid concurrency whenever possible. Do not use concurrency. Avoid it! Run! Save your soul!

Well, there are some cases where you cannot avoid concurrency. As you might not always be able to forward such jobs to your fellow teammates, you need to learn about it. A typical case for concurrent programming or multi-threading is client server communication. Client server communication usually requires to listen to a TCP/IP port, continuously, which is usually done with blocking reads. The thread that listens to the port is not able to do anything else. As your application might still need to react e.g. to user interactions, you need another thread to do this. Now you are in trouble. Client server messages may arrive at the same time when user interactions occur. Both threads may simultaneously try to change overlapping parts of your model. This may result in chaos, unreproducible effects and severe system crashes. You might try to use Java synchronization mechanisms to avoid concurrent manipulations on critical model parts. This usually results in deadlocks. To avoid the deadlocks, you increase the critical area to larger parts of your model or to the whole model. This avoids circular wait. However it most likely causes the port listener thread to block your GUI thread for a long time. Again your GUI hangs. To sort this out will cost you weeks. It is hard to debug. The error occurs rarely and unexpectedly, and even magically disappears completely[1] during debugging sessions. Thus you might try to ignore it for some time, however it will strike back when you do the most important demo of your life. Even when you have sorted out the whole thing, you will still have sleepless nights before your next demo as you will still fear an occasional failure to occur. Thus, do not use concurrency. Avoid it! Run! Save your soul!

Well, eventually powers that are stronger than you might force you to dive into this.[2] If this happens to you, we strongly recommend: use only a very small number of threads, unless all your threads are working on different, isolated data structures! Do not deliberately create a new thread because this might be done in parallel. Keep it simple. Next, define clearly separated areas of responsibility for your threads. For each of these areas, only one thread should work in it. If another thread wants to read something in that area, it shall send a request to the responsible thread, the responsible thread will retrieve the information and send it to the requester. Yes, this needs more time. However, it is thread safe and the chance of locating a missbehavior is so much easier..

If you have not yet tried to do concurrent programming, some of the discussion above might be a little bit abstract for you. Thus, let us clarify some terms and then go into an example. A program is essentially a bunch of code. If you start a program, the computer allocates a so-called process that executes the code. A computer is usually able to execute multiple processes in parallel. To avoid conflicts, the computer's operating system isolates the different processes from each other. Thus a process is not able to access the runtime memory of another process. This means, an object created by one process cannot by accessed by any other process. You are safe. Multiple processes may communicate only by exchanging files on the common hard drive, pipes, or sockets, e.g. TCP/IP. TCP/IP is often used in a fashion quite similar to files. The main difference is that if your process communicates via TCP/IP it may not only speak to other processes on the same computer but also to other processes on any other computer reachable via the local network or the Internet. Therefore, TCP/IP gives you more flexibility. However, as discussed above, sometimes you want parallel execution within one process, e.g. to keep your GUI interactive while you are listening to a TCP/IP port. Parallel execution within a single process is done using so-called *threads*. Threads run in parallel to each other, however they share the same memory. This means, an object created by one thread may easily be accessed by another thread in parallel. Thus, while you are executing a method on an object and this method changes some attributes, another thread may execute

---

[1]These errors are known as *Heisenbugs*, errors that seem to disappear when studying those.

[2]We are aware that multicore processors are the current trend and addressing the efficient programming of these is one of the current major problems of software engineering. We nevertheless, still advise the beginning developer to design a problem single-threaded or with only few threads in mind and cleanly separate out parts of the system which can be easily parallelized later.

```java
public class LostUpdateExample implements
    Runnable {

  static int value;

  public void run() {
    while (true) {
      int tmp = value;
      System.gc();
      value = tmp + 100;
      tmp = value;
      System.gc();
      value = tmp - 100;
      System.out.println(value);
    }
  }

  public static void main(String[] args) {
    new Thread(new LostUpdateExample()).start();
    new Thread(new LostUpdateExample()).start();
  }
}
```

Listing 12.1: Lost update with threads in Java

a method (the same or another) on the same object accessing the same attributes. Chaos. Unreproducible effects. Severe system crashes. See Listing 12.1 for an example of such a lost update condition, try it yourself!

This was, so far, still quiet abstract. Thus, let us go into some examples. First we will discuss multiple threads to keep your GUI responsive while long lasting actions are executed. Second we will discuss multiple threads used for a chat program.

12.1 Multiple Threads to Keep Your GUI Responsive

To illustrate how your GUI might freeze due to long running activities and how careful you must be to solve this with additional threads, we use a demonstration program for money transfer, cf. Figure 12.1. This example deploys a left bank and a right bank which provide only one account each and which run their

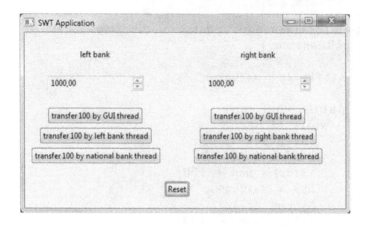

Figure 12.1: Bank transfer GUI

accounting software in threads within the same process. (No, it is not a real world example.) There are three ways to transfer 100 money from one bank to the other bank. You can do the whole transfer within the GUI thread, within the bank thread or within the thread of a third bank, the national bank. Each way has specific effects with respect to concurrency which we will discuss below.

Figure 12.2 shows the model objects behind this GUI. The left and the right bank are modeled by objects b22 and b23, respectively. In addition, we have a NationalBank object n6 that may be used to avoid concurrency. We have two TransferAction objects t28 and t36 that provide a method to transfer money from one bank to the other. The three banks each own a Timer (java.util.Timer) object. The Timer objects represent threads used by the three different banks to execute TransferActions concurrently. Finally, the GUI object c0 is shown which owns another thread.

All three kinds of money transfer shown in Figure 12.1 use the same operation to actually transfer the money. This operation is provided by the special action objects of Type TransferAction shown in Figure 12.2. Figure 12.3 shows the run method of the TransferAction objects. The source and the target bank are attached to the TransferAction object via src and tgt links, respectively. The first story diagram activity directly withdraws 10000 cents from the source bank. Then, its collaboration message 1 retrieves the balance of the target bank. To simulate, that the change of a bank account balance may involve some database access that may need some time and for demonstration purposes, the second activity of Figure 12.3 does a Thread.sleep(). After 5 seconds, the third activity adds 10000 to the target balance that has been retrieved in the first activity of Figure 12.3 and assigns the new balance to the target bank. Note, this is a very stupid and risky way to do such a transfer. We have chosen this way

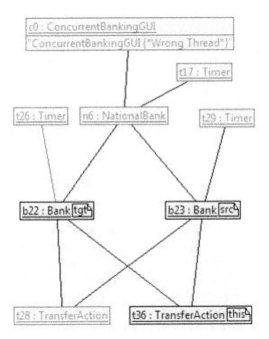

Figure 12.2: Bank transfer object model

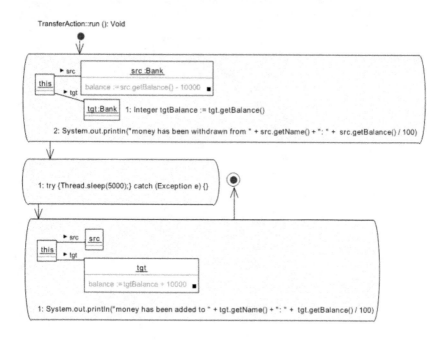

Figure 12.3: Bank transfer GUI

deliberately to be able to demonstrate concurrency risks.

Let us now see what happens, when we run the `TransferAction` within the GUI thread of our example application. To discuss the timing behavior of multiple threads in detail, we use UML sequence diagrams, cf. Figure 12.4. A sequence diagram shows a group of objects on the title line. These objects know each other somehow and are able to exchange messages. Each object has a dashed, vertical life line below it. This life line orders outgoing and incoming messages in time order from top to bottom. Messages may either be method invocations shown with solid arrows or method returns shown with dashed arrows. Actually, UML sequence diagrams have much more elements, cf. [17, 16], but for our purposes this suffices.

Figure 12.5 shows a sequence diagram outlining the timely behavior for a bank transfer done within the GUI thread. In this example, the user clicks on the left "transfer 100 by GUI thread" button of our GUI, cf. Figure 12.1. Note, users may act concurrently to your program. Thus, we consider a user to have its own process or thread. In our sequence diagram the user is represented by the stickman object. To reflect that the user owns its own thread, the sticky man and its lifeline and its activities are rendered in blue color. (Each thread will get its own color.) The GUI of your application always runs its own thread, too. In

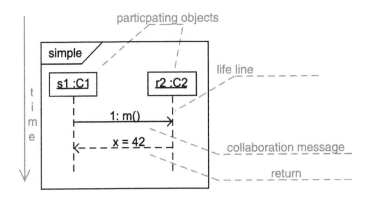

Figure 12.4: UML sequence diagram example

Figure 12.5 this GUI thread is represented by the APP[3] object. The GUI thread uses black color. When the user clicks on a button, the operating system or the window manager of your computer identifies the corresponding application and delivers an event object to its GUI thread. In our sequence diagram this step is depicted by the click() message from the user to the APP object. Basically, method click is called on the APP object (with some parameters not shown in our example). Usually, a method is executed directly and only after all its jobs are done, the method execution returns and the caller may go on with the next operation. However, the call to method click just adds an event to the input queue of the APP object and then method click returns directly. This is done in parallel to any operation that might currently be executed by the APP object / thread.

In our example, we assume that the APP thread was sleeping and it wakes up when the click event has been added to its event queue. When the APP thread wakes up, it calls method dispatch on itself. Method dispatch consumes events from the event queue, in our case the click event, analyzes them, and delivers them to their target widget. Thus, in our example, method dispatch calls method selected(ev) (like mouseDown, mouseUp) on the button object representing the clicked button. The causing event is passed as parameter ev. As discussed in Chapter 11 the button object does not handle the event directly but it forwards the event to a listener object that implements the han-

---

[3]For objects owning their own thread, we use upper case letters.

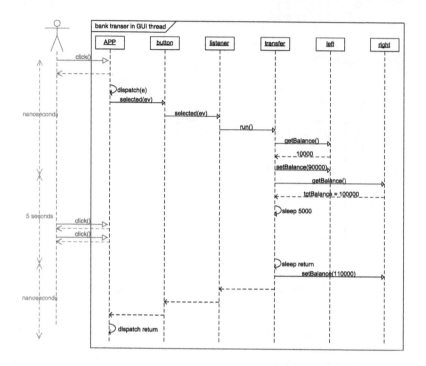

Figure 12.5: UML sequence diagram for money transfer within GUI thread

dling, cf. Figure 12.5. Our listener is programmed to call method run on the transfer object. The transfer object is of type TransferAction and its run method has been discussed in Figure 12.3. In the direct execution example the listener might have implemented the operation directly. We use it here only to facilitate the comparison with the other executions that are discussed below. As discussed above, the run method of the transfer object retrieves the balance of the left bank and sets the new balance of the left bank to 90000. In addition, the transfer object retrieves the balance of the right bank, 100000 in this situation. Now the transfer object calls sleep(5000) on itself (or on its thread).

Up to now, the handling of the mouse click uses less than a millisecond of time. Doing a double click takes some 100 milliseconds. Thus, while the APP object takes care of the first mouse click, the user has no chance to do another click. The user is just to slow. However, during the 5 seconds that the APP thread is sleeping (simulating a lengthy database access) the user may click multiple times. Such clicks create new events on the event queue of our APP object. However, the APP object / thread is still busy to execute the first click and thus, the additional clicks are ignored until the first event has been handled, successfully. Note, the events are fully ignored, the button does not even slide in and out to give visual feedback that it has been pressed. This happens not only to mouse clicks but also to resize and refresh events send to our GUI when its window is resized or when the window has been hidden behind some other window and then becomes uncovered again. The GUI will not react at all. Thus, the user might easily get the impression that the application is dead and the user might kill the application. Or the user starts to hammer on some button multiple times to cause some reaction. Actually, all these mouse events will be recorded and added to the queue and the APP will take care of all of them one after the other causing the GUI to be dead even longer. In summary, the user will not be happy with the behavior. It is just not OK to execute any action handling within the GUI thread that might take longer then some 100 milliseconds. While computers are pretty fast these days and most actions will take nanoseconds only, access to the hard drive or to some internet service may easily consume some 100 milliseconds and thus, such actions must not be executed within the GUI thread.

As discussed, long running actions need to be executed in a thread separate from the GUI thread. While there are numerous possibilities, currently we recommend to use java.util.Timer objects to add new threads to your application. Timer objects run their own thread and they deploy a task queue for jobs to be executed. You might add objects of type TimerTask to that queue via a schedule(task) method. The Timer will execute such TimerTask objects one after each other. We like Timer objects because they serialize[4] the execution of simultaneously arriving TimerTasks and because they also offer to delay the execution of a TimerTask for a certain amount of time or to repeat the execution of a TimerTask within a certain time interval. Accordingly, the object model in Figure 12.2 already employs three Timer objects, one for each bank.

Figure 12.6 shows the execution of mouse clicks to the "transfer 100 by left bank thread" button. Again the user click is added to the APP event queue and method click returns. The APP thread wakes up and calls dispatch() on itself. This results in selected(ev) calls to button and then to listener. This time the listener does not call run() on the transfer object directly but it schedules the transfer object for execution at the Timer object. Then, method schedule(transfer) returns directly and the whole reaction to the user click by the APP thread terminates and the APP thread is ready to react to new GUI events.

As discussed the Timer objects runs its own thread. Thus the Timer object uses upper case letters and the Timer object and its lifeline and all its activities are shown in red color. When the new transfer task has been scheduled, the Timer thread wakes up and calls run() on the transfer object. Then the transfer object does its job on the two banks, sleeps 5 seconds, completes the transfer,

---

[4]We mean with serialize here the process of putting events in a sequence, one after each other.

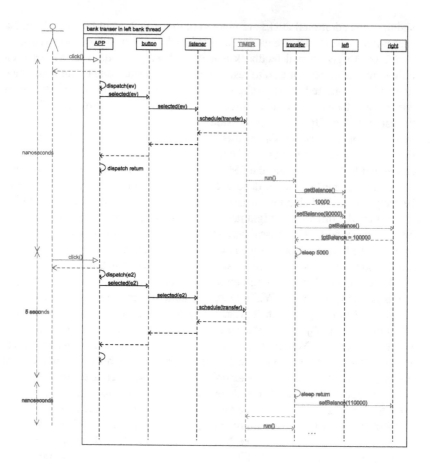

Figure 12.6: UML sequence diagram for money transfer within left bank thread

and terminates.

While the `Timer` thread sleeps, the user may click on the "transfer 100 by left bank thread" button again. This causes the scheduling of the `transfer` task for a second time[5]. However, the second execution of the transfer task waits within the `Timer` queue until the first execution terminates. After that, the second execution starts. The two executions are not executed in parallel and thus we are safe.

However, when the user clicks the "transfer 100 by *left* bank thread" button first and the "transfer 100 by *right* bank thread" button second within let us say 1 second, we are in trouble, cf. Figure 12.7. In Figure 12.7 we have omit-

---

[5]Actually, class `Timer` does not allow to reuse `TimerTask` objects. Thus, for each schedule you need to create a new `transfer` object. We omitted these details for the sake of understandability.

ted the button and listener objects in order to make space for two Timer and two TransferTask objects. Thus, in Figure 12.7 the APP thread calls method schedule on the appropriate Timer object, directly. In our example, the first click goes to the "transfer 100 by *left* bank thread" button and thus the first schedule(ltra) invocation goes to LTMR, the Timer of the left bank. (Each bank has its own timer, cf. Figure 12.2. Similarly, each bank has its own TransferAction object. Object ltra belongs to the left bank.) LTMR runs its own thread and uses red color. When recieving the schedule(ltra) command, the LTMR thread wakes up and calls run() on the TransferAction ltra. TransferAction ltra does its job, reduces the balance of the left bank to 90000 and then it falls asleep.

After about a second, the user clicks on the "transfer 100 by *right* bank thread" button. This time the corresponding schedule(rtra) command is send to the RTMR object. The RTMR object again owns another thread (the third within the application by now) and uses green color. As RTMR owns its own thread, it starts execution directly in parallel to the execution of LTMR (which is sleeping right now). This brings us into trouble.

Before falling asleep, ltra has reduced the balance of the left bank to 90000 and retrieved the balance of the right bank which is 100000. Now rtra, the TransferAction object of the right bank starts to work. TransferAction rtra reduces the balance of the *right* bank and retrieves the balance of the left bank. Note, the balance of the left bank has already been changed to 90000 (while the balance of the right bank has not yet been changed to 110000). Now rtra falls asleep.

After about 4 seconds, ltra the TransferAction object of the left bank wakes up again and completes its task by changing the balance of the right bank to 110000. Yet another second later rtra the TransferAction object of the right bank wakes up and completes its task by changing the balance of the left bank to 100000. We end up with a balance of 100000 for the left bank and a balance of 110000 for the right bank. Ups. At the beginning both banks had a sum of 200000 cents, now they have a sum of 210000 cents. We have generated 10000 cents by just sending 10000 cents from left to right and from right to left. Well, it could be worse, we might have deleted 100000 cents. Anyway, this is a severe bug. The bug occurs because we have carefully created a pitfall in method run of class TransferAction and by interleaving the execution of the two transfers[6]. All this effort just to show you that concurrent threads are dangerous.

Yes, the problem might look artificial. Unfortunately, the problem is real. Generations of developers have spend their life in fighting this. Yes, it is quite complicated to trigger this problem. However it occurs in practice. It occurs

---

[6]The created pitfall is basically the same as the "lost update" problem known from database system theory.

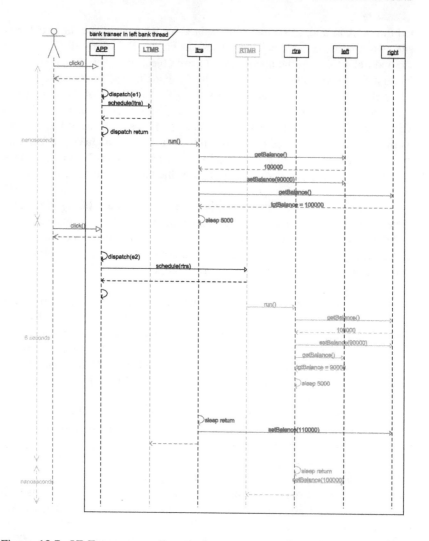

Figure 12.7: UML sequence diagram for money transfer within left and right bank thread

not immediately in small programs but later on when your program has grown complex. And, while it is complex to trigger the problem it is even much more complex to identify its cause and to fix it. This holds already for small systems and becomes worse when your program has grown complex. Thus, beware.

In our example the problem arises because the execution of two actions that operate on the same objects runs concurrently[7]. This should be avoided. Usually, you use Java synchronization mechanism to block multiple methods to enter the same object area, mutually. Unfortunately, Java synchronization has many pitfalls and we do not recommend this. We propose to use one Timer thread for each object area and this and only this Timer thread operates on the objects in that area. Then you are safe. Figure 12.8 shows a sequence diagram using a single national bank Timer NBTMR to do all the transfers. In this example the user first clicks on the *left* "transfer 100 by *national* bank thread" button, cf. Figure 12.1. This time the APP calls method schedule(ltra) on the Timer NBTMR of the national bank. It passes the transfer object ltra belonging to the left bank because we want to transfer from left to right. NBTMR wakes up and ask ltra to do its job. Object ltra changes the balance of the left bank to 90000 and falls asleep. This gives the user the chance to do a click on the *right* "transfer 100 by *national* bank thread" button of our GUI. Thus, the APP calls method schedule(*rtra*) on Timer NBTMR. This time we want to transfer from right to left. The task is enqueued to the task queue of NBTMR. However, as NBTMR is still busy to execute the first request, the new request is not yet considered.

After 5 seconds ltra resumes and completes its job by assigning 110000 to the right balance. Now, NBTMR runs the rtra transfer. Object rtra changes the right balance back to 100000 retrieves the 90000 of the left balance and falls asleep. 5 seconds later, rtra changes the left balance to 100000 and terminates. Money has been transferred from left to right and from right to left. No parallelism. No money has been generated, no money has vanished. And, the user interface is responsive while we are transferring money. Issue solved.

12.2 A Basic Chat Program

To demonstrate the usage of multiple threads for TCP/IP-based communication we start with a simple chat program named BasicChat. Figure 12.9 shows two instances of the chat window when already 4 chat messages have been exchanged.

Figure 12.10 shows an eDOBS screen dump of the objects deployed within the left BasiChat program instance. There is the BasicChatGUI object that runs the GUI thread. The BasicChatRoot object is the root of the object model. It owns 4 ChatMessage objects, one for each message that has been exchanged. The BasicChatRoot object has a Timer object that runs a thread used to control access to the object model. Finally, there is SocketThread object that owns a thread used for TCP/IP communication over a ServerSocket.

---

[7]Furthermore, when implementing such transfers in real programs, the use of transactions is recommended so the subtraction and addition of balances are one atomic operation.

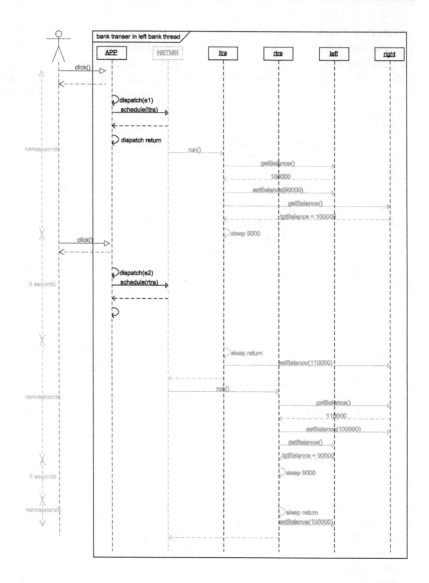

Figure 12.8: UML sequence diagram for money transfer within national bank thread

The GUI of BasicChat has been designed using Windowbuilder as described in Chapter 11. Not a too big effort. The model classes BasicChatRoot and ChatMessage have been generated by Fujaba, again easy. The tough part

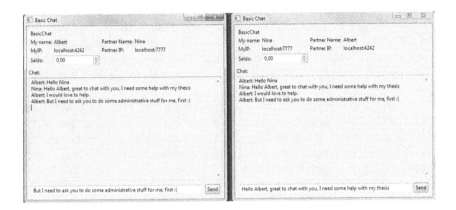

Figure 12.9: Two BasicChat windows

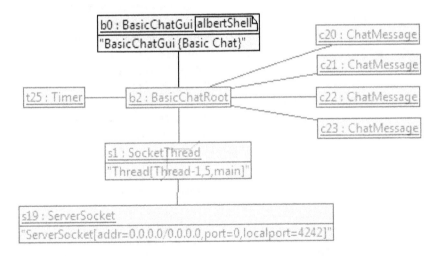

Figure 12.10: Objects deployed by one chat

is the multithreading and the TCP/IP communication. To get this right let us go through an example, cf. Figure 12.11. In our example Albert has just typed some message `txt` within the text field on the button of his chat window (shown on the left of Figure 12.9. Albert now clicks the send button. The `click()` reaches the `AGUI`[8] thread which calls method `selected(e)` on the corresponding button (omitted in Figure 12.11) which calls `selected(e)` on the attached handler object `anmh`[9]. In Figure 12.11 this is abbreviated by a direct message from `AGUI` to `anmh`.

Albert's `NewMessageHandler` object `anmh` has two tasks: it updates the model of Albert's BasicChat application and it sends a message to Nina's BasicChat application. When updating the logical model we need to beware: in parallel to the `AGUI` thread, the thread receiving messages via TCP may simultaneously add messages to the model. As discussed we solve this with a `Timer` object `AMT`[10] that sequentializes operations on the model. Thus, our handler object `anmh` initializes a `TimerTask` object `anmt`[11] and then it schedules the `anmt` to the model timer `MT`. The model timer will handle this as soon as it gets CPU time assigned, see below.

The message handler object `anmh` continues by sending a `write(txt)` command to the client `Socket` object `acsock`[12]. The client `Socket` object `acsock` opens a TCP channel to a `ServerSocket`[13] object owned by Nina's `BasicChat` application. Within Nina's BasicChat application the `ServerThread` object `NST`[14] represents the thread that listens to Nina's `ServerSocket`. In Figure 12.11 we abbreviate these details by a direct message from Albert's `acsock` to Nina's `NST` object. Note, the data transport from `acsock` to `NST` is done via some network, locally or the Internet. If the two instances of our BasicChat application run e.g. on two different smart phones, message transfer may need some second. From Europe to USA it might still need half a second. In your local network it should work in some milliseconds. From the point of view of `acsock` and `NST` the data transfer is buffered. This means, `acsock` might write to its outgoing port and then go on with other things while the message is transferred. Some time later the message arrives at Nina's `NST` object which will then process the received `txt` directly. However, Albert's BasicChat might have done

---

[8] `AGUI` means Albert's Graphical User Interface.

[9] `anmh` is an acronym for Albert's NewMessageHandler, the class that implements this handler object.

[10] `AMT` means Albert's Model `Timer`.

[11] `anmt` means Albert's `NewMessageTask`, the class that implements the `TimerTask` object that updates the logical model.

[12] `acsock` means Albert's Client `Socket`. `Socket` is a Java library class for TCP/IP communication.

[13] `ServerSocket` is a Java library class that allows to open a port for TCP communication. The owner of the `ServerSocket` object then waits for a client `Socket` to connect to this port. A connected TCP socket can be used for bidirectional communication via streams.

[14] `NST` means Nina's `ServerThread`.

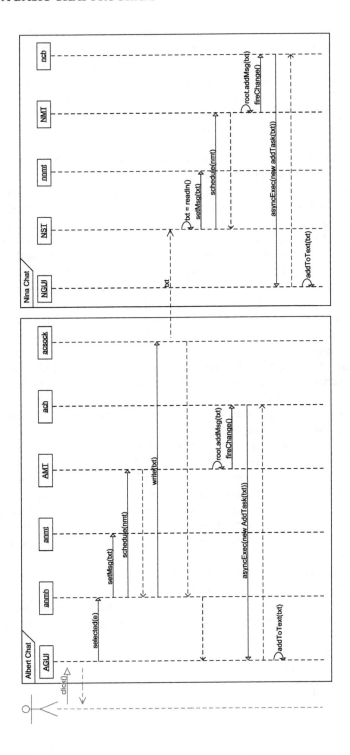

Figure 12.11: Handling one chat message

a lot of things meanwhile it might even already have sent the next message.

Once our message handler anmh has managed to send the new txt via acsock its job is done and its execution terminates. In parallel (or now), the model Timer AMT might get CPU time. When the model Timer wakes up, it calls method run() on the scheduled anmt object. The run method of the anmt object will then do the model updating task, i.e. nmt will add the new message txt to the BasicChatRoot object, cf. Figure 12.10. In Figure 12.11 we abbreviate these steps by sending a root.addMsg(txt) command from AMT to itself. This model change now needs to be reflected in the GUI of Albert's BasicChat program. As discussed in Chapter 11 updating the GUI is done by data binding mechanisms. In our example we use a so-called property change handler object ach[15] for this purpose. When the model changes, the change handler ach gets informed by a fireChange() message. This message passes additional parameters identifying the model change. This change information is omitted in Figure 12.11 for brevity. The change handler ach then tries to update the GUI to show the new txt message. Again we need to be careful: the AGUI runs its own thread and the change handler ach runs within the model Timer thread AMT. To avoid concurrent modification conflicts, the change handler must not update the Text widget of our GUI directly but it needs to create a new AddTask(txt) object and then it schedules this new task at the AGUI for execution. In our GUI library this is achieved using an asyncExec() command. After scheduling the AddTask, the change handler ach terminates. Eventually, the GUI will wake up and perform the update as shown by the addToText(txt) message in Figure 12.11 and the txt becomes visible in Albert's BasicChat window.

Meanwhile, the txt may have reached Nina's ServerSocket and the responsible ServerThread object NST has read it with the txt = readln() command. In the next step, the NST object wants to update the logical model. As the model runs its own thread in Nina's NMT[16] object, NST uses another NewMessageTask object nnmt[17], assigns the txt and schedules it. When Nina's NMT wakes up, the root.addMsg(txt) command updates Nina's logical model and a fireChange() is issued to Nina's change handler nch. Nina's change handler nch creates an AddTask and schedules it at Nina's NGUI[18]. When NGUI wakes up, the text widget in Nina's window is updated to show the received message.

This was kind of lengthy. Actually, the flow of information is not so complicated. The scenario becomes tricky due to the different threads and as sending a command to a thread always means to create a new task object that shall execute the command and then to schedule the new task object. Our scenario employs

---

[15] ach means Albert's Change Handler.
[16] Nina's Model Timer.
[17] Nina's NewMessageTask.
[18] Nina's GUI.

6 different threads and thus we have this problem frequently. However, as soon as you get used to it, things become reasonable and working according to this scheme will soon feel normal for you.[19]

As we have the overall picture now, let's have a look in some code snippets to clarify the details. Listing 12.2 shows class NewMessageHandler. A NewMessageHandler has a shell attribute, cf. line 2 of Listing 12.2, that refers to its BasicChatGui object which in turn owns a BasicChatRoot reference to the model root, cf. line 10.

As first action, method widgetDefaultSelected retrieves the typed message txt from the Text input field at the bottom of the BasicChat window and packs this txt into a ChatMessage object msg, cf. lines 13 through 16. Next, we create a newMessageTask and schedule it to the model Timer, cf. line 21.

Now we want to send the message to our partner BasicChat program. Therefore, we need the IP address of the computer that runs the partner BasicChat program. As we want to be able to run two BasicChat programs on the same computer (e.g. for testing purposes), each instance of the BasicChat program may use a different port. Note, TCP/IP communications uses different ports on each computer. Ports are numbered. There are reserved ports 0 to 1023 for operating system purposes. Port 8000 is often used for user-space web servers, and there are other conventions for ports >1024. Your program may choose any port number from 1024 to 65 535 it wants, as long as no other program uses the same number. If another program uses the same port number when you try to open it, the open operation will fail. In our example, Albert's BasicChat and Nina's BasicChat both use IP address "localhost", cf. Figure 12.9. Actually, localhost is a generic name for your local computer. When you open a TCP/IP connection with such a name, a DNS (Domain Name System) service of the internet is used to resolve the name to an IP number (127.0.0.1 in our case). Albert's BasicChat program uses port 4242 while Nina's BasicChat program listens on port 7777, cf. Figure 12.9. In our BasicChat program the TCP/IP address is provided in a single Text field of our GUI in the form "localhost:4242", which is the concatenation of hostname or IP-address and a TCP port number which gives a socket address. Thus, lines 24 through 26 retrieve the partner socket address from the model root, split it at the colon and parse the port number to an int.

With this information we are now able to create a client socket object in line 29. Such a socket object is used like a file. You may read from it or write to it. We want to write to the socket in order to send our txt to our partner. Writing to a file needs a PrintWriter that needs an OutputStream which is provided by our socket, cf line 31. Then, line 32 does the write. Now, the message is almost sent. Actually it is already in the communication buffer at this point. You need to either flush() the out object or close() it to make sure

---

[19]Well, you need to decide for yourself whether this is desirable or not.

```
 1  public class NewMessageHandler extends SelectionAdapter {
 2    private final BasicChatGui shell; {
 3
 4    public NewMessageHandler(BasicChatGui babChatGui){
 5      shell = babChatGui;
 6    }
 7
 8    @Override
 9    public void widgetDefaultSelected(SelectionEvent e)
10      BasicChatRoot root = shell.getBasicChatRoot();
11
12      // get text and add message to message list
13      String txt = shell.getTxtNewMessage().getText();
14      ChatMessage msg = new ChatMessage()
15        .withSender(shell.getMyName().getText())
16        .withText(txt).withAmount(0);
17
18      // add message to our model
19      NewMessageTask newMessageTask =
20        new NewMessageTask(root, msg);
21      root.getModelTimer().schedule(newMessageTask, 0);
22
23      // send it to partner
24      String partnerAddress = root.getPartnerAddress();
25
26      String[] split = partnerAddress.split(":");
27      int portNumber = Integer.parseInt(split[1]);
28
29      try {
30        Socket socket = new Socket(split[0], portNumber);
31        PrintWriter out =
32          new PrintWriter(socket.getOutputStream(), true);
33        out.write(txt + "\n");
34        out.close();
35      } catch (Exception e) {
36        e.printStackTrace();
37      }
38    }
}
```

Listing 12.2: NewMessageHandler snippet.

the buffer is actually sent over the network. For simplicity reasons, this simple example program just closes the connection and it will create a new connection for the next message. Actually, this is very slow and one should better keep the connection open. However, such connections may die after some time and when you send the next message you first need to check whether your channel is still alive or whether you have to create a new one. This is not too hard, but our example would need some additional 10 lines of code, which we omit here and leave as a quick exercise for the reader.

Now let's have a look on the receiver side. Listing 12.3 shows the code of class SocketThread. Class Socket extends class Thread, a Java library class for threads. An object of type Thread becomes a thread when you call start() on it. The start method adds the new thread to the operating system or to your Java virtual machine and then method run is executed in the new thread.

The first interesting line of class SocketThread in Listing 12.3 is line 16. Line 16 creates a serverSocket object on the current computer for the port number that is passed as parameter. A ServerSocket object provides an accept method, cf. line 19. The accept method listens on the corresponding port until a client Socket is created that connects to it. When a client Socket connects, method accept returns another Socket object that is used for communication on the ServerSocket side. We store this Socket in variable clientSocket.

Now we start reading from the clientSocket. As for a file this is done using a BufferedReader that uses an InputStreamReader that uses an InputStream that is provided by the clientSocket cf. line 21.[20] Now we can do an in.readLine(), cf. line 26. Method readLine collects characters from its input channel until it receives a newline character or end-of-file is reached in which case null is returned. The latter happens for sockets when the connection is closed by the sender. Method readLine returns as soon as one line of text is complete. When we have received a line, we construct a ChatMessage, put it into a NewMessageTask and schedule this task at the model timer, cf. line 36. This is important because when applying the model change directly from the socket receiving thread, we might have concurrent accesses to your model, which can lead to problems. The use of the model thread serializes all model change operations.

Our BasicChat program just exchanges plain text messages to be read by humans. However, exchanging data between programs follows just the same scheme. For example, Albert may change value of the Saldo spinner within

---

[20]Looking at this chain of streams and readers in reverse order clears this construct: A InputStream delivers raw bytes to read. The InputStreamReader converts those to characters in respect with the local encoding and locale, as we expect only text messages. Finally, the BufferedReader groups those characters in one blocking read call per received text line, terminated with a newline character.

```
1   public class SocketThread extends Thread {
2       private BasicChatRoot basicChatRoot;
3       private ServerSocket serverSocket;
4
5       public SocketThread(BasicChatRoot basicChatRoot) {
6           this.basicChatRoot = basicChatRoot;
7       }
8
9       @Override
10      public void run() {
11          // open socket and listen to it
12          String[] split = basicChatRoot.getMyAddress().split(":")
                ;
13          try {
14              String portName = split[1];
15              int portNo = Integer.parseInt(portName);
16              serverSocket = new ServerSocket(portNo);
17
18              while (true) {
19                  Socket clientSocket = serverSocket.accept();
20
21                  BufferedReader in =
22                          new BufferedReader(
23                          new InputStreamReader(
24                          clientSocket.getInputStream()));
25
26                  String line = in.readLine();
27                  while (line != null) {
28                      // handle msg
29                      ChatMessage msg = new ChatMessage()
30                      .withSender(basicChatRoot.getPartnerName())
31                      .withText(line);
32
33                      NewMessageTask newMessageTask =
34                          new NewMessageTask(basicChatRoot, msg);
35
36                      basicChatRoot.getModelTimer().schedule(
                            newMessageTask, 0);
37
38                      // read next msg
39                      line = in.readLine();
40                  }
41              }
42          }
43          catch (Exception e) {
44              e.printStackTrace();
45          }
46      }
47  }
```

Listing 12.3: SocketThread snippet.

his BasicChat window, cf. Figure 12.9. We might want to transfer the new value to Nina's window to show the same value in both windows all the time. We might use the same communication channel for usual text messages and for transfer of the Saldo value. If we do so, the receiver needs to be able to distinguish between text messages to be added to the text area of our BasicChat window and numbers that shall be shown in the Saldo spinner. A simple way to achieve this is to prefix each message with a keyword flagging its type, e.g. "msg:" for text messages and "Saldo:" for Saldo values. Next, we might want to transfer some IP addresses collected in the first BasicChat to the second BasicChat. And so on. Soon you will deal with some hundred keywords. This is tedious and error prone. To exchange complex data between two programs we propose to use a JSON-based protocol. With JSON [7] you easily transfer nested key value tables. JSON-based protocols are reasonably concise, human readable, very flexible, and somewhat reluctant in case of data evolution. In the next section we provide an exercise for a collaborative whiteboard-based on our BasicChat but exchanging modified pixels instead of text messages.

12.3   Exercise

12.3.1   Collaborative Whiteboard

Please extend our BasicChat to a WhiteboardChat. Therefore:

1. Extend the GUI of our BasicChat by a Canvas of e.g. size 500x500 and add a clear button, cf. Figure 12.12. In addition, create an Image of the same size and assign it to the canvas.

2. Add a MouseListener to the Canvas that reacts on MouseDown and MouseUp events. On MouseDown, store true in a boolean field e.g called mouseDown.

3. Add a MouseMoveListener to detect mouse moves on the Canvas.

4. Method mouseMove(ev) of the MouseMoveListener shall

   (a) call a method paintPoint(ev.x, ev.y) within the GUI thread, and

   (b) send a message to our chat partner that contains the data of the mouse event.

5. Method paintPoint(x, y) uses a graphics context GC to draw a filled rectangle with black background color to the Image that is shown in the Canvas. You will need to provide a listener to repaint the Canvas as

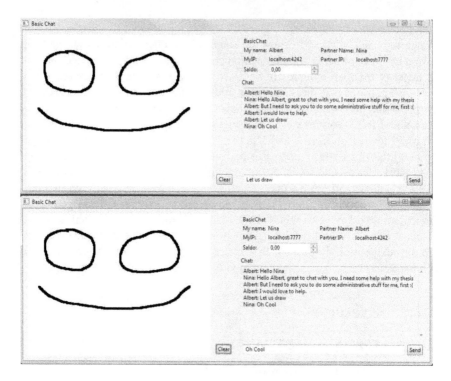

Figure 12.12: WhiteboardChat GUI

follows:

```
canvas.addListener (SWT.Paint, new Listener
    ()
{
    public void handleEvent (Event event) {
        event.gc.drawImage (image, 0, 0);
    }
});
```

In addition, method paint(x,y) needs to call canvas.redraw(ev.x, ev.y, rectanglewidth, rectangleheight, false) to actually redraw the display in that area.

6. Within the SocketThread extend the method that handles the received lines to detect the data of mouse events. When you receive mouse event

data create a Runnable object with that data and send it to your GUI thread using asyncExec(runnable). When executed, the Runnable shall call method paint(x,y) to paint the received point.

7. For the clear button add a selection listener that fills the whole image with a white rectangle and redraws the canvas.

12.3.2 Client Server Chat

To enable more than two clients for our WhiteboardChat develop a chat server that holds connections to multiple clients:

- Provide a mechanism letting clients connect to the server.

- Any message shall go from a client to the server and then from the server to all clients. As it may need time, the server should have a special thread for the sending of the messages. For communication between the thread that receives client messages and the thread that sends out messages to the clients, you may use class java.util.concurrent.LinkedBlockingQueue. Use method put to enqueue a message and method take for a blocking read on the queue. These methods are safely synchronized by experts. You do not want to deal with these synchronization issues yourself.

- Test your implementation with some five clients.

- Extend our basic chat for multiple chat groups or multiple parallel chat channels.

- You may also change the method that accepts messages such that it keeps the new socket open and spawns another thread to listen to that socket. This means on the server one thread for sending messages, one thread for accepting new clients and one thread for each client listening for new messages. On the client side, you may need one thread listening for server messages, one thread for the GUI and one thread managing access to the internal data model.

- You may extend your server with a persistence layer. For a basic chat you may just store the chat history in order to send the message history to new clients. As a next step, you might store multiple user logins. This may allow that a user terminates a chat and continues it later from another computer / location.

12.3.3   Multi Player Versions of Our Exercise Applications

Use the techniques learned from Section 12.3.2 to build multi player versions of our exercise examples:

1. Build a client server based version of our Mau Mau example.

2. Build a client server based version of our Battleships example.

3. Build a client server based version of our Mancala example.

4. Build a client server based version of our Mensch Ärgere Dich Nicht example.

5. Build a client server based version of our Towers of Hanoi example.

6. Build a client server based version of our ATM Money Withdrawal example. (Build your own bank. :)

7. Build a client server based version of our Library example.

8. Build a client server based version of our Trouble Ticket System example.

9. Build a client server based version of our Webshop example.

10. Build a client server based version of our Connect Four Game example.

Chapter 13

Story Driven Modeling

Up to now, we have learned to focus on simple scenarios, to refine them into storyboards, and to derive class diagrams from storyboards. We use code generation to implement the structural parts of our model and to generate JUnit tests that drive the algorithmic parts of the development. For algorithm development we switch to the perspective of the computer and identify the general algorithm steps. Then we refine the general algorithm steps to model-based algorithm steps and code the behavior. The latter may be done with story diagrams. In addition, we do GUI wire-frames that are implemented using GUI builders. Then, GUI and model are connected by data binding and action listeners.

While these development steps are all necessary and have proven to work for many applications, larger applications need some additional steps that have not yet been covered. Thus, this section outlines *Story Driven Modeling* (SDM) as a workflow for the development of larger applications. In addition to the discussed steps, Story Driven Modeling also employs requirements scenarios, reference architectures, and design patterns.

13.1 Iterative Refinement

As an example for the development of a small model, we reconsider our Study-Right University. For the Study-Right University we roughly followed the following process:

1. Look at example situations and small scenarios at application level.

2. Refine example situations and application scenarios with object diagrams and storyboards.

3. Derive class diagram, generate model structure implementation.

285

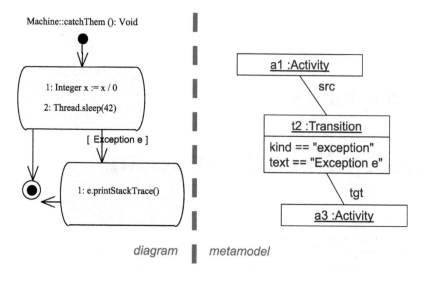

Figure 13.1: Exception handling

4. Derive / generate tests.

5. Take computer perspective and

   (a) outline general behavior / algorithm at application level,

   (b) refine algorithm steps towards object model,

   (c) and implement the general behavior / algorithm.

6. Validate implemented behavior / algorithm with example scenario tests.

7. Identify alternative scenarios and refine algorithms and re-validate.

This workflow covers the model part of an application. It might be used also for larger, more complex models in an iterative way. For example, we use this approach frequently when we extend our Fujaba tool. If we e.g. add a new kind of diagram or a new element for a given diagram, it is easy to start from the existing system and look at examples for the new features.

We tried to introduce exception handling in story diagrams. This was unsupported in Fujaba up to version 4, and needed to be added for version 5. The introduction of exception handling was triggered by an example story diagram calling Thread.sleep(42) (which throws an InterruptedException) in a collaboration message, cf. Figure 13.1. See also Section 9.1.8.

Thus, we needed to catch that exception with a try-catch block. We discussed on a whiteboard to add a special transition for exception handling coming up with an example as in Figure 13.1. We decided to introduce a new constant for transitions of kind "exception" and to use the text attribute to store the declaration of the exception variable. A more complex discussion was necessary to outline the extension of Fujaba's control flow analyzer. Fujaba's control flow analyzer iteratively groups blocks of activities into control flow tokens. This means that the control flow analyzer identifies loops and if-statements. This mechanism had to be extended by a new control flow token for activities with exception handling. With the help of this extra control flow token, it was easy to extend the template-based code generation to generate the desired try-catch blocks. This turned out to be a very tricky part for our extension. It required a profound knowledge of the algorithm used by the control flow analyzer and of its help structures, the control flow tokens.

Our Story Driven Modeling approach proved to be very helpful to tackle our story diagram extension, especially analyzing the problem with the help of a concrete example. We first analyze on the domain level, i.e. within a story diagram, then on the object level and of course also by looking into the algorithms. This worked very well although the Fujaba system was reasonably complex at that time (about 500,000 LOC). This experience shows that looking at example scenarios facilitates to identify the parts of the system to deal with. It therefore facilitates the extensions of larger systems.

13.2 SDM with Graphical User Interfaces

As discussed in Chapter 11 Story Driven Modeling is easily extended to integrate the development of graphical user interface parts. As shown for the Group Register example the plain Story Driven Modeling approach may be extended as follows (new points are in *italic*):

1. Look at example situations and small scenarios at application level.

2. *Build GUI mock-ups for scenarios or scenario steps. Run the scenarios with the mock-ups.*

3. Refine example situations and application scenarios with object diagrams and storyboards.

4. Derive class diagram, generate model structure implementation.

5. *Build GUI part with GUI builder.*

6. *Provide data binding and dummy action listeners.*

7. Derive / generate *GUI tests*.

8. Take computer perspective and

    (a) outline general behavior / algorithm at application level,

    (b) refine algorithm steps towards object model,

    (c) and implement the general behavior / algorithm.

9. Validate implemented behavior / algorithm with example scenario tests.

10. Identify alternative scenarios and refine algorithms and re-validate.

Here we describe a very GUI-driven approach. In practice, you may also focus on the model part first (using the approach of Section 13.1). You may add the GUI parts later.

To develop the GUI parts we propose to use mock-ups or wireframes. GUI mock-ups built with pencil and paper are especially helpful in discussions with customers. We do not recommend to use any kind of GUI mock-up tool in discussions with customers, not even PowerPoint. Customers are not always educated in software development. If you do a computer-based demo of your GUI mock-up, the customer will think the GUI has already been implemented. In addition, if you discuss changes of the GUI and you open some dialogs of your mock-up tool, the customer will have difficulties to distinguish between GUI elements that will be part of the desired application and GUI elements that are part of the mock-up tool. They all look the same, do they not? Thus, on software delivery, the customer may ask for the dialog to reshape the application at runtime as you have shown in your mock-up demo. The customer may also complain that the GUI elements do not exactly look like the ones in your mock-up demo. "This is not what you demonstrated". After your mock-up demo, the customer may argue: "Well, the GUI is already implemented, why does the rest need so long and why is it so expensive?" We recommend to avoid these kinds of problems with mock-ups-based on analog technologies. (Yes, pencil and paper. Whiteboards. Flip-charts. Paper snippets and glue.) Thereby, the customer will never mix up the mock-up or mock-up editing with the actual GUI implementation.

Even with the help of modern GUI builders and libraries, GUI construction remains a tedious and error prone task, especially for beginners. First of all, you deal with large libraries and a large number of predefined classes and interfaces. There are all kinds of GUI elements. There is a science on layout managers. There are all kinds of events which can be triggered by user interface elements. In addition, modern GUI libraries utilize many design patterns like composite pattern, Model-View-Controller pattern, or observer pattern. Many beginners are not used to these design patterns and in turn may have difficulties to develop classes that shall play a certain role in one of these patterns. Finally, modern GUI libraries and the design patterns they deploy make frequent use of inheritance, which again is a concept that beginners may not be used to very extensively. So, if you start with GUI building: be aware and try not to become frustrated. We all have gone through this. If you try to teach GUI building: remember, it is a lot of stuff.

In addition, there is the problem with multithreading. As soon as your application becomes slightly more complex, long running operations need to be decoupled from the GUI. Otherwise, the user interface is frozen while triggered operations are executed. Similarly, communications with other programs, e.g. via remote procedure calls may introduce parallel execution threads. In addition, multi user support may require multi threading mechanisms. As soon as your application is split in GUI threads and model threads, you have to deal with all kinds of multi threading related problems. This is another problem for beginners, even for people calling themselves professionals (cf. Chapter 12). This is a problem to be respected and not to be underestimated by teachers.

The next obstacle in building applications with graphical user interfaces is testing. GUI testing is largely an unsolved problem in Software Engineering. Especially hard are questions like: does it look as expected. Therefore, problems related to layouters are not easy to test. While it is hard to test what is going on on the screen, it is possible to test on a level a little bit more abstract than that. Tests may get access to widget elements. Thereby, tests may fire user interaction events like mouse clicks or key presses. Similarly, tests may fill input fields or validate the content of result fields. At this level, a test might provide some input data for a property editor, press the Send button and thereby trigger a model operation. As a result the object model will change which triggers property change events that trigger GUI updates. After that, the test may check the content of some other GUI fields to ensure the desired effects. Still, you cannot be sure that the result is displayed in a sufficient way (the result field might e.g. be out of scope or an image displayed to small), but at least you ensure that GUI elements and model elements are connected in a reasonable way. Unfortunately, GUI testing frequently has to deal with multi threading problems since GUI thread and model thread might be decoupled. In that case, the test needs to give the execution threads some time to provide the results before the result fields are checked. Such testing is not yet generated from storyboards.

13.3 SDM with Customers

When we go for larger, more complex applications requirements engineering aspects arise. This is addressed in the following workflow for Story Driven Modeling with customers (new points are in *italic*):

1. *Speak with customer and develop requirements scenarios.*

2. Look at example situations and small scenarios at application level.

3. Build GUI mock-ups for scenarios or scenario steps. Run the scenarios with the mock-ups.

4. Refine example situations and application scenarios with object diagrams and storyboards.

5. *Get customer feedback.*

6. *Instantiate reference architecture, i.e. choose GUI framework, persistence framework, communication framework, model framework.*

7. Derive class diagram, generate model structure implementation.

8. Build GUI part with GUI builder.

9. Provide data binding and dummy action listeners.

10. *Derive / generate GUI tests, persistence framework tests, communication framework tests, model framework tests.*

11. Take computer perspective and

    (a) outline general behavior / algorithm at application level,

    (b) refine algorithm steps towards object model,

    (c) and implement the general behavior / algorithm/

12. Validate implemented behavior / algorithm with example scenario tests.

13. Identify alternative scenarios and refine algorithms and re-validate.

Lets discuss the *"Speak with customer and develop requirements scenarios"* step with the help of an example.

SDM_Scenario for applying SDM to the project called UGrade:

> Chris is a lecturer at Kassel University. He runs the exercises for our programming methodologies course next time in winter term 2011 / 2012. This course has about 80 students. Each second week, students will get programming assignments. Students shall do their homework and send in their solutions. Chris employs a group of tutors (Theodor, Tabea, Tom) that do the grading. After grading, the students get feedback on their code via email and Chris has to collect all the grades. Organizing all this by email is tedious and error prone and thus, Chris initiates a project to construct a program facilitating this job. We build a small development team

with Dave, Doris, and Daniel. To get an idea of the project, Chris and the development team meet for a first requirements session. Chris explains his problem using examples from the last course. Dave proposes to do a requirements scenario covering the main assignment handling activities and how these activities shall be supported by the new Program.

They come up with the following requirements scenario for the assignment management system[1]:

Course Assignment Scenario:

1. At the beginning of the programming methodology course lecturer Lee opens a new web site for it.

2. At the course web site, Lee opens a student registration.

3. About 80 students register for the assignments, e.g. Stefan, Sarah, and Samuel.

4. After the first week, Lee provides the text for the first assignment in file PMAssignment1.pdf. This is added to the course web site.

5. The students do their homework. Well, most of them.

6. Students upload their solutions as zipped Eclipse projects via the course web site. In this scenario, Stefan and Sarah have done pair programming. Thus, they submit one file PMAssignment1.zip together with their two names.

7. At the end of the second course week about 50 solutions have been submitted.

8. Now the tutor team starts grading. To distribute the solutions among the tutors and to get an overview on the progress of the grading, something like a Kanban board [27] shall be used. The Kanban board shall show a table for the different grading steps. This table shall have a backlog column for the solutions that have just been handed in, a column for solutions under grading, a column for sending feedback to the students, a column for collecting the grades, and a done column.

9. In this scenario, the Backlog column shows a sticky-note for the solution of Stefan and Sarah. Tutor Theodor drags this solution

---

[1]In our overall example Chris has two roles. Chris is the customer in our software project scenario and Chris is the lecturer in the application usage scenario. To distinguish between these two roles, we name the lecturer in our usage scenario Lee.

to the grading column and downloads the PMAssignment1.zip file via the sticky-note.

10. Theodor imports the solution code into his Eclipse workspace for grading, compiles the project, and runs the JUnit tests. He digs into the test code and into the solution code. In general the solution is right. However, Theodor adds some suggestions for improvement as comments to the code. Theodor gives this solution grade B.

11. Theodor zips the project again. He revisits the Kanban board and via the sticky-note of Stefan's and Sarah's solution he opens a dialog to upload the commented version of the solution and to enter his grade plus some remarks.

12. Theodor drags Stefan's and Sarah's solution to the done part of the grading column and goes on with the next solution.

13. After three days of grading, the tutors have looked at almost all solutions. Thus, Lee sends the tutor comments and the grades to the students by dragging the corresponding sticky-notes to the feedback column of the Kanban board.

14. The system sends out email notifications.

15. Due to the email notification, Stefan and Sarah revisit the course web site. They notice their grade B and download the zip file with the tutor's comments. They dig into the comments. Unfortunately, they have problems with some of the comments. Thus, they contact tutor Theodor and ask for a meeting.

16. Stefan, Sarah, and Theodor meet in person and discuss the solution and the comments. Stefan and Sarah explain some more of their ideas and point Theodor to some parts of the code Theodor has not noticed on first reading. Due to the new insights, Theodor changes his grade to B+. Therefore, Theodor revisits the Kanban board and changes the grade on Stefan's and Sarah's sticky-note.

17. On Friday that week, Lee closes the submission of solutions and publishes an example solution on the course web site. In addition, Lee gives a lecture explaining the example solution and answering more students' questions.

18. Lee collects the solution sticky-notes and moves them from the feedback column to the done column.

> 19. Lee adds a new sprint to the Kanban board for the second assignments.
>
> 20. This goes on.

Dave, Doris, and Daniel thank Chris for the fruitful input.

If you want to read more on Scrum and Kanban, take a look at these references: [32] for Scrum, [13] for Kanban.

13.3.1 Requirements

The first step of SDM for larger applications is the development of *requirements scenarios*. This step corresponds to requirements engineering activities. SDM proposes to base the requirements engineering on scenarios. However, compared to the application scenarios we have used for smaller examples, requirements scenarios cover the usage of the desired application in a broader context. To understand the requirements of our customers right, we need to understand the relevant parts of their work. In our case, we need to understand the overall process of handling course assignments and students solutions and the grading steps. This overall process gives us an important insight on how the application that we plan to build is going to be used by our customers. Usually, such a requirement scenario will cover certain steps that need not to be supported by the planned application. For example, the publishing of the pdf file with the new assignment may still be done via the course web site as before. Still our system is affected, since it will also need to create some infrastructure to group the incoming solutions to the proper assignment in the different weeks and to enable the closing of the solution upload for a certain assignment before the example solution is published.

After developing a sufficient amount of requirement scenarios (or during that step), we may discuss with our customer, which steps of the overall workflow shall be supported by the desired application and which parts of this should be started with. In our example, we might e.g. use an existing system for the student registration step. This system might then deliver a comma separated file to be loaded in the assignment management application. Again, discussing which parts of the requirements scenarios shall be supported by the planned application gives important input for the realization, either we need to build a user interface to enable student registration or we need a data import mechanism to get the student names into our application.

In standard software engineering or requirements engineering we use use-case diagrams and use-case descriptions to document the functionality that is

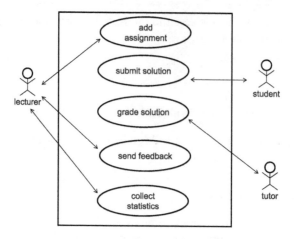

Figure 13.2: Use-case diagram for UGrade

part of our application and the borders of our application and the interaction of
our application with the outside world:

SDM_Scenario for applying SDM to the project UGrade:

> Just to get a good overview about the planned application the development
> team Dave, Doris, and Daniel develop a use-case diagram for the planned
> application, see Figure 13.2.

Use-case diagrams show functionalities as ellipses, the system border as a rectangle and the users as stick men. Double arrows depict which user accesses[2]
which functionality. In addition, each functionality is described in further detail
by a textual use-case description.

There is nothing wrong with use-case diagrams. They actually show very
well what are the main functionalities of the desired system and that there may
be multiple kinds of users which use different subsets of the overall functionalities. However, to come up with a good use-case diagram we propose to go
through a requirements scenario step by step. Do not try to come up with a use-
case from thin air. This can have about as terrible results as coming up with
a class diagram from thin air. You will model things nobody required. While
use-case diagrams give you a distilled view of your application, requirements
scenarios also document a lot of context information: why is a user going to

---

[2]Each arrow crossing the system border is a strong indication that some graphical user interface
for that use-case is needed.

use a certain functionality, how do the functionalities interact, which steps of the overall process lie outside the application, and how do these steps influence the system. Yes, you may put some of this information into the use-case descriptions, but requirements scenarios give you a broader view. If you read through our Course Assignment Scenario, you have to decide in each step "Is this a new functionality for our system not covered by an existing functionality nor an outside system?". If yes, find a verb for labeling the ellipse and draw a new ellipse. If not, skip to the next step. In our example Course Assignment Scenario (see above) step 1-3 are outside actions handled by persons or other systems. In step 4 it is mentioned that assignments are added. Therefore, we add the functionality "add assignment" to our use-case diagram. Homework is (hopefully) done by the students on their own (step 5), this one we skip. Step 6 talks about uploading solutions. This leads to the describing verb phrase "submit solution" which is a new functionality. Continuing in this manner through the steps of the requirement scenario will lead to the final use-case diagram. You also should write down the stakeholders while playing through the steps (eventually by going through them a second time) and see with what functionalities of the system they interact. This leads to the stickmen and the interaction arrows.

In our example, the development team has spoken with customer Chris, only. Usually, there are more stakeholders in a software development project. In our example, the developers might meet the tutors, too. The tutors will use the system later on and to meet their requirements, you should at least speak to them. Most likely, this will reveal more details and many additional important aspects. Again, requirements scenarios might be used in such discussions. Speaking with different stakeholders might also reveal that different people in the customer's enterprise have different views on the tool. Sometimes these requirements may contradict each other. While the management may want to cut jobs, the job holders might have a different view on this. Some experts might not want to speak to you, since their job relies on their exclusive know-how and if you put this exclusive know-how into software or just into a requirements scenario, it looses its exclusiveness. There is no simple solution here. We only claim that using concrete example scenarios facilitates the communication among the different parties and avoids undetected misunderstandings. While this sometimes will reveal conflicts, it is better to discuss these things before the software has been built and changes become expensive.

Requirements are moving targets. Usually, requirements change during a project. For example, the customers may change their minds when they see the first version of a GUI prototype. They also may change their mind when they see the planned costs. The customer's representative may change. The competencies of different stakeholders may change. The customer's enterprise may be bought. Laws may change. Competitors come with similar solutions. Now our system needs to be better than that. There is also no simple solution here. However, we will revisit this issue when we discuss money and development time later.

Requirements engineering also has the task to clarify the so-called non-functional requirements. Our requirements scenario gives you a lot of hints on these non-functional requirements. We know that a course has about 80 students. There may be a larger number of students, however, we do not expect millions of accesses per second. Solutions may be zipped eclipse projects of some megabytes size. There may be smaller or larger solutions, but we do not expect to need more than a terabyte of disk space. Thus, a usual server will suffice. Still, we need a persistent storage that deals with large binary objects. Concerning reliability, we should never lose a solution and we might want to keep track on relevant dates and operations e.g: When was a solution submitted, when was a new version submitted? Which tutor gave which grade at which date and time[3]? Who changed the grade when and for what reason. All this needs to be secured against data loss[4]. Obviously, there are some security requirements: students should not be able to manipulate their grades. And we need to keep the grades confidential such that one student cannot see another student's grades[5]. The system must never be down in the minutes before the solution submission closes. To our experience, requirements scenarios are again very helpful to address such non-functional requirements. The requirements scenario give you a much better understanding of why a certain non-functional requirement is important for your customer. This is much easier to address than a requirement like "system must be up 7 days a week, 24 hours a day, all term long".

At a certain point in time a project needs a name. Actually, you need this name quite early. As soon as you create a directory for the project on your disk, or a new entry in your versioning system or a new entry in your project management system, you need a name for it. Changing this name later is pretty hard. It is unbelievable how fast such a name replicates and spreads out to numerous places. Changing it requires to update all those other occurrences. Thus, we recommend to chose a project name very soon and than stick to it. You may easily give the application you build another name or a new name later on, if you restrict yourself e.g. to the title bar of the GUI window. Perhaps you can also rename the installer file and the script that invokes the program. Already changing the name of the main class causes trouble. It is easier to have a second main class with a new name that calls the old main class. Thus, we recommend to discuss the project name with your customer before you create the project folder and the first files:

SDM_Scenario for applying SDM to the project UGrade:

---

[3]This kind of functionality is called *logging* and easily available through libraries.

[4]*Journaling* is a commonly used technique that records all data modification operations and can be replayed in case of data loss or corruption. A underlying file-based versioning system or a versioned file system is another option.

[5]Security and authorization frameworks provide such functionality.

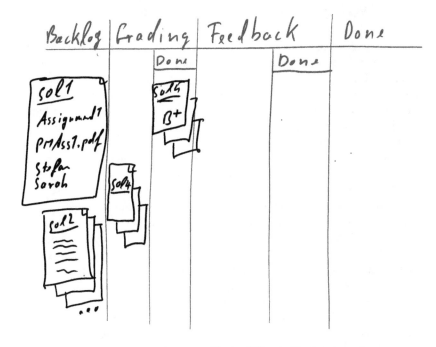

Figure 13.3: GUI mock-up for the UGrade Kanban board

At the end of their first meeting Doris does not forget to ask Chris for the project name. "Chris, we need a name for the project to be able to create the project folder. It is no big deal, we use it just as a working title. The program may get another name later on." Chris has already thought about it: "I would name it 'Unified Grading System' or short UGrade". "Cool." Issue solved.

At a certain point in time, you will develop GUI mock-ups for the planned application. This might either be done during the development of application scenarios or already during the discussion of requirement scenarios:

SDM_Scenario for applying SDM to the project UGrade:

While discussing steps 8 through 13 of the requirements scenario, it turns out that Chris wants a Kanban board as GUI for managing the grading process. To get a better idea of the whole process, Daniel proposes to draw a mock-up. During the further discussion, this mock-up helps a lot to get an understanding of the desired system. Figure 13.3 shows a snapshot of the GUI mock-up as used during the discussion.

13.3.2   Writing business software for customers

Finally, we also need to talk about money and time. If you want money from your customer you need something like an order form or a contract with your customer. In the simplest view, the accounting department of your customer will not accept any invoice if it did not send out an order for the thing or has a contract to refer to. Either way, the order or the contract need to name the product that shall be payed for. Here you basically have two choices. First, you may list all the functionalities that the new program will have and add a price tag to it. The list of all functionalities is usually referred to as formal requirements document. Requirements documents frequently rely on use-case diagrams together with textual use-case descriptions. We will discuss textual use-case descriptions in the context of application scenarios and algorithm outlines below. You may alternatively try to use requirement scenarios as requirement document. From our point of view this is much simpler for all partners. However, requirements scenarios deliberately exemplify the desired functionality, only. Thus, requirements scenarios do not exactly describe all functionality in all cases and thus they may leave room for interpretation about which extra cases need to be handled and which not. This vagueness might be a bug or a feature. If you meet your customer at court, vagueness pays off for lawyers, only. However, if your projects runs smoothly, vagueness helps to meet requirement changes. Vagueness may also help to tackle budget issues, if you run out of time. It gives you some more freedom to negotiate with your customer about the importance of certain features. However, be aware that it also gives your customer the freedom to require more. Statistically, less than half of the software projects finish in time and budget. You know this. Your customer knows this. To sue you will not speed up the project. If you just say, "OK, you do not like the software, you will not pay, thus we will not deliver.", you do not get your money but the customer does not get the program. No one will be happy. Thus, most likely, your customer is ready to accept some compromises. In this light, your customer may also accept some vagueness in the requirements document.

Actually, we are ready to argue that requirements scenarios describe a system less vague than standard textual use-case descriptions. While textual use-case descriptions try to cover all cases by describing the functionality in a rule oriented way, textual rule descriptions are known to be a source of misunderstandings and a source for court meetings for ages. Actually, social laws are textual rule descriptions and if there would be no ambiguities in them, there would be no need for courts and lawyers at all. Describing requirements with the help of example scenarios facilitates clear communication between stakeholders from different domains and thus avoid misunderstandings and court meetings. Therefore, requirements scenarios should be preferred for requirements documents. Technical customers will agree with this. Administrative customers or lawyers may have a problem with this. Note, usually the requirements are negotiated with your later users while contract and money are negotiated with administrative. Very likely, your users that want more functionality and usability do not like their own administrative people and fight them for budget issues, too. Thus, your users might be flexible in interpreting the contract and even help you to deal with or to exploit vague parts or your requirements document or contract. As long as you make your user happy, your user will be your friend.

To avoid the discussed problems with requirement documents, there is a second alternative for contracting: you follow the idea of eXtreme Programing [14] and just agree on a certain amount of man power. The idea is also called "rent a developer team". In your contract you just offer to work on the project for a certain amount of time. And then you bill on an hourly or daily rate. This kind of contract is easy to accept for administrative people and lawyers. It is also easier for you, because you have a smaller risk not to be able to deliver a certain functionality in the given time. You never promised it. Actually, in this setting the customer has all the risk. The customer has little or no means to put pressure on you to deliver something. To balance this risk a little bit, eXtreme programming proposes short development cycles of e.g. some weeks. After each development cycle the developers present their achievements or may even roll out intermediate releases. Then, the customers decide whether they are satisfied with the progress made and the project shall be continued or whether they are not satisfied and the project stops. This puts the pressure on the development team to deliver something worth to continue the project. In addition, this setting is very flexible in terms of focusing the development direction. Customer may either ask for fixes or improvement of already addressed functionality or may accept the achieved functionality and ask to go on with new functionality. Still, this setting has the problem that at the start of the project the customers do not know what functionality they are going to get for which amount of money and which budget is needed to cover a set of functionality, that actually provides a value for the customer. Well, to be honest, a contract promising a certain amount of functionality for a certain amount of money in a certain time contains just the same risk. Yes, you may have a written contract with precise requirement documentation. Still, the developers may fail. You sue them. You do not pay. You still do not get the software. After all, it depends on the level of trust between the developers and the customers how the contract is designed. Perhaps, a mixture of promising functionality and selling a certain amount of development time does the best job.

Overall, this is a textbook for beginners in Object Oriented Modeling. This is not a textbook on requirements engineering. There are much more aspects to be covered in requirements engineering. We recommend to find these details in textbooks dedicated to that topic. Here, we just want to emphasize, that the usage of requirements scenarios is an excellent help for requirements engineering.

13.4   Exercises

13.4.1   Kanban Board

Build the Kanban board application discussed in this chapter.

13.4.2   Assignment Management System

In some of the courses at your site, students may have to hand in weekly assignments or midterm assignments. Build an application that organizes this process:

- Students shall be able to subscribe for courses.

- Teaching assistants shall be able to publish new assignments and additional material to the students.

- Students shall be able to hand in their solutions, electronically.

- For the grading process, the solutions may be sent to one or more instructors.

- Feedback shall be sent back to the students.

- The grades shall be collected on a central site to be able to give an overview of a students performance in the course and of the overall performance of the course.

- At the end of the term, print certificates.

- Establish and manage different kinds of user accounts with different access rights.

- Prevent students from cheating or stealing other students' solutions.

- Log all activities and prevent this log from manipulation by any user.

13.4.3   Key Administrative App

Assume that your site introduce NFC (Near Field Communication) cards for access to the university building, the department building and / or the computer lab. Build an application that manages the administrative processes for this case:

- Manage the creation of user accounts and administrative accounts.

- Manage the handout of NFC cards to users.

- Manage which users get access to which buildings and rooms.

- Manage who has the right to grant new rights to new users.

- Manage to withdraw access rights and manage who has the right or the duty to withdraw user rights.

- Manage to grant or withdraw administrative rights.

- Manage to log a history of all actions. Do not give administrative or any users the possibility to manipulate the history.

- Discuss process, GUI, usability, and security issues with the administrative and security staff at your site.

- Get the administrative and security people at your site to use your system.

The main challenge in this exercise is to deal with administrative people and to negotiate requirements with them. The technical aspects are easy to cover, using the techniques you have learned by now. Handling people from other domains will be a very fruitful lesson. Thus, do anything to get people from other domains involved. If you are a teacher: it does not work to use some software people and ask them to fake the customers. You really need some people that think and live in other domains. Thus, really ask a security guy to come into your class for questions and requirements negotiation. Note, even administrative staff from the computer science department may already be to close to software to serve as good customers. Ask administrative staff from other departments or from the central administration. Make sure they are not used to software projects, already. It might even be a problem to use the same people for multiple years in a row.

Chapter 14

Yes, It Scales

Within this book we have demonstrated Story Driven Modeling with fairly small examples. First of all, examples for lectures and exercises must be small to be treated within some hours or weeks or text book pages. Second, we advocate an iterative agile software development work flow. Agile software development is known to be restricted to smaller projects and especially to small teams with no more than about 10 or 20 developers.

Still, we claim that Story Driven Modeling may also be used by larger projects. As an indicator, we have measured the sizes of our own software projects that have been developed with the help of Story Driven Modeling. First of all the Fujaba project itself has been developed this way. During its 15 years of development, the Fujaba project has deployed some 100 contributors and it sums up to about 500 000 lines of code. Story Driven Modeling still works for the Fujaba project. For this book, Albert and Ruben have just measured the amount of Fujaba generated code that we currently have on the hard disks of our laptops: Albert 1 080 910 lines of code and Ruben 361 482 lines of code and Leif Geiger a former PhD student of Kassel University and the Fujaba developer responsible for eDobs 562 598 (on March 8th 2012 15:26 CET). Thus, we eat our own dog food.

Generally, we claim that Story Driven Modeling scales in multiple dimensions:

- more objects
- more classes, more algorithms
- design patterns
- more installations, more users

We discuss these scaling dimensions in the following sections.

14.1 More Objects

Your application might scale just in the number of objects. Let us assume our Group Register, cf. Chapter 11, suddenly works with some 1000 people buying some 10 items a day, each. This will already totally screw up your user interface. Recall, the Group Register has a table showing all users with their balances on the left and a table with all bought items on the right. An SWT GUI table with some 1000 entries might already crash. At least, it is pretty unusable, e.g. if you try to find a certain name in it. The item table will soon contain some 10000 lines and will surely slow down the application or crash it and it is surely unusable. Note, the algorithm should still be able to deal with this number of objects: iterating through some 10 thousand or 100 thousand objects should still be doable in fractions of a second.

To deal with such a large number of objects at the GUI level you will most likely restructure your user interface to show not all but only some persons or items. You might add a search field to the persons table and show only matching persons. Alternatively, you show only the first 20 persons and add next / prev page buttons. Similarly, your might group the buys e.g. by day or by hour and show only one group and provide a search field and next / prev buttons. You may also extend your object model e.g. to support multiple (barbecue) events, and then your user interface shall provide possibilities to show only participants and bought items for one event and to switch between events. Such changes are easily done using our Story Driven Modeling approach in an iterative manner as discussed in Section 13.1.

Let us assume, the Group Register with the improved GUI grows even further. Now you have about 1 million persons in your system doing about 10 buys a day for about 100 days. This results in 1 billion (10^9 or one giga) objects. Assuming that your computer has some 10 or 100 gigabyte of main memory, you will eventually run out of memory. Well, in principle this is no problem as your operating system will start to swap some parts of your main memory to disk. The swap space on your disk will help you with some more terabytes (10^{12}). However, you will soon learn that Java programs do not deal very well with swapping. Java deploys a garbage collector that routinely goes through the whole memory to collect unreachable objects. If some memory part has been swapped to disk, the garbage collector will soon pull it back into main memory in order to search through it. This causes some other part of the main memory to be swapped from main memory to disk. Probably the part that the garbage collector wants to investigate next. The general rule is, as soon as your system starts swapping, the performance of your Java application breaks down. Actually, your whole system stands still and you will have to kill the process.

To deal with such a large number of objects at memory level finally requires that you take care of the memory management yourself. You keep only a fraction of the objects in main memory and store most objects on the disk. Next you add careful management for removing unused objects from your main memory and for retrieving new groups of objects from the disk. At first this requires some iterative refinement of your application as discussed in Section 13.1. However, the management of a large number of objects on the disk requires additional technologies that need to be chosen carefully.

First you may just serialize objects and then store a long list of them in a usual file. This is very hard to maintain, when some objects need to be retrieved, changed, and stored again. Each time you will have to read through the whole file and disk operations are usually a factor 1000 slower than main memory access. It is also pretty easy to corrupt your file and loose all your data.

The default for managing large amounts of data on the disk is a relational database. They come in all flavors and at all prices. There is a large number of frameworks like Hibernate[1] that help you to map your classes to database tables and to transform objects to database tuples and back again. These techniques are widely used e.g. in all kinds of web servers. It is the standard technique for this purpose. Using it causes some pain but works after spending the necessary effort.

An alternative for persistent storage are NoSQL key value databases like the Berkeley DB [9] or Hadoop [1]. NoSQL is the technique used by e.g. Google and Facebook. Using a key value database requires that you somehow create unique keys for all your objects. In addition you need to be able to serialize your objects. Then you may use `database.put(key,object serialization)` to store an object on the disk and `obj = database.get(key)` to retrieve it again. Keys can be simply object UUIDs (Universally Unique Identifiers) or object counters and used like references: starting from some root object, objects reference each other with the database keys. If we still refer to our Group Register, all objects would usually reside on the disk. Only those persons and bought items that are currently visible in the GUI or that e.g. belong to the current event are retrieved from the database. On change, you store the objects again. When the modified object is stored again, it will survive system crashes as in a new program run you will safely retrieve it again. When you e.g. change to another event, you remove all references to the old objects in your main memory and thus the garbage collector will take care of them. Then you retrieve the new set of objects you need to deal with and that's it. For all these chamges you may again use our Story Driven Modeling iteratively, cf. Section 13.1.

---

[1] Hibernate is a persistence framework, which maps Java objects to relational database structures. See [19].

14.2   More Classes, More Algorithms

Next your application may scale in the number of classes and methods you use. Let us assume you have programmed e.g. a small web shop and now you keep on adding new kinds of products to it. You may have started with books and now you want to offer electronic devices, light bulbs, or furniture. For each new kind of product a different set of properties needs to be stored and provided to the customers. Some new product kinds may need special handling e.g. the fresh fish you want to offer. Thus, for each new product kind you may need new classes and new methods that handle the specific issues for this product kind. You soon end up with some 1000 classes and some million lines of code.

In principle this kind of scaling is no problem for our iterative Story Driven Modeling approach. Still, for each new product you should analyze example scenarios, do storyboarding, derive new classes and new algorithms. However, when the size of your application grows beyond some threshold you will need additional help to structure your classes and code. Such a structure is usually called an architecture. The architecture will help you to find classes and methods related to your new product kind and it will help you to find and reuse and adapt existing functionality.

Bringing structure / architecture to your code starts with well-organized (Java) packages. These packages may be organized in hierarchies. This is a good start. Next you might group certain packages into something you might name a component. This grouping may manifest itself in dedicated Eclipse projects within your Eclipse workspace and in library / jar files used to distribute components. More complex components might be constructed by combining smaller components.

To get an overview about your components or your architecture you might use a component or package diagram as shown in Figure 14.1. It shows a very simple reference architecture for interactive systems. In interactive system, you usually have in the center a component that implements your object model. Obviously, you have a GUI component. This GUI component might consist of your GUI framework, the window construction code and the binding code that glues your GUI with your model. To store data you need a persistence management component, usually a database. For more complex functionality you may need a control component as shown on the top of Figure 14.1. In the context of web applications this is also called the business logic layer. Finally, your program might want to exchange data with some other programs. This might e.g. be done using JSON [7] mechanisms. Such functionality might be organized in a communication component. The communication component might also do TCP/IP-based communication.

The reference architecture of Figure 14.1 does not show any relations between its components. Usually, architecture diagrams heavily deploy various

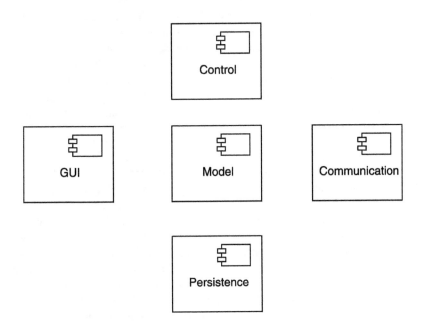

Figure 14.1: Reference architecture for interactive systems

kinds of usage, inheritance, import, include, or depends relations. While this might help you to understand your architecture, such relations are frequently misused to express certain visibility constraints that shall be enforced in the implementation. Unfortunately, software architects tend to provide only the minimal set of relations they assume to be necessary. However, during implementation you may have the need to access some persistence functionality from the control component while your architect wanted a layered architecture where control deals with the model only. Your architect wanted to decouple the components in order to improve maintainability. While this might have been a good idea in the beginning, now it forbids you to access the persistence component. If you find yourself at one point in this situation, the work around is to add some relay code to the intermediate layers. This does not really improve your application but it makes your architect happy. Overall, architecture relations are highly overrated and frequently misused. And therefore, our architecture does not use them at all. However, you still need to think about how components interact. The Story Driven Modeling way is to have a scenario for your functionality and within the scenario you identify which object does which part of the job and how the objects collaborate and how they forward information to each other and how the rely on each other and how they use each other. The implementation of these different objects might lie in different packages or components. Then you derive the relations between components from the collaboration of your objects. This usually results in meaningful architectures. However, you might feel that there is too much coupling between your components. In this case you should revisit your scenarios and consider to achieve some decoupling by changing the object collaboration. This might e.g. deploy some design patterns that are actually made for this, cf. Section 14.3.

So far our architecture just structures our code base. As discussed multiple times, design discussions based on class diagrams or code structure are futile. To address behavior aspects you should use scenarios and storyboards. As an example consider the architecture scenario in Figure 14.2. This architecture deploys a `tgui : AdminGUI` Object that represents the *whole* complex Tartu University adminstration GUI component that actually consists of multiple windows, composite structures, labels, text fields, layouters, and handlers in one single object, representing a component from the architecture's view. Similarly, the `tad : AdminData` component instance represents the whole object model of the Tartu University adminstration, i.e. the university, its rooms and buildings, its students, its staff, its courses, its grades, assignments.

Although `tgui` and `tad` represent quite complex components you can still use them to discuss their collaboration in example scenarios. For example, we might want to send the Tartu student Artjom for a student exchange to Kassel University. In step 1, Alexa the responsible administrative staff fills in the details via the `tgui` component and triggers the process by clicking a "Submit" button in the GUI, cf. Figure 14.2. As the `tad` component most likely runs its own thread, in step 2 the `tgui` component schedules a `SendTask` object to ask the data model `tad` to perform the necessary actions. In step 3, the tad component asks the `tadb : AdminDataBase` to provide a copy of Artjom's student file and forwards this data to the `tcom : AdminCom` component. The `tcom` component is in charge of sending the data to the administration of Kassel University. Therefore, `tcom` opens a data connection to the `kcom : AdminCom` component of the `kassel : UniversityAdmin` program. Please continue this scenario to model how `kassel` handles the received data, as an exercise.

To summarize, Story Driven Modeling easily scales to the architecture level, as it allows to discuss and work on concrete scenarios, which abstract from in-memory objects, heterogeneity and interfacing to coarse-grained objects representing components at system level.

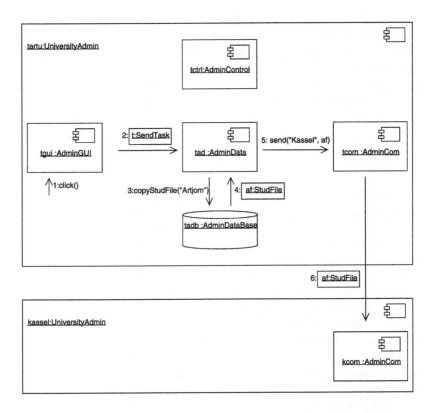

Figure 14.2: Instance-based architecture scenario

14.3 Design Pattern

When your program scales up, you will most likely use some design patterns [26] to improve your design, to decouple components, to improve flexibility and maintainability, and to facilitate communication in your team. Design patterns have proven to be an excellent design aid and thus we strongly encourage you to study this subject and to use them in your systems where appropriate. Unfortunately, in [26] the design patterns are discussed with the help of code structure and class diagrams, mainly. Actually, the design pattern explanation in [26] addresses many behavior aspects, but they do not yet use Story Driven Modeling. (Therefore, we plan to write a book on design patterns with Story Driven Modeling as soon as we have finished this book.) Still, most design patterns manifest themselves at the level of object diagrams and storyboards. Thus, the usage of design pattern is easily incorporated in Story Driven Modeling. However, you need to take some care when you derive class diagrams from the storyboards as explained in the following examples.

The most common design pattern is the Composite design pattern used to organize hierarchical data. Figure 14.3 shows an example object diagram for a hierarchical structure on locations in University organization. When you derive a class diagram from this object diagram you naturally come up with the classes Room, Building, Campus, and University. Naively, your would then derive one consistsOf association from University to Campus and a second consistsOf association from Campus to Building and a third consistsOf association from Building to Room. As discussed in [26] this design would create a maintenance problem: when you later on e.g. introduce Floor objects that group Rooms within Buildungs you need to remove the consistsOf association from Building to Room and introduce the new Floor class and two new consistsOf associations. Next, you have to adapt all places in your source code that were using the old association between Building and Room. This will be most likely spread out through your whole system. Thus, this small local change requires an effort proportional to the size of your program. That is evil. Now your architect shows up and complains about the tight coupling of your components and if you would have listened to him or her, you would have encapsulated this design decision in one small component and it would have been easy to change. To avoid this trouble, the Composite design pattern offers help.

The trick offered by the Composite design pattern is to introduce a common superclass SpaceUnit that provides a unique self association consistsOf. This allows an arbitrary nesting like Rooms in Rooms in Buildings in Universitys. While you give up some static type checking, you gain a lot of flexibility. If you now add a new class Floor, most of your code will not need to be changed. The change remains local and your architect will love you.

Similar to the Composite design patterns, many other patterns like Chain of Responsibility, Model-View-Controller, Strategy. may be used explicit or implicit in Story Driven Modeling. Sometimes, design pattern concepts become already visible in the object diagrams and storyboards. Sometimes, they will manifest during the derivation of class diagrams. Anyhow, design patterns and Story Driven Modeling blend well.

14.4   More Installations

If your program actually works well and offers some added value for your users, people will start to use it. Depending on your architecture this means that multiple copies of your program will be installed on many computers. This creates some new challenges for you. First of all, the more your program is used, the more bugs will be found. As a teacher you know this from your courses: if you

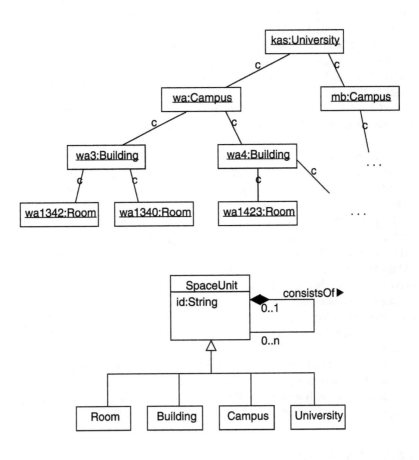

Figure 14.3: Using a Composite design pattern in Story Driven Modeling

announce something a little bit vague, e.g. the assignment is due next week, and your course has some ten students. No problem. If you have some 100 students, about 10 of them will ask you if Sunday night is still OK. If you have about 1000 Students, 100 will ask you if Sunday is still OK and about 10 of those will start a lengthy discussion with you, why you insist on Friday noon. Overall, you get 50 mails a day on this and will have no more time for anything else. Just the same happens to you if your program suddenly has 1000 users. You will be flooded by questions, remarks, change requests, and bug reports. If you grow to some 10 000 users, you will have to support multiple platforms like Windows, Linux, and MacOS. Users will ask for versions in different languages like French, Turkish, or Chinese. Users will trigger the most bizarre bugs you can think of. This goes on. If you grow to some 1 000 000 users, you will get requests for platforms like DOS, IBM 360, Siemens 9000. You name it. They ask for languages like Klingon. And they ask for new features like a coffee counter, calendar support, versioning support, time warp, teleportation, and wormholes. When you reach this level, go to the stock markets and live happy ever after.

To deal with a growing number of user requests you should setup a project website with forums, blogs, FAQ, download page, and a ticket system for bugs and feature requests. Then you add staff to your team and go for it.

However, there is another aspect to be addressed, the problem of software evolution. From time to time you will develop new releases of your software. When users install new releases, they usually expect that they can still use the old data. Thus, you need either to provide some backward compatibility or you need to provide data migration mechanisms. The longer your program lives, the bigger becomes this problem. At a certain time, you may want to give up compatibility to Version 0.1. Depending on the numbers of users you have, for sure there will be users still using that old version and complaining not to be able to upgrade to version 7.42. Ask Bill Gates about this. Story Driven Modeling can offer only little help here. You should try to use techniques that are ready for data evolution as e.g. JSON data [7]. You need to plan and discuss data migration issues with your team. Here, Story Driven Modeling will help you to analyze migration examples. Still this remains an open problem.

14.5   Exercises

1. Turn the multi player Mau Mau game we have built in Exercise 12.3.3 into an Android version. Add ads. Put it in the app store. Get some 100 000 users.

2. Build an IOS version, put it into the apple store and sell some 10 000 copies for some dollars each. (Do not choose the minimal price possible. You will need some price reserve for special offers.)

3. Come up with new versions 4 times a year.

- Follow the steps above for our Battleships example.

- Follow the steps above for our Mancala example.

- Follow the steps above for our Mensch Ärgere Dich Nicht example.

- Follow the steps above for our Connect Four Game example.

- Follow the steps above for some new game you develop yourself.

CAUTION: Some of the activities above may trigger legal issues e.g. copyright and trademark and patent topics. In principle, the idea of a game is free. However, names and look-and-feel might be protected. Also you must not just copy any game material (text / pictures). You need to build such things anew yourself. As soon as or better before you actually start making money with your games, be sure to talk to some business and legal people about these issues.

Chapter 15

SDM of Embedded Applications

Developing Software for embedded systems differs from traditional software development in various ways. First of all, the target platform or system is not the host development machine. If you're programming a washing machine control program, you cannot attach your keyboard and monitor to the machine to enter the code, neither the machine contains a compiler. This means, we need to edit and compile the program on our host computer, and then deploy the compiled software on the target system. If we want to debug our code, the target system must provide a remote debugging interface, otherwise debugging is nearly impossible.

Many important aspects of embedded software engineering are not covered by this chapter, we just give a rough overview how to implement embedded software using the SDM method. In detail, we do not deal with hard timing constraints or realtime issues here. We do not deal with low-level processing features like interrupt requests and handlers. We don't show how to program software that directly interacts with hardware like device drivers do. We don't cover machine language or other system programming languages.

Many embedded systems as e.g. a small mobile robot may easily be seen as a distributed system: these days the sensors and actors become smart e.g. an ultrasonic distance sensor is not just wired to one pin of your microcontroller and you derive the distance from some voltage level. The ultrasonic distance sensor does the measurement autonomously and it sends the distance as a digital value to your microcontroller via an I^2C bus. As a programmer you just read this value via a method call. Similarly, a motor is not wired to one of your microcontroller pins. Motor speed is usually controlled by PWM (puls width modulation). This means, you switch the motor on and off in a high frequency and by changing the

315

ratio of on and off time, you control the amount of power that the motor gets. While your microcontroller might be able to do this directly, usually the motor has its own little IC, doing the PWM and it is connected to your microcontroller via some bus. Many motors produce some pulse when they have rotated by some degrees. If you try to count these pulses directly via your software, you need to be smart not to miss one. Luckily, most motors have their own IC that counts the pulses and you may ask this IC via a bus. Thus, a simple robot is easily modeled as a group of motor and sensor objects that are connected to a microcontroller / brain object. This idea is easily extended to a group of robots that collaborate e.g. in robot soccer team. We have also frequently combined simple robots with Android-based mobile phones. At the one end, the mobile phone may be used as a remote control for the robot. On the other hand, the mobile phone may be mounted on the mobile robot and it may provide extra sensors, e.g. a camera, extra communication means, e.g. Wifi, and extra brain power, e.g. routing computations. For image recognition problems, we have combined mobile cameras on a robot with image recognition software running on the GPU of a PC. All these systems are easily modeled as a distributed, concurrent system or as a set of collaborating and interconnected objects. SDM enables you to derive an object model for your overall system and all its components and to run through scenarios that clarify how the various system components collaborate to do the overall task. Once the duties of the various components are identified, you program them for the different components using the language and approach that is most suitable for it. This heavily depends on the target platform.

For testing purposes, you may simulate the overall system behavior before deploying it on real robots in real world. Such a simulation covers not only your system components and their behavior but also the real world environment they are living in. For a mobile robot you may need to simulate its position and movements, and when it runs into an obstacle, or when it measures the distance to a wall. This "real world" model is again easily developed with the help of SDM. Thus, SDM is an excellent aid for the development of embedded systems.

15.1   What is an Embedded System?

Embedded systems are today's everywhere-hidden computers. Systems that somehow operate, process input, output data or actions, but don't really expose that they contain little computers, running little programs. But even the tiniest systems contain some kind of processor, which can be programmed in some programming language and runs code. Because these embedded systems are so different from regular personal computers, we have to face the following obstacles:

- Embedded systems have limited resources, especially for input and output

- there might be no display. There might be no hard-disk or any storage to log data to. There might be no keys or buttons or other input devices to interactively control the system. In general, the computing resources might be limited in RAM, ROM or CPU power.

- Different target language (in most cases, NOT Java), or different language capabilities plus usually a different processor architecture build a gap which is not existent in classic software development.

- Remote debugging is required as we inherently have a developer host machine and a deploy target system, which runs our code, whereas the debugger interface resides on the host. Both systems need to communicate in order to debug our programs. This debug interface might require a hardwired link between host and target like a USB or JTAG debug interface, which might be cumbersome when developing for wireless systems.

- In some cases, we are forced to use inter-system-communication to achieve some useful system behavior: For example, logged data must be transferred to some database storage system. TCP/IP networking is not always available, so we somehow have to encode our data for limited protocols and communication channels.

So, what can you do when you develop software for embedded systems and still use Story Driven Modeling:

- Develop, test and debug the overall system structure and business logic on the host machine. For a simulation develop real world models. To run tests and simulations you might need to develop some hardware abstraction, i.e. a virtual motor that on virtual power moves the robot virtually, i.e. it just changes the current coordinates. Such simulation components are worth it and a good alternative to remote debugging the embedded system on the target platform (or having no debugging at all). You will have to develop test drivers and hardware interaction mock-ups to be able to do such simulation tests, but you wanted to do that anyway, right?

- As you develop your components for simulation on your host platform first, try to avoid specific language features like Java reflection or library functions (e.g. SWT GUI) that may not be available on your target platform. Frequently such language and platform specific functionality can be replaced by local mechanisms that e.g. in the case of reflection may be generated by an (adaptable) code generator: You can generate quasi-reflective or generic accessor methods, factory classes or even meta-information of your component directly as code. In your simulations, you may replace low level components that will finally be programmed in e.g.

C by more abstract simulation components. This abstract simulation component may e.g. not accurately simulate how your microcontroller controls the motors of your robot but just simulate how the overall robot moves on the surface.

- Your overall component model will also help you to distribute responsibilities among system components. In one application, we used two robots that were traveling in a maze with narrow streets. When the two robots meet in such a narrow street, they are blocked as they cannot pass each other. Thus, our route planning had to avoid such blocking meetings. At first, we located the route planning within the robots. However, this would have required that the two robots inform each other about their plans in order to be able to avoid conflicts. Instead, we placed the route planning in a central host component that easily was able to coordinate the two robots. Later on it turned out, that the transfer of complex routes from the host to the host computer to the robots was tedious as the host runs on Java and the robots on C. To avoid the problem of interchanging complex data across language and platform boundaries, we introduced agents on the host platform that deal with the routing information by remote controlling the robots. The planning component handed the routes to the agents within the host and the agents send simple move commands to the robots what was easy to do even across language and platform boundaries. Such design issues are very well discussed with Story Driven Modeling means.

We will show some application scenarios for which we have developed software using the Story Driven methodology. Because the software for embedded systems requires a lot of background knowledge concerning electrical engineering, or hardware, we will only roughly outline our software design approach.

Usually embedded software follows a simple chain of actions running in a loop:

1. read input: e.g. sensors, (user interface) buttons, or other communication input like network.

2. process the input: e.g. calculate a control value for a heating system based on the sensor data just read.

3. act: activate the heater in case of a heating system, beep, control motors.

So, your initial code for a microcontroller component might look like this:

```
void loop ()
{
  read ();
  process ();
```

```
    act ( );
}
```

Sounds easy right? As usual, problems starts when it comes to details. Sensors want to read with a certain periodic timing: We need timers and interrupts. Same applies to actuation. Processing can be difficult as well, as data is processed with different data rates, might contain noise and jitter. So, develop your program carefully, always keeping the clear initial structure in mind. In addition, use smart sensors and actuators that require little micro management. If things become tense on one microcontroller, think about distributing tasks on multiple microcontrollers.

A commonly used software design pattern in the context of embedded systems are state machines[1]. Such a state machine consists of multiple states with transitions between them. When starting up, one entry state is active, meaning it executes (periodic) code or at least is marked active, so it can process events. Events are either generated internally (e.g. periodic timer events) or externally (e.g. certain sensor data, communication event). When a transition matches its event, a state transition occurs, so that the following state is active. Usually a state machine is implemented with concurrency, e.g. for generating events or to use communication streams which need to be read with blocking method calls. For concurrency issues, see Chapter 12. On a microcontroller, we recommend to implement the state machine, within our single main loop as a simple switch-cases statement controlled by simple state variable. Do not fumble with multiple threads or dynamic object structures and abstract state classes that are overridden by specific state classes.

15.2 Example: LEGO Mindstorms NXT Robotics System

The LEGO Mindstorms NXT Robotics System provides various sensors, some actuators / motors and a "brain", the NXT brick. It contains a microcontroller, buttons, display and a battery. The brick is capable of running a firmware supporting various programming languages. We use the LeJOS operating system or firmware, which provides a JavaVM running on the NXT Brick, which is an embedded microcontroller system. This firmware supports the direct execution of Java bytecode, so that we can use our regular tool-chain (Code generator, Java IDE and compiler). LeJOS only supports a subset of the Standard Edition Java. Most importantly, no (remote) debugging is possible, reflection is not supported and only a limited subset of the standard Java API is available. Only 64 kB RAM

---

[1]UML provides state diagrams as special notation for state machines. Details can be found in [16].

/ ROM is available, but the VM features multiple threads, so small Java programs using a restricted set of libraries are no problem.

Developing software for the NXT is difficult. Furthermore (or luckily), the platform is not powerful enough to run really sophisticated algorithms like image processing, so you might want to perform such tasks in combination with some other systems, like a data processing PC connected to one of the NXT's interfaces.

In general, we suggest to structure your code so that parts of it can be run in the host in a well-defined test environment, and you're only deploying the program build for NXT when running the real target system in its productive environment. For example, there is no need to run JUnit on the NXT, this can be done on the host, more over, doing that gives you debugging capability and all the development productivity tools available on the host machine.

The basic method to achieve this is to be able to run the same code on the NXT and on the host machine. Therefore, we decouple program logic parts from the API and provide adapters for the NXT API. As your program logic uses an abstract NXT API, it cannot tell which concrete implementation it is dealing with, i.e. whether it deals with a physical NXT component or just with a simulation component on the host. You will need mock-ups and test drivers, e.g. you will have to simulate all the NXT's I/O during testing your program logic. For example, when the logic tells an NXT Motor to rotate for one second, the test driver has to give a feedback during that period that the motor is constantly running (or not, if you are simulating a stalled motor).

15.3   Example: Android Platform (for Robotics)

The Android platform can be seen as embedded target platform and gets more and more popular. It can be used not only to write fancy 'Apps', games and gadgetry, but also as user-input device or controller in the field of home automation. It is not only feasible as remote device to control home automation functions, but Android also gets more and more popular as runtime system for embedded devices like alarm locks, interactive displays. It is perfectly suited for such applications as it has a rich programming API, is based on the Java language and supports a wide variety of target platforms. Such a platform might even be headless. The main reasons why Android is quite popular and very suitable for our presented development approach is that it is based on the Java language, so we can reuse our toolchain (for example Eclipse), it is much more powerful than traditional embedded systems (e.g. GBs of RAM/ROM, GHz of CPU clock frequency, multicore) and furthermore features a great (remote) debugger, absolutely comparable to desktop Java. Rich communication interfaces and already build-in sensors even make it an easy-to-use and yet powerful platform for be-

Figure 15.1: Example NXT robot with Android brain.

ginners. Beside home automation, which usually does not focus on rich powerful application logic but more on interfacing the various components, we also think that an Android device makes an excellent robot brain, so it can be combined with the NXT robotic system presented in the previous section. An image of an NXT robot with an Android brain can be seen in Figure 15.1.

15.4 Developing for Arduino

Arduino is a popular microcontroller platform. It is using an 8-bit CPU with very limited hardware capabilities, e.g. 32kB ROM and only 2kB RAM. It comes with its own development environment, which lowers the learning effort for beginners rapidly. Like most low-level processing units, it is programmed using the C (resp. C++) language. The Arduino IDE adds some kind of special source code preprocessor that expands the program to a form that is fed to the regular (cross-platform) GNU C/C++ compiler. This adds some of the compile time check features and editing comfort we are used from Java.

Programs are usually checking for events by reading electrical levels at the microcontroller's input pins and invoking actions by actually setting certain electrical levels at the microcontroller's output pins. Combined with some periphery electronics and hardware, sensors can be attached and motors can be actuated, like the NXT brick does. This way, an interaction in the system's context is achieved. The control programs usually consist of a main loop running at a high frequency reading and writing I/O registers. Because the main loop runs constantly, we somehow have to schedule timed events, for example for blinking an LED at a low frequency. So our main loop mixes different concerns and time constrains, and usually also logical conditions in various combinations. Programming this by hand is difficult.

Our solution to this is first not to put too much functionality on the Arduino: when there are other components in the overall system, you might consider to move responsibilities to them. Second, we try to come up with a simple systematic and code style that allows to deal with multiple interleaved tasks, easily. Third, we try to cover certain problems with code generation mechanisms: An implementation for a certain fixed-time scheduler can be generated in order to decouple timed invocations. State machines can be used to simplify logical conditions. Lookup tables make your program more efficient. All those artifacts can be generated, even for a non-object oriented language like C.

15.5 Exercises

There are numerous open challenges in robotics and engineering. Find a challenge that emphasizes collaboration of multiple robots and smart behavior above mechanical and electrical and control engineering problems. Participate.

You may also set up your own challenge e.g. your own little "urban challenge" for autonomous driving. Do it with model cars or lego cars in order to minimize mechanical problems (and risks for human lives). Do it with multiple cars to make it more interesting. Try to achieve some collaborative behavior.

Teaching Guidelines

This chapter is intended to be read by teachers. It is just a small summary of our experiences we would like to share.

A possible way to teach this course is in 8 times 4 hour sessions, but doing it in 15 weeks and distributing one point to about two lessons should work well:

1. Introduction, modeling and abstraction, user stories and scenarios, use-cases.

2. Objects, object diagrams.

3. From objects to class diagrams.

4. From model to code, Test Driven Development.

5. Method design, the Object Game.

6. Modeling in Fujaba, story diagrams, storyboards.

7. Coobra (distributed modeling), more modeling in Fujaba.

8. Simple design patterns and Test Driven Development in Fujaba, interfacing Fujaba, questions and tips and tricks

Also prepare your students to do interactive work. Even if you can deliver a lecture on the Story Driven Modeling method, letting the students do in class exercises is plenty of fun. We have provided plenty of inline exercises.

Course Projects

We have made good experiences with course projects: choose two games e.g. Mau Mau and Mancala (or add to our game collection your own favorite board game). Each week, show one development step on the first game and let the student do the same step on the second game. Each week you build upon the results of the previous week and at the end of the course, the students have developed a small game that they can actually play and that they can show their people at home.

Live Programming in Lectures

Programming is an active skill. It is hard to learn programming by looking at programs. It is much easier to learn programming by looking at programming activities. Thus, in our lectures we do live development of software as often as possible. This means, the teacher programs and each key stroke is seen on the projector. This needs some preparation and some training but it is a great method for teaching programming skills. And, there is no problem if you do some mistakes during live programming. We call this a learning opportunity. For students it is valuable to see that programs do not materialize out of thin air but are constructed step by step and that problems may occur and how to deal with them. In addition, if there is a compiler failure or a test assertion fails, this activates students to help you in solving the problem. Thereby, students are highly motivated to follow your steps and to think through what you are doing. It works great. Depending on your class sizes and equipment, you can actually encourage your students to program together with you on their computers or even let them try out some of the problems themselves. Try it.

Social Exercises / Preparations

If people have trouble working in teams the following exercise might be a good start:

- Form random teams of 3-5, e.g. by utilizing the student enrollment number modulus n.

- Define a day and time outside the course, where you meet regularly.

- Give a list of the abilities / skills and one weakness of every team member concerning a software development project.

- Add email and contact data.

- Write one abstract why this combination of abilities makes a good developer team.

- Share this document with your teammates and the teacher.

Tools Preparations

We found several possible solutions to provide the course tool software to the students. These are sorted by their complexity for the individual, average student. A more convenient way increases the initial preparation effort for the lecturer, but might pay off when you have a large number of students attending your course and cannot or you do not want to deal with individual installation problems. The suggested methods are:

- Virtual Machine Images, for example based on a Linux containing the pre-configured software, containing an Eclipse distribution ready installed and configured. Pro: really easy to run, almost nothing can go wrong as long as the virtual machine runs. Can be easily reset. Con: Resources: requires fast, virtualization-enabled machines (lots of laptops nowadays are still missing this), plenty of harddisk space, students might be unfamiliar with the provided operating system.

- Eclipse with pre-installed plugins, provided as ZIP archive for all major platforms. Pro: Easy to run, just unzip and launch. Con: Needs to be prepared each time the tools change (bug-fixes, evolution). You might want to preconfigure an update site, which also leads to the next solution:

- Require a certain Eclipse distribution, e.g. Eclipse Classic with Subversion plugin installed, and provide an update site URL to install the tools. Pro: Easy tool updates because there's a central deployment site, moderate easy to run. You should definitely provide a step-by-step installation guide, or students will fail (entering the wrong update site, installing conflicting plugins etc.). Con: It is hard to track the cause if the tool installation fails (for example check eclipse distribution version(s)).

- Take an Eclipse IDE and check out the tool's source code, then run it as Eclipse Runtime IDE. Pro: Students learn a lot about tool development as they can take a deep look into it. You could work on a certain software version of the tools, e.g. one that enables or disables certain features to match the course contents (You might want to provide a source code repository then). Exercises can be easily tool-development related. Con: Understanding the Eclipse Runtime IDE / plugin development adds another possibly hard learning step when the course begins. Be aware of that! Configuring the initial workspace can be hard, takes a lot of time per student, so does preparing the installation guide. Requires more resources to run than the previous two solutions.

Bibliography

[1] Apache Hadoop. URL: http://hadoop.apache.org/ [cited March 22, 2013].

[2] Balsamiq Mockups | Balsamiq. URL: http://www.balsamiq.com/ products/mockups [cited October 10, 2012].

[3] EclEmma - Java Code Coverage for Eclipse. URL: http://www. eclemma.org/ [cited October 09, 2012].

[4] Eclipse Tool. URL: http://http://www.eclipse.org/.

[5] Fujaba Tool, Kassel Site. URL: http://seblog.cs.uni-kassel.de/ projects/fujaba/.

[6] Inkscape. Draw Freely. URL: http://inkscape.org/ [cited October 09, 2012].

[7] JSON. URL: http://www.json.org/ [cited March 22, 2013].

[8] Merriam Webster, Online. URL: http://www.merriam-webster.com/.

[9] Oracle Berkeley DB. URL: http://www.oracle.com/technetwork/ products/berkeleydb/overview/index.html [cited March 22, 2013].

[10] SDMLib. URL: http://sdmlib.org [cited March 18, 2013].

[11] UML Tool for Fast UML Diagrams. URL: http://www.umlet.com/ [cited October 09, 2012].

[12] UMLLab from Yatta solutions. URL: http://www.uml-lab.com/de/ uml-lab/.

[13] David J. Anderson. *Kanban: Successful Evolutionary Change for Your Technology Business*. Blue Hole Press, April 2010.

[14] Kent Beck and Cynthia Andres. *Extreme programming explained: embrace change*. Addison-Wesley Professional, 2004. URL: http://dl.acm.org/citation.cfm?id=1076267.

[15] Kent Beck and Erich Gamma.   Test infected: Programmers love writing tests.   *Java Report*, 3(7):37–50, 1998.   URL: http://www-public.it-sudparis.eu/~gibson/Teaching/CSC7302/ReadingMaterial/BeckGamma00.pdf.

[16] Grady Booch, James Rumbaugh, and Ivar Jacobson. *The Unified Modeling Language User Guide*. Addison-Wesley Professional, 2 edition, May 2005.

[17] Grady Booch, Jim Rumbaugh, and Ivar Jacobson. *Unified Modeling Language–User's Guide*. Addison-Wesley Reading, MA, 1999. URL: http://www.lavoisier.fr/livre/notice.asp?id=O3OWRAALRXSOWE.

[18] Jean Bézivin and Olivier Gerbé.   Towards a precise definition of the OMG/MDA framework. In *Automated Software Engineering, 2001.(ASE 2001). Proceedings. 16th Annual International Conference on*, page 273–280, 2001.   URL: http://ieeexplore.ieee.org/xpls/abs_all.jsp?arnumber=989813.

[19] JBoss Community.   Hibernate.   URL: http://www.hibernate.org/ [cited March 22, 2013].

[20] I. Diethelm, L. Geiger, and A. Zündorf. Systematic Story Driven Modeling. Technical Report, Universität Kassel, 2002.

[21] Ira Diethelm, Leif Geiger, and Albert Zündorf.   Systematic Story Driven Modeling, a case study.   Edinburgh, Scottland, May 2004.   URL: http://www.se.eecs.uni-kassel.de/se/fileadmin/se/publications/DGZ04.pdf.

[22] Ira Diethelm, Leif Geiger, and Albert Zündorf. Mit Klebezettel und Augenbinde durch die Objektwelt. In *INFOS*, pages 149–159, 2005.

[23] Ira Diethelm, Leif Geiger, and Albert Zündorf. Rettet Prinzessin Ada: Am leichtesten objektorientiert. In *INFOS*, pages 161–172, 2005.

[24] The Document Foundation.   LibreOffice.   URL: http://www.libreoffice.org/ [cited October 09, 2012].

[25] Erich Gamma and Kent Beck. JUnit: A cook's tour.   *Java Report*, 4(5):27–38, 1999. URL: http://www.redbrick.dcu.ie/~deviant/files/Renaat/testing/cookstour.pdf.

[26] Erich Gamma, Richard Helm, Ralph Johnson, and John Vlissides. *Design Patterns: Elements of Reusable Object-Oriented Software*. Addison-Wesley Professional, 1 edition, October 1994.

[27] K. Hiranabe. Kanban applied to software development: From agile to lean. 2008. URL: http://www.infoq.com/articles/hiranabe-lean-agile-kanban.

[28] Microsoft. Microsoft Visio - Office.com. URL: http://office.microsoft.com/en-us/visio/ [cited October 09, 2012].

[29] Microsoft. Word - Document and Word Processing Software - Office.com. URL: http://office.microsoft.com/en-us/word/ [cited October 09, 2012].

[30] Nomagic. MagicDraw. URL: http://www.nomagic.com/products/magicdraw.html [cited October 09, 2012].

[31] Klaus Pohl. Requirements Engineering–Grundlagen. *Prinzipien, Techniken. dpunkt. verlag, Heidelberg, Deutschland*, 1, 2007.

[32] Ken Schwaber. *Agile project management with Scrum*. Microsoft Press, 2009. URL: http://books.google.com/books?hl=en&lr=&id=RpYX01XVMksC&oi=fnd&pg=PP2&dq=scrum&ots=ldtxnrhyGV&sig=ed_8uLAyrNSIgynYmTNEUgdH6Lo.

[33] Edwin Seidewitz. What models mean. *Software, IEEE*, 20(5):26–32, 2003. URL: http://ieeexplore.ieee.org/xpls/abs_all.jsp?arnumber=1231147.

[34] Albert Zündorf. Story driven modeling: a practical guide to model driven software development. In Gruia-Catalin Roman, William G. Griswold, and Bashar Nuseibeh, editors, *ICSE*, pages 714–715. ACM, 2005. URL: http://dblp.uni-trier.de/db/conf/icse/icse2005.html#Zundorf05.

Index

330